Praise for
A Literary Education and Other Essays

"Epstein follows up *Essays in Biography* (2012) with another collection of provocative and beguiling thought pieces. The range of his curiosity is exhilarating."

—*Publishers Weekly*

"[In *A Literary Education*] prolific essayist, biographer, and novelist Epstein . . . delivers . . . lots of erudition . . . and . . . fun."

—*Kirkus Reviews*

"Erudite, penetrating, and decisive . . . Epstein's delivery is filled with thorough analysis, delightful allusions, and outright laughs. . . ."

—Peter Dabbene, *ForeWord Reviews*

"Maybe it's time for a 'Joseph Epstein Reader' that would assemble the best work from his previous books for old and new fans alike. In the meantime, *A Literary Education* inspires hope that Mr. Epstein's good run [referring to the author's 24 books] isn't over just yet."

—Danny Heitman, *Wall Street Journal*

"[This is a] wonderful book of summer reading that's [also] . . . good for the cold, gray days ahead. . . . [Epstein is] a man of his time and above his time. . . ."

—Suzanne Fields, *Washington Times*

"Joseph Epstein turns out the best essays—of the literary or familiar kind— of any writer on active duty today. . . . Those who've reviewed Epstein's work over the years . . . praise his humor, his erudition, his vast learning, and his elegance. . . . Epstein's writing, like most French desserts, is very rich stuff."

—Larry Thornberry, *American Spectator*

"Epstein's . . . *A Literary Education and Other Essays* . . . is his 24th book. This volume confirms that Epstein is not only the greatest living American literary critic, but also the country's foremost general essayist. He is, almost singlehandedly, holding aloft the flame for what used to be the honorable calling of 'the man of letters.'"

—JOHN PODHORETZ, *COMMENTARY*

"[Epstein] writes sentences you want to remember. . . . His essays are troves of literary reference and allusion, maps between centuries, countries, genres. . . . [They] have personality and style, yes, but they also have something to say, and that's the pivotal distinction between Epstein and his bevy of imitators. . . . What's more, his wit is unkillable. . . ."

—WILLIAM GIRALDI, *NEW CRITERION*

"Epstein is an essayist of the old school—learned, productive, and available to many occasions. A man gifted with a wit both cutting and self-deprecating, and an easy command of the many syntactic variations of the periodic sentence, he also has a fearless willingness to assert a view—and this, as any reader of the essay knows, is the drive wheel of the whole business, never mind if that view is widely shared or unpopular."

— SVEN BIRKERTS, *LOS ANGELES REVIEW OF BOOKS*

Praise for
Essays in Biography

"Erudite...eloquent...opinionated...edifying and often very entertaining."
—*Publishers Weekly*

"The acclaimed essayist ... presents a provocative collection of essays that [is] ... guaranteed to both delight and disconcert."
—*Kirkus Reviews*

"[He] brings to biography a genius of discernment."
—*Choice*

"Mr. Epstein's essays are brilliant distillations. ... "
—Carl Rollyson, *Wall Street Journal*

"*Essays in Biography* ... is smart, witty and a pleasure to read."
—Jonathan Yardley, *Washington Post*

"This ... collection of biographical essays ... [is] unabashedly personal, and flavored throughout by a wit that never stays in the background for long. [What Epstein calls a] 'heightened sense of life's possibilities' is ... what a reader may take away."
—*Boston Globe*

"Joseph Epstein['s] ... style and wit make his subjects come alive.... [He is] the dean of contemporary essayists."
—*Washington Times*

"Epstein is a gifted storyteller, a discerning critic, and a peerless stylist.... It's fair to say that a variety of over-used adjectives—witty, urbane, intelligent—are in this case quite appropriate."
—*Weekly Standard*

Wind Sprints

Wind Sprints

Shorter Essays

Joseph Epstein

Also by Joseph Epstein

Axios Press
PO Box 457
Edinburg, VA 22824
888.542.9467   info@axiosinstitute.org

Library of Congress Cataloging-in-Publication Data

Names: Epstein, Joseph, 1937-
Title: Wind sprints : shorter essays / Joseph Epstein.
Description: Edinburg, VA : Axios Press, [2016] | Includes bibliographical references and index.
Identifiers: LCCN 2015035571 | ISBN 9781604191004 (hardcover)
Classification: LCC PS3555.P6527 A6 2016 | DDC 814/.54--dc23 LC record available at http://lccn.loc.gov/2015035571

For

CLAUDIA ANDERSON

The elegant, highly intelligent woman
in the doorman's coat.

Contents

Introduction

SOME WRITERS ARE DARK and some cheerful, some rely on irony and some do nicely without it, some are prolific and some are costive, some write well enough but feel no pressing need to write and some who when they don't write are filled with self-contempt and a strong feeling of hopelessness. I myself fall into the last category—those writers who feel a desolating sense of uselessness if a few days go by without their writing anything, and writing it for publication.

Any day on which I fail to write at least a few paragraphs is, by my reckoning, a lost day. Should a week go by without my writing something more substantial, therapy may be indicated. Let a month go by—and I don't think it has for many years—you had better hide my razor and any other sharp instruments that happen to be around my apartment. This pressing need to write marks the writing disease in full fever. Like all interesting maladies, it is a disease with no known cause and no known cure.

I have been fortunate, at least up to this point in my writing life, in having a small band of editors who have encouraged my scribbles for their magazines, and hence they provide a regular outlet for my scribbling fever. A few among them prefer, though I hope not from me alone, shorter scribbles, literary sprints rather than marathons. I, though I began writing longish essays, enjoy writing a piece of anywhere from eight hundred to fifteen or so hundred to two thousand words, pieces of the kind that make up the substance of this book.

Writers continue to produce six-hundred page novels and two-volume biographies and, in the case of the Danish writer Karl Ove Kanusgard, continuous autobiographical works running to six and more volumes, but the current tendency in serious as well as purely entertaining writing is for shorter and shorter pieces, books, even lectures and talks. The world has, if not perhaps run out of patience, considerably shortened its attention span. We live in the era of the telephone text, the tweet, the Instagram, and people are inclined to blame them for the jittery nature of contemporary concentration. But this shortening of the attention span set in long before these advances, if advances they be, in technology.

As a university teacher, I sensed years ago that it wouldn't do to deliver fifty-minute-long lectures to my students, lest I gently put them asleep. In an earlier day, the *New Yorker* used to run three- to four-part profiles and pieces even longer on the subjects of geology or wheat, and no one complained. In collecting my own longer essays recently, I noted that some among them run to 10,000 words; today magazines once hospitable to essays of that length set their outer limits at around three to four thousand words. Make it shorter is the watchword of the day. Less is not necessarily more, but less is distinctly what is wanted.

The majority of the pieces in this book were written for the section that appears at the front of the *Weekly Standard* magazine under the rubric of *Casual*. A casual in the *Weekly Standard* can be about almost anything: from an incident in domestic life to a current social trend to a complaint about contemporary nuttiness to a personal obituary for a friend or family member. The only constraints in a *Weekly Standard* casual are length: taking up a single page in the magazine, and allowing room for an often brilliant comic illustration, they run to no more than 825 or so words.

I have been writing these casuals, at the rate of roughly one a month, since not long after the *Weekly Standard* began publication in 1995. Some I have been able to write in two or three hours; some I have struggled over, searching for the right ending, for days. I find great pleasure in composing them. My first audience for these casuals, after myself, has been Claudia Anderson, the editor whom I can count on to catch me out in small yet if let pass embarrassing errors, suggest always useful changes, and to get back to me within half-an-hour or so after my sending a casual to her. She is every scribblers' dream of a perfect editor.

Other of the pieces in this book have appeared in the *Atlantic*, the *Wall Street Journal*, the London *Daily Telegraph*, and elsewhere. Some I wrote at my own inspiration, some were suggested by editors. Turning out pieces quickly, and on request, has allowed me the pleasing illusion that I am, so to say, working press: hat tipped back, cigarette dangling from lower lip, bottle of booze in bottom desk drawer. Doing so also encourages the notion that I am beginning to achieve command of my craft. To keep to the track and field metaphor set out in the title of this book, it is pleasing to think one can compete at different events: sprints (these pieces), the 440 (literary criticism), the mile (longer personal essays), the marathon (book-length essays), pole vault (short stories), and other events in the great decathlon that is literature.

JOSEPH EPSTEIN

The Romanian Air-Force Diet

(1996)

AN ENTRY IN MY JOURNAL of roughly five years ago reads: "I learned that my cholesterol count is a very fine 185. Must carefully cross all streets. It would be a shame to die with so splendid a cholesterol count." On the other hand, it might give my son a talking point at my memorial service. "My father," I can hear him say, "was a man well in control of his life, as witness his cholesterol count of only 185." I hope he will not mention that he often remembers me glancing down upon my plate at yet another boned, skinless chicken breast and looking gloomy at the prospect.

I am the man who coined the phrase—not yet in wide currency—"entrée envy." Entrée envy denotes that moment in a restaurant when the waiter brings out everyone's main course, and you look around the table in the hope of discovering that no one has ordered a more enticing dish than yours. In my case, entrée envy includes the hope that no one's plate has more food piled upon it than mine.

My natural voraciousness conflicts badly with my growing desire for long life. I grew up in Chicago on a diet of corned-beef sandwiches, hot dogs, sausage pizzas, steaks, chops, chopped liver, and rare roast beef, served in a series of restaurants that, if Jane Brody had anything to say about it, would be compelled to have at least two full-time cardiologists on the payroll. I used to go to a restaurant in Skokie, Illinois, called The Original Big Herm's—The Hermitage, as I prefer to think of it—which served an Italian beef-and-sausage combo sandwich with sweet peppers that required three hands and fourteen small paper napkins to manipulate and consume, and then afterward there was the dry-cleaning bill to consider. In youth, my idea of a nightcap was four fingers of salami, a dozen chocolate-chip cookies, and a pint of butter-pecan ice cream, after which I slept the sleep of the just.

I talk a big game but, wretched truth to tell, live rather a small one. To get some numbers on the table, I am 5'7" and weigh 130 pounds. A further confession: I use a Nordic Walk-Fit, treading its inclined track to oblivion for at least half an hour every other day. I am, I suppose, fit as a fiddle, an odd simile since the same cannot be said for most of our contemporary fiddlers, Perlman, Zuckerman, Stern, enviably happy, chubby chappies all.

Each meal poses the question: Is it better to enjoy one's food and die younger or live longer with considerably lessened pleasure? Every day is the Ides of March, and I await the knife—the knife not of the assassin but of the surgeon. I anticipate the procession: chest pain, stress test, angiogram, bloody blade, interior lanyards of arteries, quintuple, septuple bypasses leaving a thorax looking like a highway map around the city of Ypsilanti. Maybe I ought to order the whitefish.

The quickest way to get one's mind off the dangers that food presents for heart attack is to linger on the possibilities of cancer. Much help is provided here by the *New England Journal of Continuous Bad News*, with its regular reports of some new food freshly discovered to bring about cancer of the nasal passages, known to occur in especially high incidence in men under 5'8" and 140 pounds.

With these dour thoughts in mind, I have organized a personal diet I feel I can live with. I call it The Romanian Air-Force Diet. I don't know if Romania even has an air force, but if it does, I feel confident it's likely to be as inefficient and riddled with corruption as dieting itself deserves to be. The Romanian Air-Force Diet has a few simple rules:

1. Avoid dining with vegetarians, terribly earnest dieters, or anyone who tends to confuse the categories of gastronomy and personal virtue.

2. When cheating, don't dabble; eat vast quantities of life-threatening foods. Cheating on a diet, like cheating in love, is unsatisfactory if one goes only halfway; one doesn't, after all, invite a woman up to one's room just to neck.

3. Go a day or two every so often without eating anything that has been declared bad for you. This will give you that inflated sense of goodness that allows you really to plunge when the opportunity to do so next presents itself.

4. Think about the reward of longevity that awaits if you don't eat life-threatening food, longevity that is more or less likely to end in: one of the multiplicity of cancers, dementia, nursing homes with a roommate plainly not of your choice, not many laughs. After thinking about all this, order the cheesecake.

5. Remember that the diet craze is chiefly an American obsession. So far as we know, Europeans, on a much richer diet than ours, seem to be living no less long, while smiling more. Order that third glass of red wine.

6. Establish a clear goal. My own goal is to reach the age of 85, so that, after what will then be a 45-year hiatus, I can once again begin smoking cigarettes.

Buon appetito!

Take A Flying Focus

(1996)

THE WORD "FOCUS" has been driving me bonkers and beyond. I see it every morning all over my *New York Times*, where political candidates inevitably need to "focus" their campaigns; social programs require "focusing"; and US foreign policy, now that the Cold War is long over, must be—ah, but you will have anticipated me—re-focused. This very morning's *Times* carries two fine focus-filled headlines: "Stars Focus Their Power, and the Issue Is Abortion" and "Dying Zapatista Leader Is Focus of Only Accord So Far."

Searching for relief, I pick up the *New Yorker*, where I discover even so stalwart a critic and careful a writer as Arlene Croce, apropos of the directors of the Pacific Northwest Ballet, writing: "One of the ways they did not deviate [from Balanchine] was in their focus on female talent." They're doing it in London, too, for in the current week's *Times Literary Supplement* I read that "One of the great merits of Tadie's biography [of Proust] is the way he brings into focus an image of the young Proust as a formidably curious and active person. . . ."

Not only in the press is everyone focusing away like mad, but athletes, too, are all asquint, trying to obtain a focus. "The main thing," says Michael Jordan, more times than I care to recall, "is to stay focused." I would argue, contra Michael, that nowadays the main thing is to say "focused."

The other day I sat in a meeting with a group of successful and intelligent businessmen. We were there to discuss the future of an institution, of which we are all trustees. Had I a dime for every time the word "focus" came up, I could have paid to fly first-class to this meeting instead of the usual steerage. These guys who, unlike me, have met plenty of payrolls and are, in Henry James's phrase, "seamed all over with the scars of the marketplace" appeared to be certain that what our institution needed was to establish its focus, perhaps narrow its focus, or maybe widen its focus, but, once focused, to keep its focus, yeah brother, amen. I looked down at the notes I took during the meeting, which read: "focus-off, go focus yourself, and take a flying focus."

What is it about the propensity of certain inelegant words to catch on and spread like an upwind California forest fire? The word "impact" had a run of this kind ten or so years ago. Such good old words as "influence" and "effect" were given early retirement, and suddenly everything had an "impact" upon everything else. Then the damn word was converted to a participle, and all things began "impacting" upon every other thing. Then it appeared as a noun, so that things had "impacts" all over the joint. Thus far focus hasn't yet been turned into "focusization," though give it time. Academics have taken to using the hideous plural, "foci," as in "The foci of this paper are three." Foci, for anyone who reads with his ear as well as with his eye, as Robert Frost claimed the best readers do, has all the intrinsic beauty of the word "pinkeye."

Certain words don't just catch on for no reason. They catch on because people feel good saying them. People like to say they are "intrigued" all the time because it makes them sound intriguing. For a time they liked to say "special person," I suppose because it made them seem rather special themselves in being able to discern specialness in others. (Today, of course, one cannot buy a non-satirical greeting card without the word "special" in it; and "special" itself has become a Hallmark word.)

People must also like to say "at this point in time"—which was first brought to us by John Dean and the Watergate crew—because it so felicitously conveys a false precision. People are very hot for the word "process," from peace process on down, and my guess is they feel it makes them subtle thinkers, able to capture the flow and delicate dynamics of political and social change. What, really, could be more intriguing than focusing on the impact of so special a process as watching a language fall apart, at least at this point in time? Few freakin' things.

So let's return the word "focus" to ophthalmology and optics, whence it derives. If you are a heavy user of the word yourself and don't know what you would do without it, may I recommend replacing focus with such solid older words as "concentrate" and "emphasize"? I think you'll find they work well—swell, even. Just relax, stop focusing, kick back, and blur out.

Withholding the Facts of Life

(1996)

I HAVE A NEW GRANDSON with the admirable name of Nicholas Charles Epstein. Nick Charles, moviegoers will happily recall, is the name of the suave detective played by William Powell in the *Thin Man* movies. A friend, when told of my new grandson's name, said she hopes it won't be long before he's sitting around in silk pajamas and a Sulka robe, sipping martinis. I look forward to that day for him, too. I only hope—for reasons I shall go into presently—that my son has the good sense, in fact the decency, never to tell the boy the facts of life.

A few years ago I was sitting in a Chinese restaurant in New York with three intellectual friends, chatting away, as befits members of the chattering class, about this and that, when in the vagaries of conversation the fact arose that none of us, as kids, had been told the facts of life by our fathers. We were all of a certain age—beyond, that is, 50—and hence born in a less psychological time than the one in which we now live. Yet three of the four of us had sons, and we each admitted that we hadn't told them the facts of life either.

To do so, we all agreed, was so awkward as to be quite impossible. I thought about telling my sons the facts of life, but could not imagine taking them off into a room and, illustrated book in hand, starting to talk in a vocabulary that included such words as "pudenda," "labia," and "seminal ejaculation." These boys had been trained in humor, light-irony division, and they would, I fear, have laughed their old man out of the house.

Sex education was no part of my public education. In my high school we had something called hygiene that was part of gym class, in which we were taught—I use the word "taught" very loosely—the evil effects of alcohol and nicotine and the rudiments of first aid. In first aid, we were given large cloth bandages, which we used not for slings or tourniquets but to bind and gag one another in the back of the room. Meanwhile, sex education went on down the hall in print shop, where vocational students produced something called "eight-pagers." These featured familiar comic-book characters in brief pornographic melodramas. "Take it easy, baby," I still recall Moon Mullins more than forty years later exclaiming in an eight-pager, "I wanna use this joy stick again sometime."

I wonder if my father ever considered telling me the facts of life. I rather doubt it. He was a busy man. The only advice I can remember his providing on the subject was his invocation to "Be careful." I believe he told me this one morning on the way out of the house. It was a little unclear what I was to be careful about. Venereal disease, perhaps. Maybe pregnancy. In any case, I didn't have to worry too much about being careful. What I wanted, of course, was to be as un-careful as possible. The problem was that the girls I went out with in high school turned out to be more than careful enough for the both of us.

I can scarcely imagine my father's father telling him the facts of life. He was a scholarly man, interested in Hebrew education in Montreal. He had had ten children, which makes me think that no one had told him about the facts of life either. He was a very elevated gent, who always wore suits with vests, a watch on a gold chain, and a prettily groomed goatee. He dispensed philosophy, not sexology. Difficult—impossible, really—to imagine him instructing his eight sons in the intricacies of female anatomy.

I hope, as I say, that my son will not make the mistake of sitting my grandson down and filling him in on the facts of life. In our family, after all, we have a tradition going back four full generations in which the men have been autodidacts in these matters, and traditions must be preserved.

Perhaps not everyone knows about the Hungarian countess who asks her husband if he has yet told their fifteen-year-old son about "the birds and the bees." The count replies that he has indeed forgot, but will do so forthwith. The next day he is walking through his estate with his son. "You know, Anton," he begins, somewhat tentatively, "the time has come for me to tell you about the birds and the bees." "What about the birds and the bees, Papa?" the boy asks. "Well, Anton," the count continues, "you will recall that two weeks ago when we were walking along this same path we passed two beautiful young peasant girls." "Yes, Papa," says the boy. "Well, my boy," concludes the count, "what we did with those two girls—it seems the birds and the bees do it, too."

It Rings—You Jump

(1997)

THE STORY IS TOLD about Degas dining at the home of his contemporary, the painter Jean Louis Forain, a 19th-century gadget freak who had one of the first telephones in Paris. Forain gleefully showed his phone to the grumpy and greatly unimpressed Degas. During the meal, the telephone rang, and Forain leapt from the table to answer it. "Ah, the telephone," Degas is reported to have remarked, "now I understand: It rings, you jump." Degas was a harsh reactionary, and a pretty good anti-Semite in the bargain, but I am coming to take his line on the subject of the telephone.

Please know that I am a man who has two lines and five phones in a six-room apartment, a car phone, an answering machine, and the ambiguous little service known as "call-waiting." I do not yet walk around with a cell phone in my pocket, and, in what I am sure will be the not-too-distant future, I plan to eschew the possibility of a telephone implant.

I used to be a phone fan. I am old enough to go back to people having what were called "party lines," which weren't the position of the American Communist Party on the Scottsboro boys but the sharing between two or more families of a single telephone line. I remember a man from the phone company coming to our apartment every month to count, with great flourish and rapidity, the nickels we inserted to make our calls.

I recall, too, the mixture of pleasure and economic terror when long distance calls were made or came in. The art of the long-distance call was to say everything that had to be said in under three minutes.

But nowadays the entire phone game, for all its added convenience, seems to have got wildly out of hand. In the past few years, I have had three different area codes: the pleasing 312, the rhythmic 708, and (currently) the hopeless 847. I have yet to master the etiquette of call-waiting. No matter how charming the person I am talking to, when I hear that little call-waiting bleep, I feel I must be off, for my next caller just might be more charming still.

Although I can myself be a telephone schmoozer of major-league quality, sometimes, if a phone conversation goes on too long, I am pleased that the little bleep calls me away. Only on rare occasions, to get rid of a caller even more garrulous than I, have I straight-out lied and said, "Oh, hell, there's my call waiting. I'd better run."

Answering machines allow the strange twist of calling someone you don't wish really to speak with and hoping instead to get his or her answering machine. I get a call every few years from a woman who always begins, "Oh, Joe, you're there!" Is she, I wonder, hoping for my machine and disappointed to get me?

When I see people talking on cell phones in restaurants I find myself mildly ticked off, though I am somehow able to restrain myself from sending the waiter around to their tables with copies of *Walden*. More and more people seem to have cellularized themselves. The other day I was with a man who had to transfer his phone from his right hand to his left to shake hands with a cousin who had to do likewise with his phone. A good friend of mine used to bring his cell phone to lunch with me in a Chinese restaurant so that he could check closing stock market prices. "Ah, Mitter Rosenfield," the owner of the restaurant one day asked him, "how da mahket?"

What comes closest to driving me back to Western Union, not to say the Pony Express, however, are the new telephone menus that greet you with a long list of options, none of which, it is almost certain, is likely to fit your requirements. Banks and other large institutions seem to have this down nicely. The other day I called the *New York Times* to speak to a man named Goldberg. After being put through the menu and tapping a couple of different digits, I was finally instructed to tap in the last name of the person I was trying to reach. It turns out there are 19 people named Goldberg working at the *New York Times*. It's enough to cause a simple country boy to get rid of his touch-tone phone.

At another, much smaller firm, none of the menu items met my needs, so I was directed to tap in o for the operator. Instead of the operator, however, I kept getting the voice-mail of someone named Kathy. Discouraged, I hung up. When the woman I was attempting to reach called me, I explained my trouble in getting through her telephone system. "I tried for the operator," I said, "but I kept getting someone named Kathy." "Oh," the woman said, "she is the operator, but just doesn't like to be called that. It's an identity thing, I guess." Just then I remembered the final convenience of the telephone: the use of my twelve-foot phone cord for strangulation.

My Detested Fellow Pilgrims

(1997)

"CHRIST," THINKS THE WIFE OF HARRY MORGAN, the hero of Hemingway's *To Have and Have Not*, "I could do that all night if a man was built that way." But, of course, a man isn't. Men aren't built other ways as well. "Men don't like complicated food," says one spinsterish character to another in a Barbara Pym novel.

I would like to add another male deficiency. With the exception of those who make their living in and around the places, men don't have much museum stamina—the ability to spend hours contemplating works of art, even the greatest works of art, with anything like the same concentration women seem able to bring to the job.

I base my opinion on a by-no-means random opinion sample: my wife and I. My wife can, in the museological equivalent of Mrs. Harry Morgan's sentiment, go all night. And I? I have just returned from a week in England, where I visited only two museums: the Courtauld in London and the Fitzwilliam in Cambridge. Both have what I think it fair to call small but select collections of painting and sculpture and art objects. Yet in both places I felt my attention wandering. I longed for fresh air. Surrounded by grand works of art, I nonetheless wished to be—elsewhere. I used to say that my museum stamina extended to roughly 90 minutes. I fear it is now under an hour, and shrinking.

The energy for the acquisition of culture seems to be diminishing in me. I used to want to read—and, truth be known, own—all the world's excellent books. This desire has departed, sent packing by the realization that it can't be done. I don't care enough about opera to want to see all the world's operas, though I continue to want to hear as much serious music as possible. I once thought I wanted to see all the world's—or at least all the Western world's—great paintings and sculpture, and I still do, but I shall evidently have to do so in half-hour sessions.

The slightly alarming thought occurs to me that I may already have seen too much art, and thus have become, without my quite knowing it, jaded. Owing to the ease of contemporary travel as well as to the ingenuity of contemporary curators in putting together "super" shows, I have doubtless seen ten times the art that a man of my equivalent level of culture was able to see a century ago.

A few months ago I was in a Park Avenue penthouse once owned by Helena Rubinstein, whose walls were all but papered with Renoirs and other paintings, so little space was there between works. I found myself deeply unmoved and greatly unimpressed. If you have seen one Renoir, as the late and not-too-soon forgotten Spiro Agnew said about slums, you have seen them all. Or so I concluded, as I plowed into my dessert, oblivious to the art all around me. Let the Renoirs go hang, I said to myself, which was what they were already doing. Like I say, jaded.

This past summer I was in Philadelphia and went to the Barnes Foundation, a peculiar museum out on the Main Line. The brilliant accumulation of a most eccentric man, a physician who made his fortune selling an antiseptic called Argyrol, the Barnes Foundation contains 60 Matisses, 69 Cézannes, and 180 Renoirs, and much else that seemed to me dazzling, all mounted in the most higgledy-piggledy fashion. Taken together, it was as pleasing a museum experience as I have had in recent years, though the rooms were awash with art gobblers such as myself.

A break for lunch, then on to the super Cézanne show at the Philadelphia Museum of Art. I had written away for tickets months before. When I arrived, vast lines had already formed, and I joined what Henry James, in a not dissimilar situation, once called "my detested fellow pilgrims." (Since I first encountered it, I have found the phrase immensely useful for dealing with the problem of tourism and snobbery, or the dis-like for people who are all too identical in their interest to you: that they are fellow pilgrims doesn't mean you can't detest them.) Although the Cézanne paintings were splendid, the crowd wasn't, and my stamina, after my session at Dr. Barnes's joint in the morning, was at low ebb. I had, clearly, over-arted myself.

In viewing art, it may be that less is more. It may be, too, that I have to put myself on an art diet. No more super shows; no attempts to do large museums in one fell, or even a triple fell, swoop. Abstinence may be required.

Perhaps a year's lay-off would be helpful. After that I might be able once again to view a Gauguin or a Chagall or a Picasso as something more than very costly wallpaper, which is what these artists' paintings have pretty much become for me. A year off—who can say?—might remove the pink from the cheeks of all those Renoir ladies and put it back in my own.

Numbers on the Brain

(1997)

"THE LITTLE GREY CELLS," says Hercule Poirot, Agatha Christie's great Belgian detective, touching an index finger to his forehead, "ah, Hastings, they are what matter." Those little cells representing our brain power—who today does not worry about losing them at too rapid a clip? As early as their forties, people begin making rueful jokes about having Alzheimer's or Halfheimer's, trying to kid away quite genuine worries about memory loss.

Two possibilities here: First, many of us truly are losing our memories, or, second, we are called upon to remember more than earlier generations and therefore suffer from overload. I was thinking about this the other night when, in a fit of insomnia, I reviewed all the numbers I am responsible for knowing by heart. I have never added them up, but, were I to do so, I should have an impressively large number. My guess is that my situation—or is it a condition?—is not so different from yours.

The first among the numbers I am responsible for is my own telephone number. In fact, in my case, this means four numbers: We have two phones in our apartment (owing to our needing an extra line for the Internet), there is the phone at my office, and there is my cell phone (which I bought as much for security as anything else). Four phone numbers to commit to memory isn't so bad, but then, in the past few years the phone company has seen fit to change our area code from 312 to 708 to 847, which adds to the complication. Then there are the others I seem to have memorized, numbers of relatives, of friends, of business associates I call frequently. These constitute another 15 or so numbers. Add in here, for out-of-towners, their area codes (and, increasingly, their changed area codes).

New numbers have been added to my repertoire in recent years. Begin with the PIN that allows me entry into my checking account at ATM stations. I now live in a building whose inside garage requires a security number that must be tapped into the door lock to get from the garage into the building. The building changes this number from time to time, and I occasionally find myself tapping in the old number. Then there is my email password, which isn't a number but might as well be; roughly every four months I get an email telling me that I have to change this, too.

I long ago memorized my car's license number. I haven't memorized either my checking-account or savings-account numbers, though my bank asks me to write out the number 39000 on all my savings deposits and withdrawals. I have a vault number, which I suppose I don't have to have memorized, but which, for extra credit (what a terrific student!), I memorized anyway. I have nearly memorized my American Express card number, though there is no real need to do so.

I do have the birthdays of children and now grandchildren to remember; so, too, my wedding anniversary. Then there are all the historical dates a supposedly cultured gent is supposed to know: Bastille Day, Lee's surrender to Grant at Appomattox, the two Russian revolutions, the date of the assassination of John F. Kennedy.

Of all the theories of memory, the one I like best—I do not say believe in—is that which compares the memory to a crowded closet, so that when one puts something new in something old must go out. If this were so with numbers, I shouldn't mind getting rid of a fair amount of sports statistics that I acquired when young. I no longer need to know that Hack Wilson, who once drove in 190 RBIs, wore a size 5 shoe; or that Wilt Chamberlain had a lifetime free throw shooting percentage of only 51 percent. But, damn it, I do know these numbers and can't seem to shake them.

Meanwhile, I seem to have lost some fundamental information. Without looking it up, I can no longer tell the number of feet in a mile. I am not sure of the difference between a meter and a yard, though I am fairly sure the former is longer. I sometimes feel lucky to remember the date of the 1832 Reform Bill.

How many of what M. Poirot calls his little grey cells do I use up just trying to retain all these figures in my head? If you know the number, please, do me a favor, keep it to yourself. I haven't room for it anyway.

A Jones for Generalizations

(1997)

I HAVE A TASTE, a craving, a positive jones for generalization. Through words, generalizations give patterns to experience. Such patterns are not only necessary if you want to make any sense out of the world at all; they are inherently pleasing things, or at least to me they are. Making generalizations is, after all, one of the things writers do.

The other day I began Casanova's *History of My Life*, which begins very promisingly, with the old 18th-century roué pronouncing: "Happy or unhappy, life is the only treasure which man possesses, and they who do not love it do not deserve it." That has a nice beat; you can practically dance to it.

I tend to favor generalizations that, along with having a high truth quotient, have a fine rhythm. The danger is that the rhythm can overwhelm the truth. One of my favorite generalizations in which this occurs is one that compares women and translations. It was composed by that prolific hack Anonymous, writing this time in French: "*Si elles sont fidèles elles ne sont pas belles; si elles sont belles elles ne sont pas fidèles.*" ("If they are faithful, they aren't beautiful; if they are beautiful, they aren't faithful.") Brilliant, but, in my experience, truer of translations than of women. A shame; this generalization's thoroughly sexist sentiment only adds a touch of piquancy.

I am also partial to generalizations of nearly insane specificity. At the close of his little book *Berlin*, Jules Laforgue notes: "All Germans—all—have rings." Laforgue is writing about Germany in 1881, and so it is a bit difficult to check him out on this. Still, that second "all"—zing, right between the dashes—nails it.

The riskier the generalization, the more enticing. The British novelist Anthony Powell is the master here. In his novels he regularly uses generalization as part of his descriptions. He writes, for two examples, of "the fumes of unambitious cooking" and of the desire of neurotics "to try to make things as bad for others" as for themselves. Does unambitious cooking give off different fumes than ambitious cooking? Of course. You can smell the disappointment in the food before you eat it. Do neurotics wish to bring us down to their deep valley of unhappiness? Do bears eschew finger bowls?

Only two tests for a generalization: experience and logic. Yet some of the best generalizations seem to defy logic. Anyone—well, almost anyone—can be logical, but to seem illogical and at the same time still be right, now that takes skill. Once again I cite Anthony Powell, who says of a character in one of his novels that he speaks a number of foreign languages with facility, and, as with all people who speak foreign languages so easily, he is fundamentally untrustworthy. Quite nuts, don't you agree? I do, too, except that that statement is true of all the people I have ever met who are able to acquire speaking knowledge of a foreign language quickly. Go figure.

A generalization that fizzles brings its own quiet disappointment. "What a surprise the weather always is when one is drunk," writes John Banville in his new novel *The Untouchable*. I have thought long about this, but find it just doesn't make it, at least not for me. "Americans love singularity," writes Charles Baxter, in one of the essays in *Burning Down the House*, his book on modern fiction. I like the ambitiousness of that: all Americans! But do Americans really love singularity more than, say, Lithuanians or Laplanders? Can't, finally, be ascertained. The ping, the little jolt of recognition, isn't there.

I continue to search for handsome generalizations for my own writing. Whenever possible, I like to make my own pings. I recently came up with this: "The talented can be charming, but there is a firm kernel of selfishness at the core—perhaps it is the core—of most people with talent." Now that I reread it, I think: Not bad. Nice try. Needs a slight tune-up. Bring it back when it has the grandeur and concision of Paul Valéry's "Life is the sum of habits disturbed by a few thoughts."

The other day I hit upon an observation that perhaps will make grist for a decent generalization. Why is it that Major League Baseball, unlike the National Basketball Association or the National Football League, seems to have no players with Muslim names? I haven't yet checked all the major-league rosters, but thus far every serious baseball fan I've queried can't come up with any exceptions. If this holds up, mightn't all sorts of interesting generalizations about the sociology of American sports derive from it? At a minimum, it may allow me to change my old sports simile from "rarer than a Jew in the front four" to "rarer than a third-baseman named Ahmad." Still, as generalizations go, at this stage no cigar. Which is too bad, because all cigar smokers love generalizations.

Out for a Read

(1997)

I HAVE BECOME A MORE ATTENTIVE DRIVER than heretofore. I used to be dreamy, listening to classical music, hoping that some phrase or formulation pertinent to whatever it was I was writing at the moment would pop into my mind. Over the past decade, I have been driving BMWs, and they give a nice feeling of protected enclosure, a perfect atmosphere for such digressive dreaminess.

In this state, the mind floats, recalling odd bits, old anecdotes, scraps of information from the past. Driving along, I not long ago recalled the story I heard about a lecture that C. Wright Mills, the radical sociologist, once gave at Columbia. During the question and answer session after the lecture, a student is supposed to have asked: "Professor Mills, in your lecture you attacked the West and the East, you attacked communism and capitalism, you attacked the family, the church, and organized religion generally, you attacked the past and held out no hope for the future. Professor Mills, is there anything at all you believe in?" Mills replied, "Yes, one thing." The student rejoined, "And what is that?" Mills, pausing briefly, leaned into the microphone and whispered, "German motors."

I, too, believe in German motors and have indeed required them to keep me out of accidents both in my dreamy driving stage and in my new, more attentive phase. I pay no more attention to the road than before, but

I have become very alert to license plates and bumper stickers. As I drive along Chicago streets, and especially on the city's beautiful Outer Drive, my mind is nowadays usually engaged in reading the license plates—the vanity plates—of passing cars. Wit, pretension, unfathomable obscurity is to be found there in profusion. Yesterday I came upon a license plate that read LP FAITH. What can it mean? Does the man still have faith in his old long-play records? Or is Faith his family name, Lawrence and Peter his first and second names? Another car, heading toward me on Sheridan Road, had a license plate that read RR TIES. RR, I assume, stands for railroad. Does this guy have railroad stock? Mystery again, as mysterious as the out-of-state plate—from Pennsylvania—that read MYSTIC 1.

As for pretension, there is a van in this city carrying the license plate GOETHE and a Cadillac with L OPERA. For years I have noted an older, yellow Rolls Royce bearing a plate reading SNOB. Snob, as I learned a year or so ago when I finally saw the car's owner get into it in a downtown parking lot, is a small, older Jewish woman who might be your Aunt Sylvia.

In Illinois, vanity plates cost $75 above the normal charge and an additional $10 above the regular fee every year thereafter. People are apparently willing to pay for their little jokes, which reminds me that a woman who parks in the same garage I do has a plate that reads MISHUGA. Someone in the license-plate division of the Illinois Secretary of State's office must have to serve as censor, for no profanity on license plates is allowed. Censors exist, of course, to be eluded, and so, occasionally, is our man in the license-plate division. The other day a Mercedes passed me on the right whose plate read BATESOME, which is an old Chicago high school slang word, perhaps no longer in use, for the male sexual reproductive unit.

License plates are the big-print version of car literature. Bumper stickers present more of a problem of the kind suggested by the sticker that reads, "If you can read this you are too close." Many have philosophical pretensions: "Question Authority" is by now, I suppose, a golden oldie. "Change the Paradigm" is rather more recondite. One day, in my own neighborhood, I found myself following an ancient Volvo station wagon, driven by an aging hippie, a fuzzy, perfectly Korenesque character, on whose sticker-crowded bumper I noted "Prevent Circumcision." Some sort of deeper vegetarian reasoning, perhaps.

Among bumper stickeristas, dialogue of a sort goes on. Or at least some people seem to feel the need to reply, bumperistically, to earlier stickers. The long-established "Visualize World Peace," the other day I saw answered by a produce firm with "Visualize World Peas." The mawkish "Have You Hugged Your Child Today?" has been met with "Have You Hugged Your Motorcycle Today?" On the subject of religious debate, conducted on a lower level than Cardinal Newman and T. H. Huxley might have done, perhaps the oldest of bumper stickers, "If You Love Jesus, Honk," has been riposted, a friend in Colorado reports, with "If You Are Jesus, Honk."

What does it all mean, this strange need to express oneself through the vehicle, so to say, of one's vehicle? "The truth is out there," written in small white letters on the black T-shirt of a young man who passed me near my apartment only last evening, may be the slogan of the age, but, in this instance, the truth is less likely to set you free than get you in a car wreck.

Please Sam, Don't Play It Again

(1997)

THERE IS A TIME IN LIFE when civilized tact checks out and dangerous candor checks in. Usually the time is late in one's seventies or in one's eighties. The condition seems to afflict men more than women. The grave yawns, further suppression of long repressed views no longer seems to have much point; what the hell, one says, let 'er rip, and, swoosh, the dam bursts with the opinion held back for so many years.

A close friend of mine, who is in the mortgage business, reports this happening one day to his 80-year-old father in the office of an important vice president of a bank with whom they had long done business. Sitting there, exchanging the standard pleasantries, my friend's father suddenly said: "You know, Grossman, you are a pompous ass, and always have been. If you had any courage at all, you wouldn't have wasted your life working for a bank." Cold silence. General embarrassment felt by everyone except my friend's father, who looked as if he had just committed a splendid public service. I asked my friend what he did. "Tried, without success," he said, "to find a place to hide my eyes."

Precocious in a number of ways, I worry about whether I myself may be hitting the stage of dangerous candor well ahead of schedule.

The other day, standing near one of the cash registers in a large book store, a young man, maybe 23 or 24, with a mustache and goatee, asked the clerk if she knew where he might find a copy of *Naked Lunch* by William Burroughs. He asked in a tentative way, as if he had only learned about the book himself in the past few days. Ever the helpful guide, I stepped forth.

"Excuse me," I said, "but I don't think you need to read that book. It's full of ugliness, stupid violence, odious philosophy, and other dreary stuff. Take my advice: Save your money and take a pass on this loathsome tome."

He looked at me as if to say, "Who is this guy?" Quite right, too. Who was I to offer such opinionation? I wished I had a badge showing him that I had published four books of literary criticism, but I'm fairly certain it wouldn't have helped. In any case, he turned away, pretending I wasn't there, obvious kook that I was, and waited for the clerk, now consulting her computer, to tell him in which section of the store he might find *Naked Lunch*. So much for vigilante literary criticism in our day.

As I recollect this emotion in tranquility, I recognize that what triggered my outburst is my sense that there is, looming even as I write, a revived appreciation of the Beat generation as precursors of the 1960s in all its (presumably) glorious tumult. Seeing signs of this everywhere causes my blood to boil, my bile to bubble, my brain to burn.

The recent obituary press for Allen Ginsberg was just the beginning. Ginsberg, whose verse today remains largely unreadable and whose every political utterance was wrong, died with the kind of praise that might have seemed heavy-handed had it been applied to Walt Whitman (to whom, inevitably, he was compared). The only good story I've ever heard about Allen Ginsberg had to do with his one night receiving an award from some cultural organization presented to him by a man named Henry Geldzhaler. The audience was clearly carriage trade, men in black tie, women in blue-rinse hairdo. By way of introduction, Geldzhaler thanked his good friend Allen for his courage in coming out of the closet so early and so fearlessly, and went on about this at great, sentimental length. When Ginsberg finally spoke, he thanked Geldzhaler, but said that, after this introduction, he wasn't clear whether he was being given this award for poetry or fellatio, though he used the much rougher word.

More. In a course in prose style I teach at Northwestern University, three students in a class of 25 brought in sentences from Jack Kerouac as examples of prose they much admire. Only the greatest exertion of self-control allowed me not to ask them why they thought so well of such dreck.

A new wave of '60s envy looks to be upon us—an emotion that entails the strong feeling among the young that they missed something momentous, that great days have passed them by. Worship of the Beats, I sense, is a way of getting back to the '60s (even if the Beats' own beginning was the '50s). The Beats' literary legacy is just below negligible, their politics chiefly about druggery and buggery. Why, some 40 years later, is this still not clear to all?

The threatened reappearance of the '60s is what has put me in my current mood of dangerous candor. Should I happen upon you in a bookstore inquiring about a Hermann Hesse novel or in the street carrying an old Kurt Vonnegut book, please don't take it personally if I start telling you off.

Overbooked

(1997)

IT'S HAPPENED AGAIN, I won't say against my best efforts, but there it is, or rather there they are, books all over the joint with my bookmarks in them. Do I have more than 20 books going at once? I am a bit nervous about counting them, for they are all-too-vivid a sign of the lack of organization, control, order in my life.

This isn't going to be a very sexy piece, so let's begin in the bedroom. On my night table, I note that I have seven books going. The one I'm reading most intently just now—that is, at the rate of 10 or 12 pages a night—is *His Father's Son: The Life of Randolph Churchill* by Winston S. Churchill, the son of Randolph. I am a sucker for all things Churchillian—I recently bought from a firm in Vermont a blue bow tie with small white polka dots advertised as the Blenheim—and this book doesn't disappoint. When Randolph marries, his father remarks that "all you need to be married is champagne, a double bed and a box of cigars." When the young Randolph loses his third parliamentary election, Noel Coward remarks, "I am so very fond of Randolph; he is so unspoiled by failure." Irresistible.

The Churchill biography is 510 pages but is easily surpassed by Albert Cohen's *Belle du Seigneur*, an English translation (despite its title) of a novel of 974 pages. I seem to have read 354 of them; it's rich stuff, and I hope to get back to it for another hundred or so pages, then perhaps drop it again for another few months. It is brilliant, though in a satirical vein. But brilliance, perhaps, like confession, is best when brief. Mae West was wrong in saying that one can't get too much of a good thing.

Cigarettes Are Sublime by Richard Klein is the other non-fiction on my night table. I had heard good things about it, and, as a serious ex-smoker, I wanted at least to read about smoking since I can no longer do it. But the book is too much summary of what others have written about smoking, and thus left me more let down than the last cigarette of a long night in the bad old days.

As for my other night table books, I see that I've got to chapter 16 of Nabokov's *Transparent Things*, which is far enough to realize that this book isn't first-class Nabokov, but probably worth finishing anyhow. I note that I've read 366 of 500 pages of *The Portrait of a Lady*. I hadn't read this great novel for more than 20 years, and when the movie version of it came out not long ago, I thought I'd reread the novel instead. It's as great as I remembered, and the only reason I haven't finished it is that I've found myself too tired of late to stay up with James, the reading of whom requires one's greatest alertness. I've made little progress with John O'Hara's *The Big Laugh*, which I bought purely on the basis of a single blurb from Fran Leibowitz: "The greatest Hollywood novel ever written." The O'Hara may be better as a bathroom book, and I may soon transfer it there.

Just now I have two bathroom books going. One is *St. Petersburg* by Solomon Volkov, a cultural history of a great city and another bulky tome (598 pages). The other is *Dinner with Persephone* by Patricia Storace, which is about Miss Storace's year in Athens. Bathroom books should be readable in short takes, and both these books are. I read the better part of Anthony Powell's *A Dance to the Music of Time* in the bathroom. I consider it no insult to an author to read him in the House of Commons, as the Welsh used to call it. An editor once invited me to write for his magazine, saying he couldn't pay me anything, but he wanted me to know that the magazine was intensely read. "They take it to the john," he said.

Other tenth- and quarter- and half-read books are spread throughout my apartment. Allow me a quick inventory: *The End of the Line*, the final memoir of Richard Cobb, the richly idiosyncratic historian of France, a book I ordered from England; a collection of what turn out to be quite brutal stories by Angela Carter; a biography of Walter Winchell by Neal Gabler; the art criticism of Henry McBride; *Six Screenplays* by Robert Riskin; the poems of Wislawa Szymborska; some letters from Janet Flanner, the *New Yorker's* one-time Paris correspondent; a book on the 1950s by Peter Vansittart; *Light Years*, a novel by James Salter, whose impressionistic writing I find especially readable on sleepless nights; and the most recent collection of essays by Isaiah Berlin.

What's going on here? None of this makes any sense. It causes me to look up, for maybe the eighth time, the word desultory. Its first definition is "marked by lack of definite plan, regularity, or purpose." Its second definition is "not connected with the main subject."

Plan, regularity, purpose? The main subject? I wonder if I could get back to you a little later on all that—once I've had the chance to finish a few of these books.

Bio-Degradable

(1998)

I RECENTLY PICKED UP A COLLECTION OF POEMS by a writer named Ann Carson and was happily struck by the simplicity of the biographical note—or bio, as it's called in the trade—written about the author. In its fine stark entirety, it reads: "Ann Carson lives in Canada." Not even the province in which she lives is given. Miss Carson, it turns out, has written other books, but these, too, get no mention. I am greatly impressed by Miss Carson's absence of vanity, her refusal to attach the prestige of institutions or previous achievements to herself in this splendidly economical bio. "Ann Carson lives in Canada."—a lean, clean writing machine, Miss Carson.

Styles in the writing of bios have changed over the years. When I first began noticing them, bios for male writers, especially novelists, on the dustjackets of their books tended to emphasize the sweaty, heavy-breathing masculine. "Jack Clark," such a bio might run, "has been a lumberjack, dishwasher, magician's assistant, short-order cook, and Marine officer in the Korean War. *The Onyx Urinal* is his fourth novel." Often there would be an accompanying photograph of the manly Mr. Clark in corduroy jacket, a pipe clenched in his square and rather pompous jaw.

Bios for female authors in those days tended to be homier. They might mention a woman writer's interest in gardening, or sailing in the summer, or having three daughters all of whose names begin with the letter Q.

Today I am sure this treatment would be considered vicious sexism. But now an even cozier, more odious change is on the way. The change is to use first names in a writer's bio.

In the "NB" column in the January 2, 1998, *Times Literary Supplement*, it is reported that Lucy Ellmann's new novel has a bio with sentences that begin, "Lucy was born in Illinois. . . . Lucy's first novel was published in 1988. . . . Lucy now lives in Hampshire." Nicknames or diminutive names, surely, will be next. "Chip's [or Muffin's] new novel is his [her] first since. . . ."

As every editor who has had to write them knows, sometimes there is a paucity of things to say about a writer in his bio, particularly a young writer, and so a bit of padding has to be done. The *New York Times Book Review* used to solve this problem by calling a reviewer about whom there must have been nothing else to say "an observer of the contemporary scene," which always seemed to me rather a pathetic thing to be. Any self-respecting writer, I used to think, wants a few italics in his bio, the titles of books he's written or the names of magazines to which he contributes.

When I was young, I remember, I used to feel what I can only call bio-envy at reading, in the *Commentary* of the late fifties, the heavily italic-laden bio of F. R. Leavis or Sidney Hook. Once an editor myself, I would occasionally describe a contributor in his bio as "distinguished," but I used this sparingly, saving it for writers of the stature of Jacques Barzun or Arnaldo Momigliano. For myself, I am thankful for never having been "an observer of the contemporary scene"; and I would like to go out without ever being described in a bio as a "national treasure." Don't ask me why, but you never want to be called a national treasure.

To fill in their bios, writers will occasionally promote things that they have in the works: "He is currently at work on a trilogy of novels about the founding of Levittown."; or, "His series of connected screenplays about the life of Buddha is nearing completion." This is all very well, except that these "works in the works" frequently never get done. A writer named Wallace Markfield used for years to have it noted in his bio that he was working on his first novel; and he did, after a decade or so, eventually complete it. (The book turned out to be a comic gem called *To An Early Grave*.) The critic James Wolcott, some while ago, began to advertise himself in his bios in

Vanity Fair as working on a novel. So far the novel hasn't materialized. No hurry, kid, I have other things around the house to read in the meantime.

I once claimed, in a bit of bio padding, that I was working on a novel, which resulted in my getting letters from two publishers asking to look at it. Unfortunately, I hadn't written a page of it. (The only thing he disliked about the writing life, Peter De Vries used to say, was the paperwork.) If two publishers were interested in that vague entity, "a novel," what might have been the reaction had I baited my trap with something a great deal more enticing: "He is currently at work on a book on double-jointed courtesans of the belle epoque."? When younger and not yet married, it occurs to me only now, I might have used my bios to promote dates: "Joseph Epstein, a smooth dancer and an easy conversationalist, is an observer of the contemporary scene, but not too close an observer." Damn. Another opportunity lost.

Neologism, the Name of My Desire

(1998)

ONE AMONG MY SEVERAL IMMODEST AMBITIONS is to leave behind a word or two of my own invention before departing the planet. I want to leave a precise word, a useful word, a good word, a word that absorbs a sweet bit of truth. Neologism, not socialism, is the name of my desire.

The only person I have ever met who accomplished this was the late journalist Henry Fairlie, who is credited with the word "Establishment," usually used with a capital E. Fairlie didn't quite invent the word—there had long been an Established Church in England, and hence a Church Establishment—but he made it immensely more widespread by applying it to power structures generally. So successful was this that the very word "Establishment" became one of the shibboleth words of the 1960s.

My dear friend Edward Shils didn't, so far as I know, invent any words, but used language as well and to as brilliant comic effect as anyone I have known. By appropriate little twists and turns—"tweakings," the kids in computer science might call them—he came awfully close to the golden land of Neologia. I once described an acquaintance to him as rat-faced. "Yes," Edward replied, with his great adjective-making power, "he is rather rodential." He could also put a fine ironic spin on words, so that, for example, when I began to call what was formerly the University of Illinois Circle Campus (the campus in Chicago) "Vicious Circle," Edward took it a fine stride further and never referred to it as other than "Ol' Vish." Linguistically imaginative as he was, he forgot, alas, to invent any new words.

New words do get invented all the time. Technological and medical invention requires them. So, too, does social science. But they seem to me, for the most part, the wrong words, or at least not very amusing words. I was in a meeting recently where, in connection with a discussion of policy, two new and fairly empty portmanteau words were introduced. The first was *intermestic*, meant to show the connection, in our brave new world, between the international and the domestic. The other was *glocal*, meant to show the connection between the global and the local. Neither seems to me to deserve a cigar, and glocal has serious problems, not only in being difficult to pronounce but in sounding awfully like cloacal. ("It's alimentary, my dear Watson.")

I've invented three words that I thought might have had a shot at staying in the language. I've used all three in my own writing, but thus far only one looks to have a chance. My first gallant entry was not a word but the phrase *youth drag*, meant to describe all those older players—guys with sad gray pony tails or motorcycle jackets, women in their seventies in miniskirts—who try to pass themselves off as young in spirit through their garb. Youth drag—I sent it up the flagpole, as they used to say in the advertising business, but no one saluted.

I tried again with *Bayarrea*, my word for too much talk about the delights of living in or near San Francisco. Much of this talk is about good living, food and wine, and fine views—and I find I soon get a snootful of it, which makes me want to heave sun-dried tomatoes at anyone engaging in it. The word may have been too specialized, too particular, like W. C. Fields's neologism squeemudgeon for a director who calls actors down for early-morning appearances but doesn't use them until later in the day. As for Bayarrea, I did what I could: I put it out on the doorstep, but the cat refused to lick it up.

My one possible contender is virtucrat, a word I first used in an article in the *New York Times Magazine* and which I have actually seen others use in print. George Will has used it, with generous attribution, in his column in the *Washington Post*. A few years ago, *Newsweek* actually had a cover story under the rubric "The Virtuecrats." They added the letter e, gave me no credit for it, and used the word not to mean, as I did, those people whose politics lend them the fine sense of elation that only false virtue makes possible, but instead those people—William Bennett and Lynne Cheney chief among them—who were stressing the need for virtue in the conduct of public and private life.

I've pushed hard for virtucrat over the years, but, somehow, I don't think it is going to make it either.

I may have to settle for inventing a phrase. Thus far, I can think of only two phrases that I can lay some claim to having invented, and both are really spinoffs. One is "In for a penny, in for a pounding"; and the other is "You live and you yearn." I've used both in print, and even more in conversation, but so far no call from the editor of the excellent *Brewer's Dictionary of Phrase and Fable*. Depressing. What do you have to do around here to become immortal, anyway?

A New Nobel

(1998)

HAS ANYONE THE AREA CODE FOR STOCKHOLM? I need to call the Nobel Prize Committee, fast. I've got an idea. It's time they added a new prize—one that, in my view, ought to have been instituted from the beginning of the Nobel Prizes in 1901.

It's always been a bit capricious, the way the Nobel Prizes are set up. Prizes for physics and chemistry, for example, but not for mathematics, on which so many advances in physics and chemistry absolutely depend. Why a Nobel Prize in literature but none in music or visual art? Why a Nobel at all in economics, that most contentious and tendentious of subjects? And speaking of contentious and tendentious, what about the Nobel Peace Prize? When a friend of mine once asked Tom Lehrer why he no longer wrote brilliant comic songs, Lehrer told him that, ever since Henry Kissinger won the Nobel Prize, nothing seemed funny anymore.

The new prize I would like to see instituted by the Nobel Committee is one for marriage. As the Peace Prize is meant to encourage peace-making in a war-ridden world, so might the Nobel Prize for Marriage do likewise for matrimony, an institution that, all the statistics on divorce make plain, is itself in great peril. A Nobel Prize for Marriage would have, as they say in advertising, a fine reinforcing effect.

As for the grounds on which the prize ought to be given, these, it seems to me, are fairly self-evident. The prize ought to be given for sticking it out, for perseverance, for endurance, for—to capture it in a single, if hyphenated, word—long-suffering. (Not that, in marriage, short-suffering is any picnic. Consider the first five of the six wives of Henry VIII, short-sufferers all.)

To launch the Nobel for marriage, it might be best to begin by giving out a few prizes posthumously, to great long-suffering husbands and wives of the past. Countess Tolstoy, surely, ought to be an early winner, having had to listen to all the count's utopian guff, to make sure that he didn't give away the copyrights to *Anna Karenina* and *War and Peace*, to compose so-called fair copies of his many novels and religious tracts, and then, at the very end, to be put to the humiliation of his publicly deserting her in the hope of dying alone.

What about Prince Albert, whose lot could not have been an easy one? Victoria, true enough, wrote gushily in her diary about her German husband, especially after his death. But I keep thinking of that famous phrase of hers, "We are not amused!" Difficult to imagine she never used it on him. Did she ever use it to devastating effect, one wonders, in the bedroom? Put the prince consort down as a Nobel contender. Then there is the marriage of the Carlyles, Thomas and Jane, of whom Tennyson said, "By any other arrangement, four people would have been unhappy instead of two."

Does Leonard Woolf qualify? Virginia Woolf, in her snobbery, was not above remarking on her husband's Jewishness, establishing her social superiority over him. With the most fragile of egos, she required vast attention, solicitation, endless reassurance, all of which Leonard supplied. She was, in the end, of course insane. Did Leonard know this to begin with? And, knowing it, oughtn't he, of all people, to have been afraid of Virginia Woolf? The man has to be reckoned a candidate for the prize.

I always thought that Lionel Trilling deserved a Nobel for marriage. Diana Trilling, his wife, combined neuroses with aggression. And now it turns out that we can add resentment to the mix. In her memoirs, all written after Lionel's death, Diana portrayed her husband as a depressive, a drinker, a snob, a gloom-spreader of the highest power. In the course of doing so, she would seem to have made herself out as deserving of a Nobel for marriage. But my sense is that it was Lionel and not Diana who deserved the prize.

As for the other Diana, the late princess, ought she or her husband to be up for a Nobel? Diana had Camilla and that frightful *mishpacha*, the Windsors, to deal with—no small packet of aggravation there. Charlie, though, took on himself all the problems attendant upon acquiring a younger, somewhat air-headed wife, with eating disorders, wretched taste in men, and the rest. It was a marriage made in hell, which is always rich soil for the Nobel Prize for Marriage, and therefore a tough call.

But a piece of cake, if not exactly wedding cake, next to the Clintons. Everyone now knows what Hillary has had to put up with in Bill. Not yet known is what Bill has had to put up with from Hillary, but, even discounting the charmless speculations of Dick Morris (whose own wife, surely, is another, a very strong, candidate for a prize), it cannot be minor. No, in the First Couple we have the possibility for the first shared prize: two people, each put on the earth to make the other suffer, lengthily and intensely. Impressive stuff.

Let's hear it for our laureates.

Gotcha

(1998)

WHEREIN LIES THE PLEASURE of catching someone out in an error? It gives one, no doubt, that little touch of self-congratulatory superiority that helps one get through another day. It's finest when one catches an enemy or adversary in an error, but catching a person one is quite neutral about will supply the necessary *frisson*—and, in a pinch, catching even a friend will do.

I was reading the *New Yorker*, a magazine known for its careful fact checking, when, in the middle of a piece by George Plimpton about a man who wished to send himself aloft in a chair held up by helium balloons, I came across the following sentence:

> The original idea was that Larry would rise to approximately a hundred feet above the Van Deusen house and hold there, tethered by a length of rope wrapped around a friend's car—a 1962 Chevrolet Bonneville, down on the lawn—to get his bearings and to check everything out before moving on.

Chevrolet, I remembered, never had a model called a Bonneville. Pontiac did. The smallness of the error, combined with the fact that perhaps few people under 50 would know it was an error, greatly cheered me. That it had got by the famous *New Yorker* fact checkers put the cherry on top.

Even better, only last evening, reading along in a brief profile in my college alumni magazine, I encountered a professor of rather extravagant intellectual pretensions quoted as saying: "He [Tolstoy] said people are either hedgehogs or foxes. Hedgehogs ball around and hold onto one idea, while foxes run from one to another. Well, I'm a fox."

"Kiddo," I muttered to myself, "you are more like a turkey. Tolstoy never said any such thing. The Greek poet Archilochus said it." (He actually said: "The fox knows many things, but the hedgehog knows one big thing.") The quotation is correctly given in the first sentence of Isaiah Berlin's famous essay on Tolstoy, "The Hedgehog and the Fox." The beauty of this little screw-up is that you can see just how it was made.

It reminded me of one of the recent mayors of my city who, on the Fourth of July, announced that he was pleased to be at Grant Park where the Chicago Symphony Orchestra was getting ready to play, as it does every year, Tchaikovsky's Twelfth. He meant, of course, Tchaikovsky's *1812 Overture*. Further piquancy was added by his pronunciation of the composer's name as if it were Chick Kowsky.

I thought about writing an amusing, only mildly malevolent letter to the editor of my alumni magazine about the hedgehog-and-fox *faux pas*. I could have written directly to the professor, pointing out his little mistake, adding that my own motives here went no further than wishing to prevent him from lapsing into the same error again. Or I could have written to him, on a typewriter and under a pseudonym, informing him that, since he wishes to come off as a pretentious horse's ass, he ought to get his facts straight.

I decided to do nothing. My problem is that I have had too many errors of my own, in various degrees of viciousness, pointed out to me. In a national magazine, I once referred to the Danish Kierkegaard as "that gloomy Swede," which enlivened my mail for weeks. (If you want lots and lots of mail, I am told, just misquote Shakespeare in print.)

More intricate but graver in its implications, in the *Times Literary Supplement* I once assigned an anti-Semitic remark—"Literature is what one Jew plagiarizes from another"—to the man who quoted it (Alfred Pfoser) instead of to the man who in fact made it (Herman Bielohlawek). Mr. Pfoser, an Austrian, wrote a quite properly angry letter to the editor;

I, in turn, wrote an abject apology for my error. I normally don't mind apologies, but those abject ones are hell to make.

I get a fair number of letters in which readers point out typographical errors in my books. They do so, I believe, good-heartedly, thinking that I can arrange to correct them in future editions. I get kindly and otherwise generous letters from time to time from a dermatologist who cannot resist, usually in a postscript, pointing out some error in grammar, spelling, or semantics in some piece I wrote years before. I finally had to write to inform him that this habit causes me to open his otherwise charming letters with a heavy heart.

I not long ago had a splendidly complimentary letter about something I had written, and it, too, was followed by a correction or two, to which the man appended a postscript, asking whether I had ever noted the tendency of people, even when praising, to want to point out errors. I wrote back to say that yes, actually, I had.

It's all, I suppose, as Dostoyevsky said about the owl and the pussycat: The owl gets one big thing wrong and the pussycat several small ones. Keep those cards and letters coming.

Literary Tippling

(1998)

TIPPLER I TAKE TO BE SOMEONE who boozes in small quantities but regularly, stopping just short of actual drunkenness. Your tippler tends to operate on the sly, if not the sneak. He ducks into a bar for a quick one. He keeps a bottle in the office, maybe a flask in the car. The thought of being cut off makes him ill. He can't, poor devil, help himself. He needs his drink.

Exchange the word drink for the word print, and I am, as I have long known myself to be, a classic tippler, literary division. I do not—cannot—leave the house without reading material. Living on the sixth floor of an eight-story building, I usually manage to get in a paragraph on the elevator. I read in bank and supermarket lines. I read during television commercials, and, in the battle between telly and text, seven times out of ten text wins. When driving alone, I keep a magazine or book on the empty seat next to me. I get in a paragraph or two at a stoplight and am usually interrupted by a honking—and slightly ticked—fellow driver.

The families of literary tipplers, like those of alcoholics, do not have it easy. All they can do is go along with the program. Too often they turn into literary tipplers themselves. My wife, a woman of great natural refinement and hence lovely manners, I notice has begun to read with her breakfast and, sometimes, lunch. My own tippling over the years, which cannot have been easy for her, has driven her to tippling on her own.

Naturally, I tipple in the bathroom. Practicing silence, exile, and cunning of a kind perhaps never dreamed of by the young Stephen Dedalus, I recently read the better part of *A Portrait of the Artist as a Young Man* there, not to speak of innumerable long magazine pieces. "I am sitting in the smallest room in my house," wrote the German composer Max Reger to a hostile critic. "I have your review before me. It will soon be behind me."

My literary tippling often but not always entails prose I do not need to read with the keenest concentration. I don't tipple with things I have to make notes upon or that I shall myself be writing about. Some genres are more tipple-worthy than others: letters, diaries, novels for which one hasn't the highest expectations. I can also tipple with fairly serious books: I mentioned Joyce, and my current bathroom book is Suetonius's *Twelve Caesars*. Poetry, however, doesn't tipple well. Nor does philosophy. Movie criticism makes a nice tipple.

At its most intense as a pure addiction, literary tippling takes the form of reading while walking. In Evanston, Illinois, where I live, one of the local sights is the writer Garry Wills walking the streets, his nose in a book or magazine. An acquaintance of mine claims this is a very great affectation—that it can't really be done. He is wrong; it can be done. I know because I have done it, and on quiet streets sometimes do it still. The great historian Macaulay is said to have been able to read while threading his way through the most crowded London streets. A good man, Macaulay.

What is the meaning behind this need—this insistent and incessant need—for taking in all this print? So much to read, so little time, might be one answer, though it would not be mine. Reading beats actual experience, might be another, though here I seem to recall Wallace Stevens writing to a young poet that he ought to read less and think more—probably good advice, even though I myself read it and didn't think it up on my own.

No, my pleasure in almost perpetual reading has to do with the love of the sentence as a tranquilizer. Something there is about an elegantly turned sentence or a well-made paragraph that calms me and makes me feel that order is possible and life is, against all strong evidence to the contrary, perhaps just possibly manageable. So pleasing is this sensation that

I feel, like the alcoholic tippler, that I really must have another one—and as soon as possible.

You wouldn't by any chance, happen to have a spare paragraph on you, would you, pal?

Great Talk

(1998)

O N APRIL 11, 1819, John Keats, on his way to meet his publisher, ran into one of his former medical-school teachers, Joseph Green, who introduced him to his companion, Samuel Taylor Coleridge, one of the famous talkers of his day. Sad to report, one of the means to becoming a famous talker is being an infamous nonlistener. On this count, too, Coleridge qualified. Keats joined the two men for a two-mile walk toward Highgate, during which time he failed to get in a word edge- or any other which-wise. In a letter to his brother George in America, Keats wrote: "I heard his voice as he came toward me—I heard it as he moved away—I heard it all the interval—if it may be called so."

Many of the world's great talkers have been men whose minds were overstuffed with erudition and general information. It is as if they must find a way to release it, lest they burst from sheer overload. My own list of great talkers includes Samuel Johnson, Coleridge, Lord Macaulay, and, closer to our own day, Andre Malraux, Edmund Wilson, Sir Isaiah Berlin, and the art historian Meyer Schapiro. A man I know reports that Schapiro once stopped him in the street and detained him for a little more than forty minutes with an uninterrupted one-way flow of talk, before remarking, as they parted, "I can't tell you how much I enjoyed our conversation."

The great talker is generally also a fast talker. Samuel Johnson didn't need to talk so quickly, but then, in Boswell, he had the perfect straight man—a human appliance no great talker should be without—feeding him subjects and eliciting opinions. Macaulay was described by a contemporary as a talking book, but, unlike a book, he couldn't be shut up.

Edmund Wilson, no un-Sanfordized violet himself, wrote of Andre Malraux's conversational style that "he likes to talk on his feet and jump around. His expositions are punctuated by *bon*! and *bien*!, nailing the point just made before rushing on to the next step." One imagines Wilson himself as more sedentary, more relentless, at the head of a table, pouring out booze and talk, neither with a light hand. Everyone who knew him speaks of the speed of Isaiah Berlin's talk, a veritable Gatling gun—rat-a-tat-tat—of chat.

The only great talker I have known well, my late friend Edward Shils, also had a speedy and unhesitant delivery. Well into his eighties, he never needed to stop to recall a name or the title of a book. He spoke fast for the obvious reason that he wanted to get everything in—or, rather, out. Like the few truly great scholars I have known, Edward had a powerful memory. One thing led to another and that to yet another. Lest he monologize through the night, I had to learn the not always gentle art of breaking-in. He never upbraided me for doing so.

The combination of powerful memory and high intelligence makes for the rapid speech of the great talkers: Their minds, so well stocked, work quickly. Information must be released speedily, for more is on the way. They tend to be polymathic, knowing not one but several things well. Great talkers are tolerable—and at their best, of course, much more than tolerable— because they really do have great talk, comprising wide knowledge, deep insight, brilliant formulation, wit, and impressive anecdotes.

Great talkers may already be a thing of the past. Men with the intellectual power, conversational style, and social energy to set up as great talkers may soon become rarer than authentic 1960s heroes. There are still some amusing talkers, whose whimsy and original point of view confer pure pleasure. But amusing talkers are vastly out-numbered by bores— if I may shift abruptly into diatribe here—heavy-breathing, preening, world-class bores.

I dined out twice last week and ran into two such bores. The first was a dirty-joke-telling bore. Mixed company causing him to lose not a step, he gurgitated an endless stream of Viagra, lawyer, and fellatio jokes. He seemed to take a certain pleasure in making everyone else at the table edgy: the bore melting neatly into the boor. He at least seemed greatly to approve of his own performance.

My other bore was of the academic variety, a man to whom, it soon became plain, one could tell nothing. He was the evening's designated teller. He pretended to listen, but one sensed that he really was only waiting—waiting to continue his own endless campaign to bring us the real lowdown, the truth, the gospel, his version.

One's heart went out to his wife, who revivified the term "long-suffering." No doubt he returned home and, in bed, before turning out the light, remarked to her that the other people at dinner had seemed to him, on balance, rather dull.

Confident bores give talk, even great talk, a bad name. Should Dan Aykroyd ever choose to make a movie called Borebusters, he'd have my eight bucks in a flash.

Stop and Smell the Prose

(1999)

REading along in *My Name Escapes Me*, the diary of Alec Guinness, that most subtle and modest of modern actors, I came across Sir Alec's avowal of his shame at being a slow reader. In his mid-eighties, he notes: "I think it stems (apart from slowness of the brain) from the fact that when I come across dialogue in a novel I can't resist treating it as the text of a play and acting it out, with significant pauses and all." Ah, thought I, *mon semblable*, soul brother, as one slow reader to another, I greet you with a salute after the long descent to the bottom of the page.

Alec Guinness's would be an excellent name to include among the charter members of a Slow Reading Program I have long wanted to start. V. S. Naipaul, who claims one cannot really hope to comprehend more than twenty pages of a serious book in a single day's reading, would make another good member. Robert Frost, were he alive, would be a third. Frost thought fast readers were the poorest readers. They were what he called "eye readers," whereas the best readers read with both the ear and eye, attentive to the rhythms and sounds—and, I would add, even the shape—of the words.

The Slow Reading Program would be a natural counter to the Evelyn Wood Speed Reading program, about which, it is good to report, these days one hears less and less. ("Sped read my way through *Ulysses* last night," the old joke about speed reading has it. "A book about Dublin, isn't is?") Speed reading has its place, especially given the bumf that makes up most of our daily reading diet. I use my own version of it to blast through the *New York Times* in fewer than thirty minutes every morning—obits, cultural chit chat, Clinton scandalogy, letters, Miss Scornucopia (as I think of the columnist Maureen Dowd)—over and out, never breathing heavily.

Otherwise I am a slow reader, almost a slow-motion reader. As Sir Alec has the actor's tic in reading, so I long ago acquired the editor's tic. I tend to do a check for error of most of what I read, and I not infrequently find myself, mentally, editing if not rewriting even quite good writers.

In John Updike's recent *Bech at Bay*, for example, I felt the following sentence, somehow, needed work: "They had gone, to the same summer camp and private school, come out at the same country-club cotillion, and dropped out of the same year of Oberlin, to marry their respective Republican husbands." Syntactically, is the placement of "Oberlin" correct; or would it be better to have said "dropped out of Oberlin the same year"? I took two or three minutes to think about this without reaching a firm conclusion.

My reading is slowed down even further by my being a writer. Most reasonably scrupulous people reading a sentence take the following quick inventory: Was it clear? Correct? Precise? Interesting? If they have the least esthetic sense, they will perhaps add, Beautiful? But the writer, when confronted with an interesting or beautiful sentence, must ask two other questions: First, How was it done? Second, How, properly camouflaged, might its magic be stolen for my own writing? This, too, can slow a fellow down.

I also sometimes copy out sentences from my reading, wise or amusing or merely striking ones. "Education is atmosphere," writes Thomas Mann in his diary. "Since happiness is impossible in this world," writes Flaubert in a letter, "we must strive for serenity." I am a sucker for this sort of thing. I lose more time looking up words whose meanings have slipped away from me. The definitions of certain words won't stay in my mind: fungible, for instance, or irrefragable. Yet even without these minor afflictions—the editor's tic, the writer's tic—slow reading seems to me a good idea, at least when the reading matter is stylish and substantial. Like any sensual experience, it ought to be attended to in a carefully paced and thoughtful way.

In the *Confessions*, St. Augustine has left one of the few prose portraits of a man reading, the man being the excellent Ambrose, bishop of Milan, a potent teacher and one of the most penetrating readers of his day. "When he read," Augustine writes, "his eyes traveled over the page and his heart sought out the sense. . . . No one was bidden to approach him, nor was it his custom to require that visitors be announced, but when we came to see him we often saw him reading, and always to himself; and after we had sat in long silence, unwilling to interrupt a work on which he was so intent, we would depart again."

Reading is that rare satisfaction, a pleasure that is deep yet happily harmless. While we are doing it we are taken out of ourselves, in the company of people usually smarter than we, building up no bad cholesterol. Why rush it? Why miss the music? Read on—but slowly, friend, slowly.

Can't Take That Away from Me

(1999)

THE CULTURAL LITERACY MONSTER first raised its ignorant head for me some fifteen or so years ago, when I gave a lecture to several hundred freshmen at Denison University in Granville, Ohio. It was a lecture no doubt too heavily peppered with proper names, and even as I gassed away, I saw that what I was saying was sailing right over the heads of my youthful audience. One sentence ran: "We see this phenomenon in the journals of the Goncourt brothers, taken over by Edmond after the death of Jules in 1870." A faculty member, commiserating with me afterwards, had a good chortle over this. "You have to understand," he said, "it's not that they've never heard of the Goncourt brothers, which of course they haven't, but that they've never heard of 1870."

Professors love to tell stories about the amusingly ample blank spots in their students' knowledge. ("This kid thought that the greatest achievement of the Ottoman Empire was the invention of the footstool.") As a quondam university teacher who was never much of a student himself, I try not to add to the stock of such stories. But I must say that I was amazed, appalled, aghast, and a little saddened to learn last week, from a contemporary, that two highly intelligent young editors with whom she works had no notion that the phrase "the last time I saw Paris" comes from the Jerome Kern song of the title. Everybody in the West, I thought, knew that. I can hear Maurice Chevalier—no, fellas, he didn't play goalie for the Montreal Canadiens in the 1940s—singing the next phrase, "her heart was young and gay," and feel pity for those who can't. How, I ask myself, can anyone not know that lovely, lilting song? Sacrebloodybleu!

One of the things that separate generations is the popular culture that each has grown up with. As a boy who grew up listening to radio, I was perfectly content to leave much of early television culture to Beaver. Which may explain why a show such as *The Simpsons* has never, to quote The Doors, "light[ed] my fire." I long ago made the decision to retain my pristine ignorance of Bruce Springsteen—and it hasn't taken much character on my part never to have wavered on this point. I know only slightly more about Billy Joel—and am, in any case, too old to go changing—whose real last name, I have long suspicioned, must be something like Hochberg.

Most of the songs that play in my head were written before I was born or when I was a child. Cultivated folk of the generations before my own carried reams of poetry in their heads. My generation carries instead the tunes and lyrics of the Brothers Gershwin, Jerome Kern, Cole Porter, Irving Berlin, Richard Rodgers, Lorenz Hart, Oscar Hammerstein, Sammy Kahn, Irving Caesar, Yip Harburg, and a few others. And they continue to give pleasure.

The great difference between the popular culture under which I grew up and that of subsequent generations is that—apart from comic books and certain radio shows—popular culture had not, in my time (the 1940s and '50s), been divided into youth and grown-up culture. A national popular culture existed, shared by all. The middle and late 1960s and the advent of rock 'n' roll changed all that—and changed it for the worse. Popular culture is richer when the audience for it is large and non-exclusionary.

My own self-imposed exclusion from popular music came soon after the early Beatles and Simon and Garfunkel. After this, I pretty much lost interest in contemporary music; and the super-sensitive sentimentality of Paul Simon's songs was already pushing it. Far from wishing to keep up, I went backwards, hugely enjoying some American songs from well before my time. Most amusing of all, I discovered, Louis Armstrong, Jack Teagarden, and Louis Prima sang songs with the proper spirit of wit, parody, and mockery of show business. With some laboriousness, I typed out the lyrics of some of these songs—"Stars Fell on Alabama," "Softly as in a Morning Sunrise," "I've Got a Right to Sing the Blues," "Just a Gigolo," and the never-popular "I Guess I'll Get the Papers and Go Home"— and attempted to commit them to memory, for the simple satisfaction of rehearsing them in the shower.

Knowing the same songs is one of the things that draws one closer to people. I don't believe I could live with a woman who didn't know, say, "A Foggy Day (in London Town)," "Tenderly," and "They Can't Take That Away from Me." Unthinkable. Bruce Johnston, who I am reliably informed sang with but was not an original member of the Beach Boys, composed a song with the memorable line, "I write the songs that make the young girls cry." I myself wouldn't care to do that. If it's all the same— and it isn't—I much prefer to sing the songs that make the older girls smile.

A Sad Case of Mono

(1999)

MY PITY GOES OUT to the monolingual, those poor devils trapped in the prison of a single language, their linguistic horizons occluded by knowing only the language of their own country. My pity, I had better quickly insert, is self-pity, for I am such a prisoner—a lifer, it is beginning to become clear.

I have dabbled in other languages, but with nothing approaching success. I speak just enough Yiddish to fool the Gentiles but not enough to speak to real Jews. My spoken French—I can read the language with the help of dictionaries—still falls a mite short of being despicable.

Once, on a trip to Italy, I believed I was getting the hang of that nation's glorious, sonorous language. Yet it turned out that I'd learned it just well enough to board the wrong train from Florence to Milan, causing me to miss my bus and have to pay a cab driver the equivalent of $80 to get me to the airport, during which we spoke to each other about Frank Sinatra in execrable French.

Many years ago, I tried to teach myself Russian. I carried a little Russian-English grammar about with me, which finally didn't help me learn the language but caused one of my co-workers to start the rumor that I was a Communist. On another occasion, I enrolled in a course in Ancient Greek, and found myself spending something like four hours a day (including classroom time) on it, and had to drop out.

Only the other day I saw, in a bin of 50-cent sale books at my local library, a handsome German edition of the plays of Gerhart Hauptmann, and wondered if I oughtn't to buy it. I would acquire a German grammar, flash cards, the rest of the language-learning apparatus. I had some free time—why not fill it up by failing to learn yet another new language?

The one language I am extremely glad not to have to attempt to learn is English, which provides, or so it seems to me, almost no help whatsoever by way of clear rules about syntax and a vocabulary full of homonyms, nonsensical idioms, and other words and constructions that have no connection that I can see with logic. Foreigners who seem easily to master it impress me greatly.

Every so often I get a German exchange student in one of my classes and am astonished at how adept he or she is in writing and, often, speaking English. One such student, whose written was much better than her spoken English, early caught on to the phrase "No problem"—the American all-purpose equivalent of the Italian "Prego"—and was beating it into the ground with overuse. Listening to her answer "No problem" to nearly everything I had said to her one day in my office, I thought that any immigrant to America today can probably survive with mastery of only three idioms: (1) No problem, (2) Go screw yourself, and (3) Have a nice day.

To be in a land where you do not speak the language can be an unnerving, even a harrowing feeling. I have felt it, in a modified form, when I was a tourist in Turkey and in the cities of the Dalmatian coast. Without a common language, one feels almost of another species, rather as if one didn't have prehensile thumbs. As a writer, I often wonder how I would have fared if I had been born in a country whose politics forced me into exile and, with it, into another language. Not very well, I suspect.

My aged father recently returned from the hospital, requiring someone to watch him full time. I hired a woman from Ukraine, in (I should guess) her late forties, with a most intelligent face, a refined manner, and either not enough English to say "no problem" or too much sense not to recognize that the English language is for her a momentous problem. Her last name is a bit of barbed wire, chiefly comprising the letters, i, y, and u, which I have not attempted to pronounce even to myself. I call her by her first name, Erica; she does not call me by any name at all, and she calls my father "Mister." Her business card has after her name the initials MD and PhD, which she is, in Ukraine. Here, with no English, she is reduced to tending to the needs of my father, and she does it with a kindliness that has touched both him and me.

They spend days together with perhaps two hundred words of English between them. While he naps, she sits in his kitchen, listening to classical music and working on an English-Russian grammar book, at which she seems not to be making much progress. He is aware of her devotion, and returns it with affection. He calls her, in a sturdy old American cliché, "a diamond in the rough." Neither ever tells the other to "have a nice day," but they seem to get through the weeks without language quite nicely anyhow.

Political Shopping

(1999)

OWING TO THE FACT that my normal five o'clock shadow had of late begun to appear around noon, three weeks ago I bought a new safety razor, a Schick, with a red handle, called, in good pseudo-macho manner, the Protector. This may not at first seem significant, but my buying a Schick razor marks a political Rubicon I have taken a very long time to cross. Twenty years ago I would never have bought a Schick razor, or a Schick anything else—no careful political shopper with even a lingering shred of liberalism would.

Political shopping involves boycotting those products whose owners have politics opposed to one's own and are thus, ipso facto, injurious to the common weal. Robert Welch, owner years ago of a candy company, was a major figure in the strongly right-wing organization known as the John Birch Society, and this required my taking a pass on all Welch products, which I did. Other products were similarly taboo. I don't recall exactly what Schick's political connection was, but it was generally agreed that he, too, was dangerously on the right, which for those of us then on the left meant on the wrong, side of things, and so *verboten*.

Today a political shopper is more often exposed to the products of the left than those of the right. The politics of the hippie generation of the 1960s always tended toward retailing—and now, through retailing, they have arrived, in a smashing big way. One sees it in all the New Age products, in the outdoor-clothing madness, in the Holistic medicine vitamin-and-herbal biz, in the healthy-eating gastronomic *putsch*.

Hippie living at upper-bourgeois prices has infiltrated the quotidian life of the so-called educated classes. It's the way we live now. If you don't like it, there's nothing for it but to take the hemlock, perhaps nicely chopped in a salad of arugula, watercress, cilantro, basil, maybe just a touch of tarragon, lightly dressed with balsamic vinegar and canola oil, and commit low-cal, no saturated fat, absolutely cholesterol-free suicide.

Apart from the hemlock, all the ingredients for this salad and many more are available in a supermarket that opened across from our apartment a year or so ago. I go into it regularly, even brandish a card at the check-out that allows me a 10 percent discount on items from the frozen food and dairy sections. I pass on the grains and on the vegetable cocktail bar, also on the trout jerky and sprouts, and instead buy Granny Smith apples (never organic ones—that organic stuff will kill you), milk, cereal, flavored yogurt, treating the place as if it were a convenience store.

Even though I have been there hundreds of times, each time I enter I feel myself a tourist—but on another planet. One enters at the produce section, yet the fauna is much more striking than the flora. Among the customers, pallid desiccation seems the dominant look, causing me to think of the joke about the new anorexic restaurant that's opened in town—the one that's closed twenty-four hours a day. Many mangy male gray ponytails are in evidence; the women seem to favor hats that have what I think of as Laplander chic. One day I saw a woman there wearing a lush mink coat. I told her to depart the premises promptly before they killed her.

Most people are eager for longevity, but these people, I feel, go in for it a good bit more ardently than the rest of us. I judge this by the intensity that they bring to their shopping; it is an intensity that precludes even perfunctory good manners: excuse me; thank you; no, please, you go ahead—this sort of thing goes unanswered here. Men pick out their green beans one at a time. The herbal section draws big crowds. Massage is offered on the premises. No one smiles. This is a serious place.

So serious that, at the check-out portals, there is no *National Enquirer*, no *Star* or *Globe*, but instead *Mothering, Mother Earth News, Mother*

Jones, Organic Gardening, Yoga Journal, Veggie Life, Herb Quarterly, Natural Cat, Sage Woman, and *Out!* Many of the checkers are refugees from that strange country, the Sixties, or the sons and daughters of refugees. Not a few nose rings, flowing manes, dreadlocks among the employees, a high proportion of whom, I note from their standing out behind the store in coldest winter, smoke cigarettes. The other day I saw one of the checkers, a chubby young woman in her twenties, walking away from the store eating what looked suspiciously like a Twinkie. My heart warmed. Go for it, kid!

Meanwhile, my right-wing Schick razor seems to have pushed my five-o'clock shadow two or three hours forward, so that now I don't seem to need a second shave until two or three in the afternoon. As for what caused my beard suddenly to grow less quickly, your guess is as good as mine. Do you suppose it's the yogurt?

The High Miles Club

(1999)

I AM A BIT SURPRISED that Miles isn't showing up more nowadays as a name for boys. Not that it has ever been a wildly popular name. The only boy I knew named Miles was Miles Uritz, with whom I went to grammar school and whose father was a bookie working out of a cigar stand in a building on Lake Street in the Loop. But the reason I am surprised that there are few boys named Miles is that so many people these days have miles on the mind. By miles, I mean, of course, air miles, which, as every middle-class person knows, allow us to fly for nothing or upgrade our seating on plane trips.

I think about air miles a fair amount myself. A few weeks ago, for the first time, I actually used 40,000, of the nearly 60,000 I have acquired over a very long period, to travel Business class instead of Economy from Chicago to San Francisco and back for two. Owing to a minor ailment, I wasn't able to partake of the booze, and the chicken dish going out was dry and the pork dish on the return was inedible. Still, for a total of nearly eight hours, I was, and felt myself, upgraded: "carriage folk," as Max Beerbohm called Malcolm Muggeridge when he showed up at Beerbohm's Rapallo home in a broken-down buggy driven by a swayback horse wearing a hat.

Yet my thinking about miles is negligible compared with that of several people I know, including members of my family, who seem to think about them almost perpetually. My son, who travels a lot on business, is a member of just about every airport and car rental club going. With his mileage and various upgrade coupons, he is rarely reduced to flying Economy—that is, with the rabble of passengers among whom is to be found his father. I have a sister-in-law so relentless at arranging mileage deals I used to say that, if you called American Airlines, you would get a phone menu that, after directing you to press One for queries about domestic flights, Two for queries about international flights, and Three for those about arrival and departure times, ended by announcing, "And if you are Louise Epstein, please press Four, and we'll be with you in a minute, Louise."

A few years ago, I read about a man who rented five cars at low prices in a single day because the bonus air mileage he received for the car rentals allowed him to end up saving money on a flight from New York to the Coast. Some people are able to add handsomely to their mileage by arranging on a flight, say, from Kansas City to Milwaukee, a brief stop and change of plane in Hong Kong or the South Pole. One of the real disadvantages of being president of the United States is that, flying exclusively on Air Force One, you get no mileage. Four—possibly eight—years without air miles! Unless this is soon changed, how can we expect to get first-rate people to run for the office?

I seem to have no aptitude for adding to my own miles. My last two trips to Europe were made on Swiss Air and KLM, neither of which added a single city block to my mileage account. I have turned down other opportunities. MCI recently sent me an invitation to betray my current long-distance phone service, for which it offered me 7,000 free miles and yet more miles each month for the calls I make. For a $60 fee, various credit card companies have offered to get me miles for everything I charge. Lots of people, I have discovered, pay all their bills, grocery and medical included, by credit card, thus piling up the miles.

Miles, it's the name of the game—it's what it's all about. Should the economy ever crash, miles may one day become the basic unit of economic exchange. ("What a beautiful engagement ring! I understand he paid a cool quarter-of-a-million miles for it.") Mileage cannot be passed on from generation; you cannot, in other words, leave your miles to your family, which, though cruel, has a right feeling of even-handed distributive justice about it. Otherwise some families might fly for nothing forever. Still, what death could be more untimely than that of someone who pegs out with a couple of hundred thousand or so miles in his account, leaving his poor widow for the rest of her days to fly Economy.

Not long ago, at my father's funeral it was suggested that, if I paid the costs—roughly $11,000—with a credit card, I could get miles: 11,000 big (or, should I say long?) ones. Fortunately, I don't have a credit card that gives me mileage. Had I the right credit card, would I have done it? Would I have been ready to fly, in effect, over my father's dead body? Better not to think about it, especially when I, no doubt like you, have "miles to go before I sleep."

Rolodeath

(1999)

I OWN A ROLODEX THAT I INHERITED—took, really—from someone dear to me after his death, nearly a decade ago. It is black, plastic, hump-backed like a 1942 Plymouth coupe, and made by a firm called Zephyr American Corp. I don't know how long ago it was manufactured, but it already has that lovely obsolescent look about it, strictly BC (Before Computers), as if it came from the age of adding and mimeograph machines. I must have used an address book before I acquired it, and now I use a computer to record all my email addresses. I should probably toss it out, but find I cannot bring myself to do so. Even though barely a decade in my possession, it contains too much of my history.

I wish I could tell you that it is a power Rolodex—powerful in the sense of recording many of the great names of the past half century. Mine does have a few good names—mostly of writers, editors, and intellectuals, with one famous painter—but no really knock-out, this-one-will-get-your-attention-Howard names. The Rolodex of a man or woman who has lived any sort of public life ought to provide a preview, or coming attraction, for the rich index of his or her autobiography. Mine, I fear, disappoints. No cards for Cary Grant, Mme. Chiang Kai-shek, Sir Georg Solti, Picasso's last wife, Paul Valéry's grandson, though it does have a card for one English lord (alas, a mere life peer), one United States senator, and one person who has had a sex-change operation.

In fact, my Rolodex has cards for a number of people whose names I do not myself recall: ephemeral sub-editors of the *New York Times Book Review*, men who install stereo equipment, a shop (long defunct) that sold juggling equipment. As a quondam teacher, I have too many students in this Rolodex. I'm not sure why I bothered to record their names and phone numbers, since no one is more difficult to reach by phone than students, that transient class which is also, in my view, easily the world's most unreliable ethnic group.

This Rolodex reveals a man no longer in the flush or rush of youth. The names of several doctors are in it: cardiologists, rheumatologists, internists, dentists, but not yet (touch wood) any oncologist or shrink. (Physicians heal thyselves, is my motto, but, if you don't mind, heal me first.) There are too many nice people whom I haven't called in several years, a harsh reminder that I am not the most constant of friends, and a few with whom I have had what now begin to look like permanent fallings-out.

I have the former office phone number of a man with the perfectly appropriate name of Hope who used to work for the MacArthur Foundation. Whenever he left his name on my answering machine, it got my blood running. He has long since left the job, and hope of large windfalls, as well as of a number of other things, has run out for me.

What most impresses me, though, is the number of subtractions, through death, that a run through the cards of my Rolodex shows. Henry James somewhere says that, when one reaches 50, someone one knows dies every day. Not quite statistically true, at least in my case, though as a habitual reader of the *New York Times* obituary pages, I am regularly brought up short by how many people seem to be taking the ten-count that I have either known directly or know about through their connection with friends of mine.

In my own Rolodex, kept over less than ten years, seventeen cards ought to be withdrawn, or at least have black borders drawn around them, to mark the decease of old friends, strong acquaintances, family. I haven't the heart to do either. Quite the reverse, I rather like to come upon these names, allowing memories of these people to wash over me. For some reason, my Rolodex often opens to the card on which is written the name

Erich Heller, the continental literacy critic, who was hard of hearing and who used inevitably to answer, in his strong Teutonic accent, my phone calls by saying: "Denk you, denk you, very vell—und you?" when in fact I hadn't asked him how he was but had merely announced my name.

One card in particular I cannot remove has the name of a young girl, written in green ink in her own small and elegant hand, a student of mathematics, brilliant and pretty, who turned up in her early twenties a manic-depressive and who, one night, unable to discern any charm in the world whatsoever, leaped from a ninth-story window to her death.

I have no plans ever to write an autobiography. My letters, though great in number, tend to be laconic and not very intimate. But I wonder if there mightn't be a publisher out there wishing to bring out my unexpurgated Rolodex. Interested parties are invited to write to my agent, Mr. Georges Borchardt, Georges Borchardt Inc., 136 E. 57th St., New York, NY 10022.

Confessions of a
Craven Materialist

(1999)

I DON'T EXPECT EVER to write anything that will gain me less sympathy than this, so I might as well get right to it: I bought a new car this week, rather a grand car, I'm afraid. It's a Jaguar, something called the S-Type sedan, with the smaller of the two engines offered, and I would like everyone to know that I chose not to have the telephone that comes with a system that allows one to turn on the radio, adjust the temperature, and do other things in the car by voice; I also eschewed the computer-screen navigational system, though I did order a CD player, and they seem to have thrown in heated seats without my asking for them. The car's color is sapphire blue and its interior is ivory white with something called Connolly leather. It drives the way a butterfly floats—effortlessly, lyrically.

Why, it seems fair for you to ask, is this man telling us this? To incur our envy, possibly hatred? No, he is telling it because, sad to report, he is ever so slightly edgy about owning so elegant a machine. A crass materialist is one thing, a craven materialist—yo, friends, that's me—quite another. The day I bought this car I thought perhaps I ought to keep it covered in our building's garage during the day, taking it out only late at night, driving it wearing sunglasses and a slouch hat through sleeping suburban neighborhoods.

My dear mother would be ashamed of my feelings. Her own taste ran to fancy cars, the fancier the better. Her last car was a maroon Cadillac Seville, with a boxy back, produced in the middle 1980s, very swank. Driving with her once at O'Hare Airport, we were caught in heavy traffic, and I suggested that she put her arm out, in the hope that another driver would give her a break and let her into the moving line of traffic. "With a car like this," my mother said, "no one gives you a break. They assume that you've already had your break."

In the short stories I have written, whenever I have characters in cars, I always specify what make of car it is that they are driving, designating not only the make (Buick, Chrysler, BMW), but the series within the make (Park Avenue, New Yorker, 328i). The kind of car a person drives tells you a fair amount about that person's wealth, aesthetic inclinations, his interest in status, and his actual status. It isn't the last word about the person, but it isn't, I believe, a bad first or second word.

One of the reasons I am nervous about my new Jaguar is that I don't want any word out about me at all. The extreme form my vanity takes is, above all, not to wish to appear vain. I was not reared but later educated to take a dim view of such small but obvious delights as a swell car gives. If one were an intellectual—yo, me again—one was supposed to be above such things. I recall being with Saul Bellow in the garage of his rather expensive building in Hyde Park, the neighborhood of the University of Chicago, where I noted a large number of dismal cars: dreary Dodges, tired Buicks, Volvos that had seen better days. "Ah," said Bellow, "Academic motors," his point being that it was of course considered unseemly for academics to drive expensive cars.

Until the past decade or so, my own program with cars was that of a strict reverse snobbery. When I could afford to buy new cars, I deliberately chose dull ones: first Chevys, then Oldsmobiles, middle of the line both. At some point, Oldsmobile jumped its prices up roughly five grand, and I said to myself that for another few thousand dollars I could get a small BMW. Which I did. And then, after four years or so, I stepped things up to the next size BMW. I became a leather-seat man. Two BMWs later, ready to buy a fourth, I saw this new Jaguar S-Type (the English not only pronounce but put heavy emphasis on that U in Jaguar), whose grill reminded me of the lovely, old bright red Jag that the actor John Thaw drives in the English television show *Inspector Morse*.

My worry is that the sheer elegance of the machine will draw attention to me, its owner, who may not be up to a comparison with his car. In the less than full week I have thus far owned it, people have stopped me on the street to ask how it drives. A number of pedestrians have pointed at the car as I have driven past. People stare at it. On the South Side, a young guy in a beater looked over at me at a stop-light in a way that made the word askance all too vivid. I accelerated, leaving him at the light, astew in his combined envy and contempt.

"On second thought," as W. C. Fields is alleged to have said on his deathbed, "screw 'em." I have taken the cure. My new motto comes from a bumper sticker I saw the other day, which read: "Get In! Sit Down! Shut up! Hold On!"

Hats Off

(1999)

I HOPE IT ISN'T TOO EARLY to begin predictions for the new millennium, because I have a small, modest, even parochial one to make, and here it is: Before the first decade of our third millennium, a Jewish high holiday service will be led by a rabbi—I do not say an Orthodox rabbi—wearing a baseball cap. Whether that cap will be worn backwards, I cannot predict. It will, though, be one-size-fits-all.

This vision came to me roughly a month ago when I saw a man—in his middle sixties, I would guess—come out of a nearby synagogue in a dark suit. In his hand was the small velvet bag in which Jews keep their prayer shawl, prayer book, and sometimes phylacteries, and atop his head sat the black cap with white lettering of the Chicago White Sox. In his look I noted not the least glint of humor, playfulness, irony. It was evidently his standard headgear, part of his regular get-up.

I own a few baseball caps myself—one a replica of the old Gas House Gang St. Louis Cardinals of the 1930s, another with Stanford written across the top, a third with the name of the town of Stonington, Connecticut—but I tend not to wear them on religious holidays, at funerals, to circumcisions, or while lecturing at the Johns Hopkins University School of Medicine. I wear them, in fact, infrequently and mostly to keep off the sun, for I find that they do not increase my natural beauty.

I do not know exactly when baseball caps went ubiquitous, as they now are, but I do recall my first memory of one being worn indoors. I was teaching a course in a seminar room in the library at Northwestern University when a student entered wearing the black cap with orange logo of the San Francisco Giants. "Mr. O'Brien," I said, "that hat, are you perchance wearing it for religious reasons?" When he allowed that he wasn't, I gently suggested he remove it, which he did, without argument or obvious resentment. Not long after, when I suggested another student remove his baseball cap, he did so, displaying a fierce bramble of hair, and told me that he was wearing it because he hadn't a chance to shampoo that morning and was having what we should now call, in our nicely nuanced psychological age, "a bad hair day."

I continued to ask male students to remove their baseball caps in my classrooms. But when female students began wearing them, with their ponytails sticking out the back, I knew the game was up. All that is left for me now is occasional sniping. When recently teaching a class on irony, I said that the ironic method entails saying one thing and meaning another, and offered as an example that "I find nothing so invigorating as teaching about the meaning of evil in the novels of Joseph Conrad to a group of students wearing their baseball caps backwards." No baseball caps showed up in that class for another three weeks.

A salesman at Brooks Brothers once told me, with great chagrin, that he had a 26-year-old grandson who didn't know how to tie a necktie. Many more people, much older than 26, apparently are unaware that men aren't supposed to wear hats indoors, let alone that they used to be doffed or at least tipped outdoors in the presence of women. Anyone who does remember such things can only have exulted at that scene in *The Sopranos*, the HBO soap opera, when Tony Soprano, dining in a respectable Italian restaurant, goes up to a youngish man wearing a baseball cap and suggests that, if he doesn't remove it, he will at the very least maim him. I myself could, as we say, "identify."

The spread of the baseball cap is part of the large trend toward the informalization of American clothing. A friend who has a men's shop tells me that nowadays his only customers for suits are lawyers. I myself buy fewer suits. I still teach in a necktie, for I like the distance it puts between the students and me. I also prefer to fly wearing a necktie, perhaps because, should the plane go down, I wouldn't want to meet my Maker underdressed. Yet, great stiffo that I am, I nonetheless find myself more and more lapsing into the informal. Not long ago I proposed to a friend, quite as formal as I in these matters, that, at dinner that evening with our wives, we forgo wearing neckties. A longish pause ensued. "Audacious," he said.

Joe DiMaggio was perhaps the only man of intrinsic elegance whose looks were not diminished by a baseball cap. Impossible to imagine Cary Grant, Fred Astaire, or Noel Coward in one. Coward it was who once discovered himself, in a business suit, at a party in which every other man in the room was in white tie and tails. "Please," he said, "I don't want anyone to apologize for overdressing." I don't believe he could have quite brought that off had he been wearing the cap of the Arizona Diamondbacks.

A Taxonomy of Bores

(1999)

MELANCHOLY HAS ITS ROBERT BURTON (author of *The Anatomy of Melancholy*), Snobbery has its Thackeray (author of *The Book of Snobs*), but Boredom, a much more capacious field than either, has no one similar. Boredom needs help. It awaits its Linnaeus, the great taxonomist, someone to classify the bores now walking the earth in such plenitude.

Many are the kinds of bores, even though in the end their dark and dampening effect is everywhere the same. Some days, it seems, they all call me. I am a magnet for bores. I have large ears that stick out, and quite possibly bores sense they make excellent receptacles into which to pour their soporific verbal potions. I have been told that I am a good listener. I am not sure that this is true, but at least in conversation I tend not to break in, which is perhaps a weakness. Whatever the case, bores find me, and go about their charmless work, leaving me, some days, feeling quite as assailed by bores as Henry James was said to be assailed by perceptions.

As to how they bore me, let me count only a few of the ways. I have among my acquaintanceship a number of what I call Solipsistic Bores. These are bores who, whatever the subject up for discussion, turn it to themselves. "I have to be tested for liver cancer," you announce. "I think I may have dandruff," the Solipsistic Bore replies, a worried look upon his

face. Solipsistic Bores suffer—or, more likely, they enjoy—the Coperni-
can Complex: They believe that the solar system rotates around them.
Lucky fellows, self-love in them never goes unrequited.

I do a fairly brisk commerce with what I think of as Good-Parent Bores.
The Good-Parent Bore makes plain how much time he is investing in his
children. He can be counted on, before long, to point out how splendidly
it's paying off by bragging about these children. One of my Good-Parent
Bores bragged for years about his first-born son's athletic prowess. He
had a great arm, he could hit anything that was thrown at him, he was
headed for the Show for sure. When this didn't pan out—didn't really
come close to panning out—my Good-Parent Bore switched attention
to his second son, a boy who is an astonishment of intellectual precocity,
it seems. Took calculus in pre-school, broke the bank on the SATs, read
Proust at 14. My heart goes out to these children—and also to myself for
having to listen to these too proud parents.

I run into more than my share of Professor's-Disease Bores. In what
other job but teaching, it has been said, can a man talk for 50 minutes
straight without being interrupted by his wife? The Professor's-Disease
Bores do not so much converse as deliver lectures. They have had a cap-
tive audience for too long. They mistake their small power over students
for charm. They think everyone must want to know the five reasons for
the Renaissance. Village explainers all, may they acquire white-lung disease from being around so much chalk.

Failed-Wit Bores are among the most difficult with whom I have to
deal. These are fellows—they are always men, never women—who seem
to believe that I go in for their turgid irony. A Failed-Wit Bore I run into
on the street likes to fill me in on his latest aphorisms. I would provide an
example, but I have blocked them all out. What I cannot block out is the
look of deep self-approval that accompanies his delivery of these inept
verbal contraptions. As I hear him out, I fear the franchise-donut-like
glaze that must be in my eyes.

My-Brilliant-Career Bores like to tell me how very well they are doing.
Onward and upward, that's how it always goes for them, bought the right
stock, sold the house just as the market peaked, yo, the Viagra is doing
its job, amazing stuff. They don't so much talk as make progress reports.

Often, at the end of these reports, they might query, "Everything okay with you?" I sometimes want to reply, "Not bad, if only I can just get this boa constrictor off my neck," since they aren't really listening anyway.

Of Single-Subject Bores, I encounter Obsessed-with-Clinton Bores, But-Is-It-Good-for-the-Jews? Bores, Diet-and-Fitness Bores, the Past-Was-Infinitely-Better-than-the-Present Bores—Johnny One Notes all, who somehow can't even manage to play that one note on key. You don't know what a sinking feeling is—but then perhaps you do—when, just as you're about to sit down to dinner, the phone rings, you pick it up, and, through the static of his car phone, you hear your Obsessed-with-Clinton Bore begin the next installment of his unending tirade on our Saintly Billy.

I could go on—my happy bores do—to mention the Grievance-Collector Bores, the Let-Me-Tell-You-My-Dreams Bores, the Freudian Bores, and Slipping-Standards or Decline-and-Fall Bores, ah so many fine bores, and so little—damn these bores—so very little time.

Send in the Clowns

(1999)

EVERY SATURDAY MORNING, from early June until late October, I go to the farmer's market in our town and feel as if I have stepped into a Koren cartoon. People look a bit shaggy, strange, rather as if they were themselves animated fruits and vegetables. While there, I myself sometimes feel a bit arugulish (funny, I don't look arugulish. Ka-boom). Something there is about fresh produce amassed in vast quantities that brings out the goofiness in people.

Nearly everyone at this market seems in a state of dishabille. Lots of feet in sandals, women without makeup, men unshaved, hair flying. Baseball hats are ubiquitous. And T-shirts everywhere, T-shirts asking that we save this or that animal, or testifying that one has been in this or that bicycle or marathon race, or commemorating one's trip to Paris, Key West, Vegas, or Martha's Vineyard.

Across the back of the T-shirt of a young man I note eyeing the portobello mushrooms is written "Tofutown." Not that I am dying to go there—I exceeded this year's tofu budget by January 2—but nothing on the shirt reveals where Tofutown might be. (Boulder, Colorado, it turns out.) A woman of a certain age wears a T-shirt that reads, from top to bottom, "I am Woman, I am Invincible . . . I am Tired." An older dude wears a T-shirt bearing the legend "Whatever . . ." A man with a substantial alderman (as they used to call pot bellies in Chicago) wears a black T-shirt with white cursive lettering that reads, "Bad Spellers of the World—Untie." On the yellow shirt of a pudgy, smiling woman is written the question: "Does Anal Compulsive Need a Hyphen?" Only when it's an adjective, Toots, I want to tell her, now go home and change that silly shirt.

Having a playful yet, I like to think, quietly malicious mind, I cannot help inventing a few T-shirt messages of my own. Here is a sampler: "Hard Rock Cafe—Purgatorio"; "Bet You Don't Know Me," with "Federal Witness Protection Program" on the back; "CCCP—The Party's Over"; "I Survived The Joyce Carol Oates Literary Oeuvre"; and "Space for Rent, Owner Has Forgone All Attempts at Original Wit." I don't see any surefire big sellers here, but you never know.

What is the meaning of people walking around in these T-shirts? It is one thing to wear one's heart on one's sleeve, quite another to wear someone else's humor on one's chest. Has it to do with that central casting director within each of us, who instructs us on how to present ourselves to the world? All these people in their comic T-shirts have clearly answered the call to send in the clowns.

There ought—to devise a less than fresh transition—to be clowns, but I'm not sure they ought to appear in T-shirts with other people's jokey lines written on them. A quick inventory of my own shirt drawer reveals a sweatshirt with Dartmouth on it, another with Illinois written in Hebrew, and yet a third with "Runyon's Travelling All-Stars"—Runyon's being a bar in Minneapolis owned by a friend—which advises, in small print, on its back: "There is no free lunch."

My T-shirts tend to carry straight-forward messages: "Evanston Public Library," "98.7 WMFT Chicago's Classical Music Station," "Chicago Joe's" (a restaurant and sports bar), and (this sent to me by a friend who was in the OSS during World War II) "Central Intelligence Agency." I sometimes wear my Central Intelligence Agency T-shirt to *epater les liberals* at the university gym where I exercise, though, near as I can make out, I don't seem to have *epated* too many.

As a kid, I owned a jacket that had KoolVent Awnings written on its back. KoolVent in those days sponsored one of the best softball teams in Chicago—I came into the jacket through a friend, whose father ran the local franchise—and I thought that, wearing it, I might be taken, by the less than fully cognizant cognoscenti, for a better athlete than I was. This jacket was the only item of clothing I wore to which my father ever objected. "Why the hell do you want to be a walking advertisement for someone else's company?" he would say. Or: "Why don't you just walk around in sandwich boards instead?"

Today a large portion of the middle class is a walking ad for Ralph Lauren, DKNY, Calvin Klein, Tommy Hilfiger, and the rest of the designer mafia. Decades ago I wore Lacoste tennis shirts with the company's small alligator over the breast, but I have long since forsworn wearing any garb with a designer logo, and, in agreement with my father, have come to feel it's stupid to offer oneself as a human billboard for another person's goods. Maybe the time is ripe for a T-shirt that reads, "'Let's Kill All the Designers'—Nietzsche." You don't suppose anyone will check the quotation, do you?

No Acknowledgment Needed

(1999)

YESTERDAY'S MAIL brought a book from a friend—not a close friend, but someone I like a lot—and I was pleased to see that my name wasn't mentioned in his acknowledgments. Instead the book bears an inscription that states "Thanks very much for your help and good advice during the past couple of years." My help consisted of my reading and commenting on 30 or so pages of his manuscript; and my advice about dealing with an editor who had moved on to another publishing house—a common enough occurrence nowadays—while this book was in mid-composition. Save the print. A free book with a nicely proportioned inscription felt just right.

I have been acknowledged in several books, and, sad to have to report to those who haven't been, as pleasures go, this one is minimal. I would rate it as roughly equivalent to my having won a good-conduct medal in the Army, which is given to everyone who has not been in a car accident or acquired a venereal disease. (I have to add here that, while in the Army I had no car.) Often I have been acknowledged for things I had no real hand in; on occasion, my name has appeared in a list with at least two other people I genuinely despised. This has caused me to imagine, with a deep shudder, my name showing up in the acknowledgments of a book by a Skinhead: "For their help during a difficult phase in the composition of this book, the author wishes to thank Joseph Epstein, Jeffrey Dahmer, and Hermann Goering."

As a careful reader of acknowledgments soon enough recognizes, writers, already a bit high from having recently finished a book, are here playing with Monopoly money—handing out lavish tips that finally cost them nothing. In my own books, I have always attempted to keep acknowledgments short and precise. I have been greatly aided in this by not incurring too much in the way of literary help. I do like to dedicate my books to family and friends. A dedication seems so much grander than a mere acknowledgment. As long as we are playing with Monopoly money, why not, I say, build hotels? But best, I think, never to acknowledge the help of one's wife, husband, or children, which, no matter how much any of them may actually have helped, is inevitably going to sound phony. "And, finally, to dear Sylvia, our pit bull, my thanks for not eating this manuscript, especially in its early stages; I owe you one, sweetie."

Acknowledgments can have other purposes. They can be useful as a depository for serious name-dropping, providing the hint that one knows famous people rather more intimately than one in reality does. Nothing in the rules that says one has to know someone at all to put him or her in one's acknowledgments. "I want to thank Bunny Wilson, Lizzie Hardwick, and Red Warren, even though none of them actually saw this book during its lengthy preparation, for providing useful models of the literary vocation at its highest power. Hey, thanks, guys."

I'm currently reading a charming memoir, *The Sorcerer's Apprentice*, by John Richardson, that has as fine a roster of acknowledgments as I've seen in decades. "I would also like to express my gratitude to the following," writes Mr. Richardson, and there follows a list of 48 names that speak to the widest—and toniest—intellectual and social connections. I shall copy down here only 10 or so of the names that, for me, have the most zing, even though I don't know who all of them are: Sid and Mercedes Bass, Bill Blass, David Douglas Duncan, Maxime de la Falaise, Lucien Freud, James Lord, Sonny Mehta, Claude Picasso, Annette de la Renta, and (*voden?*) Robert Silvers. If he can't dedicate a book to William Shawn, now long dead, the least an author can do is mention Bob Silvers in his acknowledgments.

If I seem a little nutty on this subject, it is because I have a grudge against acknowledgments, having lost a friend through them. I have felt a certain sourness at being exaggeratedly acknowledged, or acknowledged as one among a select circle of creeps, but no acknowledgment quite got to me so much as one offered by a former graduate student who had become a friend. When his dissertation, extensively rewritten as a book, arrived in my mailbox, I noted that both I and a man whose intellectual career I had come intensely to dislike were thanked in the exact same terms. We were both credited, as I recall, with independence of mind and courageousness of thought. My feeling was that if this other fellow had these qualities, I didn't want them. When the author next called, I told him how powerfully ticked his acknowledgment left me, and went on about it long enough to constitute telling him off. I must have been very convincing, for we haven't spoken since and that has to have been more than two years ago. This isn't a book, but I would nonetheless like to end here by making a different kind of acknowledgment: I was a jerk.

Dear Editor

(2000)

EACH MORNING, when the *New York Times* arrives, after checking the obituaries, I go right for the letters to the editor. What I am looking for is a man or woman after my own heart: someone publicly announcing a heterodox opinion that is courageously, elegantly congruent with one of mine. I am searching for people, in other words, whose perceptions are as subtle, whose cast of mind as impressively independent, whose intelligence quite as radiant as my own.

Occasionally I find them. Such a person is Sheila Feit, of Syosset, New York, who nicely blasts a *New York Times* writer for fearing technology, then adds that she has "chosen from the beginning not to spend much time online, to play computer games or to use the computer for daily activities," and adds further that, though she wrote her letter in longhand, she is sending it by email. Another is V. A. Carney, of Stowe, Vermont, a black American, who feels it "a supreme insult to any decent, fair-minded black American" to suggest that blacks "should be held to lower ethical standards because they cannot comport themselves properly." Can you see my fist come down, my thumbs go up, my little touchdown dance commence?

Someone who does not qualify is Walter Cronkite, the man with a face only a nation could love, who recently bestirred himself to allow that he feels all presidential candidates "could show true leadership by agreeing to one or more genuine debates to set forth their foreign policy." And since you'll never guess why, I'll let Walter, the old clichémeister himself, tell you: because "foreign policy has never been more important to the future of the United States and the world." Do you suppose he knocked off for the rest of the day after squeezing out that brilliant missive?

A good letter to the editor should never, Cronkitically, pontificate. It should instead show anywhere from mild to entirely out-of-control exasperation. On his television talk show, Steve Allen used to put on his hat and shift into the highest possible dudgeon to read angry letters from the *New York Daily News*, doing a man who had had it up to here (just above the eyebrows, I believe), was ticked to the max, wasn't going to take it anymore, was being driven just short of insane and maybe a little beyond.

Not all letters to the editor need be angry, or take on the burden of straightening everyone else out. Some of the best provide a charming addendum. I once wrote an essay titled "I Like A Gershwin Tune" that elicited a lovely letter from a man who told an anecdote illustrating the genuine modesty of Ira Gershwin, to whom it never occurred to use his own celebrity to acquire a reservation at a crowded restaurant. I almost wish someone other than I had written the Casual on acknowledgments in books in these pages a few weeks ago, so that I could send in an addendum letter having to do with an author acknowledging himself, as Philip Horne, in his *Henry James: A Life in Letters*, does for his use of a Henry James letter that he happens to own: "Only one of these letters is in a private collection; I thank myself for my permission to publish it."

One way of judging a magazine is by the quality of the letters it prints. Magazines that print letters in praise of themselves ought to be distrusted. Any magazine with intellectual pretensions ought to garner letters that are disputatious and probably tendentious. The etiquette is to allow the writer under attack to answer all such letters; and if he is any good at polemic, he will usually be able to apply to his unhappy correspondent the intellectual equivalent of the Cobra Twist, a hold devised and applied by the former wrestler Cyclone Anaya—a combined half nelson and reverse leg twist—that left his opponents briefly writhing before falling unconscious to the mat.

Like the Manhattan attorney who, when asked whether he had ulcers, answered, "No, but I give them," I do not now write letters to the editor but answer them. Many moons ago I had a man named Edwin R. Newman, the television broadcaster and self-appointed language expert, stalking me in the letters columns of intellectual magazines. I did my best to greet each of his letters with a smile and a karate chop, until, finally, he desisted. Long before that, living in the South, I wrote an occasional letter to the *Arkansas Gazette*, arguing with the foreign policy of President Charles de Gaulle. Odd, but he never answered.

Letters to the editor in too great number can weary a writer. Dying of cancer, Lucy Dawidowicz, the historian of the Holocaust, when handed the printed version of what she knew to be her last article for *Commentary*, remarked on her deathbed to Norman Podhoretz that, while she didn't especially look forward to death, "At least I won't have to answer any more letters of complaint from rabbis from Passaic, New Jersey." A great woman, I think. Wish I had thought to write a letter to the editor to say that.

Don't *Tutoyer* Me, Pal

(2000)

I WENT TO THE UNIVERSITY OF CHICAGO, which is considered, as the world reckons these things, a fairly serious place. Heavy, grey, false yet nevertheless massively impressive Gothic architecture. First atom split in a handball court by Enrico Fermi & Co. Enough Nobel prize winners to field a weak softball team. Great books all over the joint. Students determined, in several polls, to have less fun than at any other school in the nation. So why is it that, when the chairman of the university's Board of Trustees sends me an announcement of the appointment of the school's new president, just about everyone in the accompanying press release refers to the new president—a musicologist named Don M. Randel—as "Don"? Call him by his first name, and all that is august in his new office slips right off him. Perhaps I ought to be grateful that they don't refer to him as "Donnie," or perhaps (who knows?) "Skippy." But even "Don" feels all wrong. Gravity—it ought to be a law.

The French have the useful verb *tutoyer*, which means to address another person in the second-person familiar; usually to do so suggests intimacy, but it can also suggest contemptuous familiarity. Since we don't have a second-person familiar in English, we go to first names. Too readily, in my view. I may be a bit raw here. I've been getting Joe'd around a lot lately—better, I suppose, than being Jack'd around, but still more than a little irritating.

I send a fax to a software company, addressed "Dear Sir or Madam" and I get a letter beginning "Dear Joseph" back. Young men with strong New York accents and soft names have been known to telephone me, early in the day, to say, "Joe, Tyler Ginsberg here. Have you heard about these 791 high-yield, tax-free bonds? Now's the time to make your move." "Tyler, sweetheart," I reply, "have we met before?" "No, not really, but these bonds are a terrific. . . ." "Tyler," I say before hanging up, "go *tutoyer* yourself, pal." Lots of telemarketers seem to go to my first name. "Is this Joseph?" they ask. So, increasingly, do merchants and artisans in face-to-face encounters. "Pleased you could come by, Mr. Nelli," I recently said upon meeting a house painter who had come in to give us an estimate on painting our kitchen. "Call me Chuck, Joe." I found I couldn't do it. Henceforth I compromised and called him nothing.

As a university teacher, I continue to call my students by their last names, always preceded by Mr. and Miss. Almost all my colleagues call their students by their first names, and many of them are perfectly happy to allow the students to call them by their own first names. A charming student whom I had befriended dropped by not long after his graduation and called me Joe. I told him I preferred he wait three full years before doing so. Good kid, he did. Another student of mine, whom, after his being out of school for many years, I invited to call me Joseph or Joe, said that he couldn't do it, and if I didn't mind he'd like to continue calling me Professor Epstein. Despite the fact that I think of the title "professor" as one best accorded to the guy who plays the piano in the bordello, I didn't argue the point, and "professor" I remain to him.

I wish I gave off sufficient high dignity to prevent being so often "first-named" by people I would prefer to "mister" me. But I'm not sure anyone today does give off such dignity. I've become less convinced, in fact, that a yearning for familiarity, or an attempt to establish fake intimacy, is always at the heart of calling strangers by their first names. In many instances, the persons doing so—telemarketers especially—cannot pronounce a last name of any complication, and so using a first name becomes not a gambit but a necessity. Going at things the other way round, if you ask someone you are dealing with for his name, and he answers "Bob," he is giving away a lot less than if he had answered "Robert Ortacelli," his last name at least permitting one to place him ethnically. Insisting on plain "Bob" is perhaps as close as one can come to retaining one's anonymity; it can be damn chilling, in fact.

The first person to note this tendency of Americans to call one another by first names on short acquaintance—or no acquaintance whatsoever—was an English writer of immitigably highbrow taste and great social hauteur named Vernon Young, whom I met only once. We exchanged perhaps 30 letters, with neither of us ever coming close to addressing the other by his first name. He once wrote to me about how deeply he detested being called Vernon by people who scarcely knew him. "My way of dealing with this," he noted, "is really quite efficient. I say to them, 'My close friends call me Mr. Young. Won't you do likewise?'" A good thing, of course, that the narrator of *Moby Dick* wasn't of a like mind, else that great novel would have begun, "Don't—whatever you do—call me Ishmael."

Don't Ask, Multitask

(2000)

FASTEN YOUR SEATBELT, KIDDO, we're going over a bumpy bit of language, another little pot-hole on the rocky road of thought, this puppy yclept—no hyphen, please—"multitasker." The word is popping up of late with a fair regularity in that thesaurus of *faux pas*, that ample warehouse of wretched excess, the *New York Times*. "I'm a great multitasker," Monique Greenwood, the new editor of *Essence*, recently announced in the business section of the paper. Miss Greenwood also runs an 18-room bed-and-breakfast and a 72-seat restaurant in Bedford-Stuyvesant, in Brooklyn, and she has no intention of dropping them because of her new job. *Essence* has more than a million readers, but, hey, no sweat, the woman is, as she herself says, a great multitasker.

The test for a new word seeking entry into the language is need; I would also allow beauty and simple amusement. In a recent collection of Henry James's letters, I note that James, that great unitasker, refers to an American visitor who arrived for a visit at his house in Rye at 1:30 and stayed until 6:30 as "New Yorkily conversing." Adverbing New York is swell, and I intend to do it myself the first chance I get. I also happen to like "oojah-cum-spiff," which stands for sheer perfection in the world of Bertie Wooster, though I haven't as yet found many uses for it.

But, somehow, I don't think we need multitasker. I say this despite the fact that I come from a long line of the dudes. More than a mere multitasker, my dear mother was a simultasker. On the phone with her, I would sometimes hear a metallic sound and, on inquiring what it might be, learn that she was stirring soup. Once she carried on a phone conversation with me while typing a letter, and as I recall it was a serious conversation. A very smart woman, she didn't require all her powers to talk to her son, so why not, she figured, put some of them to other uses?

I may, at one point, have been a multitasker myself. I once had three different jobs: I edited a magazine, I taught at a university, I published enough of my own writing to come perilously close to qualifying as what Edith Wharton called a magazine bore. I had no notion at the time that I was a multitasker; I thought I was just trying to make a living. But my multitaskesqueness had quite as much to do with my intellectual *modus operandi*—or MO, as they say down at the station—which is always to have a big project going, then do six or seven other things to avoid doing what one is supposed to be doing on the big project. By evading taking on first things first, I have found, you can get a tremendous amount of work done.

Multitaskers interest me less than do what I think of as chaos merchants. These are those people—most of them, in my experience, men—who can keep on going when their lives are under attack from several quarters. These are the fellows who are in Chapter 11, being audited by the IRS, have been served with papers for non-payment by ex-wives, are cheating on their mistresses, have the mafia on their tail for juice money, couldn't help noting that for the past 10 days they have been urinating blood—and yet seem, as near as one can make out, to be getting a great deal of pleasure out of life.

The hideous "multitasker"—it has a bad sound and a bad look (mul tit, ask 'er)—is probably a digibabble-age replacement first for "moonlighting," then for "Renaissance man." Renaissance man was hugely, comically overused a decade or so ago. A physician who could write a clear English sentence on a non-medical subject, a baseball player who read a book, anyone who could watch television and breathe evenly—all were Renaissance men. When I heard Dick Cavett described as a Renaissance man, I found myself longing for the Reformation. One of the nice things about having been born during the Renaissance is that at least no one could call you a Renaissance man.

What distinguishes the junk language of our day from the junk language of earlier days is that it is so quickly taken up by people who are supposed to—but of course don't—know better: journalists, public figures, academics in high places with low tastes. Glimpsing a recent book about Henry James, I came across the phrase "James's take on this question." Henry James had a point of view, insights, observations, *aperçus*, a striking *pensée* or two, yet I am certain that he didn't do "takes," ever. Before long I expect to find Leonardo or Michelangelo described as a multitasker.

Multitasker may be around for a while. For one thing, people enjoy the novelty of new words, especially—as multitasker surely is—self-congratulatory ones. For another, with more people working at home, I suppose there is likely to be more opportunity for spreading oneself over more than two or even three jobs and adding to the multitasker army. Multitasker is a word made for a certain kind of person, rain-makers, paradigm-shakers, out-of-the-box thinkers—serious jerks, in other words— and I wish them joy of it.

HMS Punafor

(2000)

ARISTOTLE, IN *THE RHETORIC,* describes the metaphor as the joining of dissimilars to show their similarity. He offers a number of examples from Homer, the franchise player of Greek literature, at one point noting his choice of the dawn as "rosy-fingered" as so much better than "crimson-fingered" or, worse, "red-fingered." Metaphor, Aristotle thought, "gives style, clearness, charm, and distinction [to speech and writing] as nothing else can." He also thought that, like the gift of a good singing voice or of swiftness afoot, metaphor-making "is not a thing whose use can be taught by one man to another." He neglected to add that, for your jollily perverse pedant (hey, Bo, that's me!), a really dopey metaphor can light up the sky.

I thought of Aristotle last week when two handsomely ill-constructed metaphors came my way. The first was hand-delivered by an earnest woman who said that she had read an article I had written in the *New Yorker* about bypass surgery and that she found it—you will have to believe me here— "heart-rending." The second, popping up a few hours later, appeared in the pages of *Beast and Man,* the excellent book by the English moral philosopher Mary Midgley, who, following hard upon a discussion of the animal-behaviorist Konrad Lorenz, writes that "Lorenz and his party have, however, a difficulty about method which also dogs me constantly in this book." In a discussion of animal ethologists, dogs is almost exactly the wrong metaphor, akin to saying that a broken toe can be a terrific pain in the neck.

Very common though such metaphors are—they are the metaphorical equivalent of unconscious puns—so far as I know, they have never been given a name. Aristotle provides a brief list of "inappropriate metaphors," which includes those that are too grand or theatrical or ridiculous, but these metaphors do not quite qualify under any of his categories, except loosely under the ridiculous. They're not good old-fashioned mixed metaphors. Nor are they those comic *faux pas*, such as William C. Carter, in his recent biography of Proust, falls into when he writes of his subject's *lycée* days: "Another piece of work, written for M. Claude Courbaud's literature class, showed that Marcel was making up for lost time."

No, these metaphors are in a class of their own; they are metaphors that forget that the function of the metaphor is to show the similarity of different things and instead end up showing the similarity of similar things, but always askew, invariably with unintended comic effect. Inept metaphors with the quality of unconscious puns I hereby name them— call out the minicams, this is a press-conference moment—punaphors.

Sex is of course plentiful in its punaphoric possibilities. In the *Weekly Standard* of some while back, someone (the guilty here shall all go nameless) wrote about Bill Clinton's "attempts to skirt the truth." But that is nothing—"a mere bag of shells," as Ralph Kramden used to say—next to the unconscious comic genius who wrote, "We'll only know the effect of passing out condoms to teenagers four or five years from now, when the rubber meets the road."

Sports is rich in punaphors. I recently heard a sports announcer say, "Using injured players as an excuse for a loss is, in my opinion, nothing more than looking for a crutch." Writing about the Johns Hopkins psychiatrist Paul McHugh, a journalist remarked that he is "never one to shrink from skewering the cults of Freud and Jung." A television weatherman in Chicago, in great fatuous seriousness, announced that "differing tolerances among people for the cold is really a matter of degree." In a *New York Times* obituary, a deceased woman who owned a button shop was described as "hooked on buttons." (Put a zipper on that punaphor.)

"These new socks," I once heard a man say, "fit like a glove." In *Commentary*, a writer, talking about teenage suicide, lapsed sadly into punaphor when she wrote: "Perhaps rather than being cases of copying, all these suicides have something grave in common."

Food is another fine field for punaphors. "The butcher, in giving us this chili recipe," someone once said in my presence, "didn't give us a bum steer." At a restaurant that served especially large portions, I heard a novelist I know say, "They certainly don't spare the horses here," to which his companion, quite properly, rejoined, "Let's hope they do." A supermarket in my neighborhood ran an ad in the local press that announced, "We want your feedback." (Would it, if we returned it, give us back our money?) A friend not long ago said that she "could eat salad till the cows come home." As a carnivore, I felt called upon to reply that "I on the other hand could eat cows till the salad comes home."

Ain't language a gas, a groove, the very first wonder of the world? No one, surely, is ever likely to develop a more efficient form of miscommunication, no way.

Jervis

(2000)

I OPENED THE *NEW YORK TIMES* the other day to discover that Jervis Anderson, "*New Yorker* Writer and Biographer of [Bayard] Rustin, is Dead at 67." I realized, with a stab of hopeless sadness, that we hadn't spoken for nearly three years—a long time for someone I liked as much as I liked Jervis. "Joe," he would say when he called, his part-English, part-Jamaican accent able somehow to extract two syllables out of my first name, "Jervis Anderson," adding his second name, as if I knew—or had even heard of—another person named Jervis.

His calls always pleased me, though they came too seldom. Often they would begin being about baseball, about which he was a knowledgeable fan, and then go on to other, larger things. Sports was one of many interests we had in common. He had grown up playing cricket, about which he also knew a vast deal and on which he wrote a brilliant essay, "Cricket and C. L. R. James," for the *American Scholar*, one of the few things that succeeded in making that highly mysterious game intelligible to Americans, or at least to this American. He also knew boxing, in both its glory and its gory aspects, and he wrote well about it, too.

Jervis had a generous smile and an explosive laugh, which it was always a pleasure to evoke. I don't think I knew anyone who had less meanness or side. Through the worst period of black-white relations in America, he never, in my presence, even hinted that, as a black man who had doubt-less suffered his share of prejudice, he existed in a state of moral superior-ity. He was what my friend Edward Shils called "a sweet character."

Not without his mysteries, Jervis was, to use an old-fashioned word, personable without being in the least personal. In all our meetings and conversations, he told me almost nothing about his private life. Once he adverted to an early marriage, long ago ended and with no children. About his life in Jamaica, he rarely spoke. We never discussed anything about the arrangements necessary to everyday existence: apartments, food, clothes, money.

Although he wrote mostly about black subjects—producing biogra-phies of A. Philip Randolph and Bayard Rustin, *New Yorker* profiles of Derek Walcott and Ralph Ellison—Jervis read much more widely than his writings might suggest. He read as a writer reads, with an intense interest in the little secrets of how it is done. He read vast quantities of novels and stories. So far as I know, he never attempted to write fiction, but, nearly twenty years ago, he mentioned that he would love to write about his boyhood in the Caribbean, and I gather he had begun to do so before his death.

Jervis was an immensely patient worker. Before writing his biogra-phies, he put in years of reading, leg-work, interviewing, holding back on actual composition until he was fully prepared. I don't know if he wrote about black subjects because they most closely interested him—he also wrote a fine book on the Harlem Renaissance—or because, as a black writer, he felt called upon to do so.

What I do know is that Jervis seemed to need subjects he could admire, even though he first appeared on my own intellectual map with a quietly devastating attack in *Commentary*—written in 1968, when it took cour-age to write such a piece—on Eldridge Cleaver, then a radical who jus-tified violence on racial grounds. Subjects worthy of his admiration did not come cheap. He may have sensed the world running out of them.

Jervis was almost too nice a man to be a writer. Neither strong criti-cism nor self-assertion came easily to him. The put down was not a form he practiced. He was deeply respectful, but in a most discerning way. His admiration for William Shawn, under whose editorship he was first invited to write for the *New Yorker*, was complete, and he never referred to him, in my hearing, other than as "Mr. Shawn."

Now that he is dead, what impresses me most about Jervis, apart from the seriousness with which he practiced his craft, was his loneliness. Not that he himself ever suggested he was lonely. Still, as a West Indian black in America, he had to have suffered some of the prejudice against blacks without the compensatory feeling of full solidarity with American blacks. As an intellectual, he was essentially an appreciator, an isolated position among people—journalists, artists, intellectuals—happiest on the attack. Greatly good-natured though he was, I'm not sure he was able to extend the gift of intimacy to many people.

Jervis lived and died alone. His neighbors, the *New York Times* obituarist noted, only suspected something was wrong when his newspapers and mail began to pile up. The delayed knowledge of his death speaks more profoundly to his isolation than anything else could. I hope he had some awareness of how attractive a man he was. Montaigne writes: "There is no sweet solace for the loss of our friends other than that which is given us by the knowledge that there was nothing we forgot to tell them." I, alas, forgot to tell Jervis that he was a gent, the real thing, and a member of that best of all minority groups, the good guys.

Foot Fop

(2000)

I COULD BE WRONG ABOUT THIS, but I'm guessing that not many
readers know who Chad Muska is. Let me quickly break the tension
by reporting that Chad Muska is a big name in skateboarding—a kid
of 22, long turned professional—and, yo, I'm wearing the dude's shoes.
Not his actual shoes, but the shoes he personally helped design for Circa
Footwear, Inc., of San Clemente, California; I purchased these shoes this
past spring for $85, plus tax, from a mild-mannered, lavishly tattooed guy
in Petaluma, California, in a shop called Brotherhood of the Board. The
shoes are gray and red and white, and made of leather, suede, mesh, plastic,
rubber, and, for all I know, plutonium. Like all skateboard shoes, they are
heavily padded, to give the feet added protection against scrapes and colli-
sions. I call them my Chads—actually, ma Chads—and I'm entirely nuts
about them.

They haven't been getting much press, ma Chads. I wear them for long
walks, and mostly in the neighborhood. A stock boy with a missing tooth
in a local supermarket told me he thought they were very cool. A few
friends have stared at them, with a look suggesting that this time I may
have gone too far and might next show up in a plumed hat. But for the
most part, they go unnoticed. People nowadays are very tolerant, at least
about one's clothes, though I recently received an invitation to a cocktail

party that noted, Dress: Business Casual: no jeans or tennis shoes. That night ma Chads stayed home.

When R. H. Tawney (1880–1962), the great economic historian, was asked if he noted any progress in his lifetime, he replied, yes, in the deportment of dogs, who seemed better behaved than when he was a boy. My own answer to the question of notable progress in my lifetime is, yes, in the manufacture of gym shoes, as they were called when I was young and as I still think of them, though in a pretentious, slightly preppy phase I used to refer to them as sneakers. When I was a small boy, two gym-shoe manufacturers, US Keds and PF Flyers, dominated the market; both turned out ugly pieces of business made of canvas and rubber and sold in black or brown and in white for girls.

By the time of my early adolescence, things began to look up. As a boy tennis player, with strokes more elegant than effective, I would wear only Jack Purcells, a low-cut white canvas shoe with a rounded rubber toe across which ran a blue line. As an aspiring high-school basketball player and general gym rat, I wouldn't wear anything other than white Chuck Taylor All-Stars, with red and blue trim. Even now, more than forty years later, I can recall buying my first pair, at a walk-down sporting-goods shop in Chicago at the corner of Damon and Foster near Amundsen High School. I wish I could say that they improved my game, but, Chuck Taylors and all, I never went beyond playing on the frosh-soph team.

I put in perhaps twenty years without owning any gym shoes. During this period, which I used to catch up on my reading, I entered no gyms, played no games, had need of none other than street shoes, which in my case meant various kinds of loafers. But around the time when I began playing racquetball, a sporting-goods shop roughly a block from my apartment began selling gym shoes at an annual sidewalk sale at impressively low prices. I bought a pair of Nike high-tops there for ten bucks. The following year I bought another pair, this time low-cut Converse, in purple—purple and white being nearby Northwestern University's colors—for six bucks. When the salesman asked what activity I intended to use the shoes for, I replied, "Napping."

Ma Chads are my second pair of skateboard shoes. My first were purchased at another so-called "extreme sports" shop—extreme sports, I gather, include skateboarding, wakeboarding, snowboarding, surfing, and roller blading—this one called the Shred Shop in Skokie, Illinois. Every salesman in the place wore a baseball cap on backwards. None seemed close to 30 or even imaginable at 30. I tried on a pair of elegant bone-colored shoes with grey, apricot, and blue trim made by a company called Gravis. Very comfortable kickers, these. As the salesman watched me test them for fit, I told him that I thought they would work well enough for my specialty, which was jumping off buildings of fewer than six stories. For a thirtieth of a nanosecond, he may have believed me.

Which leads smoothly into the question of what sort of shoes one ought to select for one's own burial. I'm not sure whether one goes to the grave shod. If so, it would be a shame to have to live through eternity with shoes that pinch. But which shoes to choose? Loafers? Plain-toed Cordovans? Well-padded Chads? Nothing, certainly, from the shoe company called Mephisto. The answer is obvious: wing-tips, so that you get the chance to discover if those babies really fly.

You Got Attitude?

(2000)

I DON'T BELIEVE I HAVE ATTITUDE, but I do own at least one bow tie that does. Some readers will wonder if that sentence isn't missing an indefinite article. Shouldn't it be "an attitude"? For anyone who feels the want of that indefinite article, I can only say, in the mortal words of Mr. T., from the old television show *The A-Team*, "I pity the fool." Mr. T., in his Mohawk haircut, his ample, well-defined muscles festooned in gold, had attitude in sweet excelsis.

The word attitude has undergone a big change. The word's core meaning used to be "a mental position in regard to a fact or state," with that position often charged with feeling or emotion. The word probably showed up most frequently in one of the following two sentences: She has a good attitude. And: I don't like his attitude. A certain malleability was also implicit in the old meaning of the word, the assumption being that one could alter, change, perhaps completely reverse one's attitude. Only human beings—certainly not inanimate objects—had attitudes.

No longer. "The most important thing today," says the designer Stefano Gabbana, "is attitude." In *Harper's Bazaar*, the blurb for a piece called "Party Favor" reads: "What does it take to pose as the latest girl? An invitation, some attitude, and two gutsy dresses." At a Texas Rangers-Chicago White Sox game in early August, a fan held up a sign reading, "Attitude Is Everything."

That is the problem: Semantically, the word is all over the place, popping up everywhere and meaning everything. No two people seem to agree on its meaning, or at any rate on its new meaning. "Wonks with attitude are scarier than the rich," runs a sentence in an op-ed piece in the *New York Times*. In *Wired*, a new basketball shoe is said to turn "on-court attitude into courtside casual." In Mark Gauvreau Judge's book *If It Ain't Got That Swing*, "the beboppers had attitude." What can all this mean? How should I know? English is only my first language.

Does Michael Jordan have attitude? Do the pro football players Brett Favre and Warren Sapp? I suspect all three do. In its new meaning, attitude is perhaps the reverse of understated. It's the bold, the *outré*, violating convention and propriety, but doing so by design, unashamedly. It's taking joy in outrageousness. It's calling attention to yourself: Yo, look at me. It's in-your-face arrogance, deliberately unchecked, but arrogance in a (somehow) winning form.

That objects—cars, clothes, shoes, wristwatches—can have attitude is a help in locating the word in its new meaning. The novelist John O'Hara promised himself he would buy a Rolls-Royce if he won the Nobel Prize. When it became clear he wasn't going to win it, he bought the car anyway, a four-door Silver Cloud III, dark green, with his initials on the driver's-side door. A few of his wealthy friends owned the more understated but not much less expensive Bentley, but O'Hara decided: "None of your shy, thumb-sucking Bentley radiators for me. I got that broad in her nightgown on my radiator and them two R's, which don't mean rock 'n' roll." That, I do believe, is attitude.

One can of course bemoan the sloppiness of standards that allows a long-established word suddenly to take on a new meaning. Yet in doing so one is engaged in an enterprise likely to be as effective as delivering a sermon on the need for more temperate behavior to a flood. By its nature, language, as in the Paul Simon song, has this tendency to go slip-sliding away. The questions to ask when a new word enters the language, or an old one is radically changed, are why? why now? and who needs this?

The current meaning of attitude is useful in denoting a new, in most cases rather mild, sort of non-conformity at a time when it isn't so easy to step out of all the ready-made patterns of custom and style. Niche-conformity, another new phrase, implies that all groups, no matter how ostensibly far out, have their own strict rules. And so they would seem to have. One passes a green-haired, heavily tattooed, multiply pierced youth in the street and, after a brief wave of revulsion, yawns. That's not attitude—that's merely conformity to something deeply repulsive.

Attitude is my Jelly-Belly red and white, unevenly polka-dotted, giant butterfly bow tie. It was given to me by a friend, and I wear it with pride, regretting only that, it being a bow tie, I cannot look down upon it myself to derive the small pleasure it seems to give others. When I wear it, strangers have been known to smile as I pass. "Like your tie," a woman said to me in New York. "Wild tie, man," a kid remarked in Chicago. "That's great," another woman said, pointing at my tie in Bozeman, Montana. A bit of colorful silk around my throat enlivening an otherwise standard get-up may be as far as attitude goes with me, but, hey, when it comes to attitude, you have to take it where you can get it.

The Game of the Name

(2000)

I FANCY MYSELF A CONNOISSEUR of the naming of Americans, and as such have discovered that we gringos do a few things in this line that no one else does. George W. Bush—whose middle initial has all but become his last name—may be mildly amused to learn that only Americans go in for middle initials. Henry James does a nice bit on the comedy of American middle initials in *Daisy Miller*, where Daisy's brat brother Randolph cites each member of his family with his or her middle initial included. Thank goodness that Europeans don't go in for middle initials, or we might have had to refer to Dante R. Alighieri, William C. Shakespeare, or Marcel G. Proust.

Apart from monarchs and popes, Americans are also alone, I believe, in using the ennobling suffix, in which one adds roman numerals to one's name, as in J. Bryan III, or George Frazier IV. A tough thing to stick a kid with, an ennobling suffix. I went through basic training with an entirely unpretentious guy named Daniel Thomas III, whose suffix was a fat pitch right in the kitchen of every sergeant he encountered: "You, Third, get you ass down there and give me twenty of your best or there ain't going to be no Fourth."

Much of the pretension in naming today seems to be invested in first names: all those Whitneys, Kellys, Camerons, Brittanys, and Tiffanys;

those Tylers, Travises, Zacharys, Lucs, and more Scotts than you can shake a Fitzgerald at. One sighs over the yearning for elegance on the part of parents who pinned those names on their children. How long this has been going on is not clear. The philandering husband in Nora Ephron's novel *Heartburn* (1983) claims to have gone out with the first Jewish Kimberly, though he doesn't, if I remember correctly, give an exact date.

The first names of my co-religionists have undergone a number of alterations over the years. The Jewish men of my father's generation were given rather stately names: Sidney, Bernard, Louis, Saul, Maurice, Irving. ("If you're named Irving," I once heard a man say upon introduction to someone so named, "you must have been born in 1920. All Irvings were born in 1920.") Occasionally, things would go awry, and the stately became comically grandiloquent. The poet Delmore Schwartz claimed that his parents, in naming him, must have had a Pullman car in mind.

The mothers of my own generation of Jewish boys tended to give their sons first names that were Anglo-Saxon last names: Arnold, Norman, Sheldon, Marvin, Barry. Put a definite article in front of any of these names and it sounds like a hotel. The slightly comic oddity of many American Jewish last names makes it a bit tricky to lash up a fit first name to them. How many first names go easily with, say, Blumenthal or Birnbaum I am not prepared to say, but Lance and Schuyler aren't two of them.

For the same reason, Jews cannot, as certain old-family Wasps could, supply a family last name as a first name. Townsend Hoopes and McGeorge Bundy seem to work well enough; Goldstein Ginsburg and Pinsky Epstein do not. We are now emerging from a period of giving Jewish boys soft names. In my class lists at Northwestern, lots of Jonathans, Jeremys, Joshs, and Jaimies still turned up. The reversion to older names had a brief fling, and for a while many a newly minted Max or Sam or Ben felt the mohel's blade. Some old Jewish names—Melvin, Isaac, Myron—appear to have become African-American first names. Others—Maurice, Seymour, Barney—do not seem destined for immediate recycling.

English professors from olden days used to have triple-barreled names, like George Barrow Woodbury, names that all but put a wing-collar under their possessors' chins. Jewish men and women, I note, are now three-naming themselves. They are probably attempting not so much to add distinction to their names as to make themselves distinguishable from other Jews.

This might be the motive for Suzanne Jill Levine, the biographer of Manuel Puig, for there are innumerable Sue, Susan, and Suzanne Levines. Steven Lee Meyers, a reporter, must have wanted to be more than just another Steve Meyers. John Burnham Schwartz, author of *Bicycle Days*, perhaps wished to establish that he is the child of a mixed marriage. Barry Alan Shain, a political scientist, and Louis Daniel Brodsky, a poet, and Stanley Myron Handelman, a comedian, must have liked the rhythm that adding on their middle names gives, though Mr. Handelman, surely, plays his Stanley Myron for a small laugh.

None of these names can lay a glove on my own favorite of all public names, that of the writer who calls herself Pepper Schwartz, PhD. I've never read any of her books—they are chiefly on marriage and sex—but I shall always revere her for her unconscious comic genius in placing Pepper and then PhD around the name Schwartz. Others, doubtless, have made fun of her name. Poor Dr. Pepper, so misunderstood.

Upsizing

(2000)

THE WORD DOWNSIZING, both an excuse and not a very happy euphemism for firing people, needs, I have decided, a mate: upsizing. The country seems to be in a serious upsizing phase. When and where and how it began, I don't pretend to know, but I have a lurking—as opposed to a somersaulting—suspicion that it may have begun with the naming of the size of cups at Starbucks.

A Dunkin' Donuts man, I don't often go into Starbucks. But when I used to frequent the joint I found myself charmed by the comedy of the language of ordering, all that decaf, double espresso, steamed, skimmed, mocha, capu-frappo-Americano, and the rest of it. But what I couldn't get my (admittedly) literal mind around was the naming of the sizes of Starbucks cups. A small cup there is known as a tall, a middle-size cup is a grande, and a large cup is a venti, the Italian word for twenty, which must stand for twenty ounces. Let's go through this again: A small is a tall, a medium is a grande, a large is a venti. Got it? If so, perhaps someday you will explain it to me.

America now being the world's lone superpower, perhaps the word small is no longer permitted to us. At 5′7″—if I stand up straight—and 130 pounds, I have a personal stake in this matter of the disappearance of the word small. I'm not sure which gets lost first, the word or the thing it describes, but I do know once a word is lost soon the thing itself departs. Now that the word disinterested is gone, for example, so are the men and women who once possessed the fine impartiality the word connoted.

In the upsizing revolution, even I rarely any longer wear size small, but have been promoted to a medium in polo shirts and a large in T-shirts and sweat shirts. It is mildly amusing, if too late to be confidence-building, to think of myself as a large. Lots of casual clothes are now unisex, so sizes have everywhere jumped up, and the fact that much fashion calls for a baggy fit increases this propensity. Clothing catalogues often mention that an item is "oversized." So an average-size man often wears not merely large but extra-large, while a large man can wear clothes with as many as three Xs before the "L."

I was sitting at a baseball game in Wrigley Field in Chicago this summer with a friend from Los Angeles. Two rows in front of us sat two beefy guys, pure Chicago characters, each of them well over 250. Such bodies, I said to my friend, were likely to be deported from California, where everyone, I assumed, worked very hard to stay in starved-to-perfection shape. Not so, he replied. A new physical type was in the land, large, wide, slightly menacing, the human equivalent of the Sports Utility Vehicle.

In football, the 300-plus-pound lineman is commonplace, the 250-pound running back not much less so. Lots of high-school basketball players are showing up at 6'8". What is discouraging to a small fellow is that these huge guys, in football and in basketball, can be whippet quick and nearly Astaire-ish in their coordination. When I was a boy athlete, really large players had the common decency to be ill-coordinated and generally hopeless. That this is no longer so is hell on the sports fantasies of a man like me—slender but slow, small but without any notable moves.

The national average height of Americans is increasing along with the national figures for longevity. So many tall men nowadays walk the streets that the term "six-footer" seems to have gone the way of the word "millionaire"—neither, that is, is a term that any longer commands interest. Lots of taller women about, too. In tennis, three of the great pros, Maria Sharapova, Venus Williams, and Lindsay Davenport, are, respectively, 6', 6'1" and 6'2".

The old ideal in feminine beauty was the shortish—5′1″ to 5′4″—bosomy woman, on the model of the young Elizabeth Taylor or Julie London. Gone without the wind. Woman-watching in airports I note many more women pass by whom I'd describe as tallish rather than shortish, lots of them wearing platform shoes that, putting them on their own pedestals, raise them even higher. Tallish, even quite tallish, no longer seems odd but has come to seem attractive. In the recent Olympics, players on the women's volleyball teams appeared rather elegant, most of the chunky little women gymnasts a bit grotesque.

A clothing store designed for small men, the reverse of the Big and Tall men's shops, has begun to advertise on the classical music station I listen to in Chicago. It calls itself Napoleon's Tailor. I may one day drop in to check out the threads. I assume that it, too, has oversized clothes for the smaller man. The next time you see me I could be wearing a new suit from Napoleon's Tailor, a size 54 small, relaxed fit. Stop me, please, if I suggest we march on Moscow.

Singing (Sort of) in the Rain

(2001)

I HAVE A FRIEND WHO SCORED HEAVILY early in life and became a venture capitalist. Over lunch one day he entertained me by recounting the nutty projects that people brought to him for financing: a geriatric dog food, an electric fountain pen, cell-phone implants. I wish he were still capital venturesome, for I have an item that needs a backer—not yet invented, true, but one I long for: a karaoke machine that you can take into the shower.

The Sharper Image, Hammacher Schlemmer, Brookstone, and other consumer old-boy-costly-goofy-toy catalogs sell radios you can take into the shower, but thus far no waterproof karaoke machines. Pity. I can so easily see myself, shampoo in hair, soap on bristly cheeks—I am among the small but happy minority who have learned the art of shaving in the shower—microphone in hand, belting out "I've Got a Right to Sing the Blues" or "I Guess I'll Get the Papers and Go Home" or "Mack the Knife." Oh, Bobby Darin, thou shouldst be alive not at this but at that hour!

Older generations of literary men and women have had yards of poetry by memory. I envy people who can keep the vocabularies of four or five languages in their heads. I have had only bits of popular songs boppin' around in mine. But of late I have taken to memorizing entire songs. I do so partly as a stay against the inevitable loss of those little grey cells that

Hercule Poirot so often refers to, and partly for the sheer pleasure of singing them to myself, on long walks but more often in the shower.

I'd like to be able to report that I've just about mastered the Gershwin song-book; or committed all of Cole Porter and Rodgers & Hart to memory. But aside from Porter's "You're the Top," which I do have by memory—"You're the nimble tread of the feet of Fred Astaire, / You're an O'Neill drama, you're Whistler's mama, / You're camembert"—my taste has run to simpler, more off-beat tunes. Among them have been "Ain't Misbehavin'," "I'm Late, I'm Late," "Fine Spring Morning," "You've Come A Long Way from St. Louis," "Comment Allez Vous," "Stars Fell on Alabama," "The Way You Look Tonight," and "Sweet and Slow."

I began with mnemonically more difficult songs. One of the first was Noel Coward's "Mad Dogs and Englishmen," which I love for its intricacy. I later memorized his "Regency Rakes"—"Complacency never forsakes / roistering Regency rakes"—which shows the clear line, at least in this strain, between Coward and W. S. Gilbert. But these songs need fairly frequent rehearsal, lest whole chunks of them slip from my mind, which they inevitably do.

I do better with shorter songs. And it came as a surprise to learn how short some songs are. "The Way You Look Tonight"—"Keep that breathless charm," etc.—is two lines shorter than a sonnet; Tom Lehrer's "Hanukkah in Santa Monica"—"Roshashonna I spend in Arizuna, / And Yom Kippa way down in Mississippa"—is only one line longer; and "Miss Emily Brown"—that lovable, huggable girl who's coming to town—is precisely sonnet-length. "Send in the Clowns," Stephen Sondheim's one entirely memorable song, took a bit more work, but was worth it.

Above all I've come to prefer the songs sung by my idols in this realm, Louis Armstrong, Jack Teagarden, and Fats Waller. All three could take the dopiest of lyrics and make them amusing by ironically undercutting them even while singing them. "My Very Good Friend the Milkman" contains two lines that may be as wretched as any ever written—"Then there's a very friendly fellow, who brings me all the latest real estate news, / And every day he sends me blueprints of cottages with country views"—and yet Fats Waller, even while mocking them, is able to make them charming.

I often use one or another of these songs in the morning as a mental calisthenic—"cloak and suiters by the oodles, say it to their cute French poodles"—a way to ease my little grey cells into the day. But they have other uses. "I'm stepping out, my dear, to breathe an atmosphere that simply reeks with class" is especially useful to have in mind when stepping out into an atmosphere—an academic conference, say—that doesn't. Sometimes the sheer throwaway cleverness sends me: "I'm a supper-club fanatic, / thunderstorm electrostatic, / from three points I'm automatic, / I'm your guy." Yo.

Donald Tovey, the great English music critic, once claimed that he had enough music by heart to play at his piano for seven, possibly eight weeks. I now have enough song lyrics memorized to last, maybe, twenty minutes. A waterproof karaoke machine, I feel, would encourage me to expand my repertoire greatly. To own such a machine would be heaven. Or, as in the punchline to the old joke about Nikita Khrushchev making love to Marilyn Monroe, heaven for me, hell for my neighbors.

The Eppy and Other Jackets

(2001)

M**Y IDOL IN MATTERS SARTORIAL** is that great villain of American literature Gilbert Osmond, of Henry James's *Portrait of A Lady*, who, James tells us, "was dressed as a man dresses who takes little other trouble about it than to have no vulgar things." Searching my own wardrobe for vulgar things, I come up with a bright red shirt I sometimes sleep in, size XL, that reads "FUBU Sports, Since 1992, Varsity Athletic, Basketball," all in raised letters, with an orangeish chenille basketball in the center. It's a shirt whose putatively short sleeves are so long as to make my arms while wearing it seem slightly thalidomidic. This, I do believe, might qualify as just a touch vulgar.

Otherwise I am a perfect fop of respectability. I buy most of my clothes at Brooks Brothers, a store that was practically a cult when I was young and has by now been so long on the slippery slope of mediocrity that it ought to require its salesmen to carry a set of piolets. I also buy clothes at a local haberdashery called Huntley's, which has the world's best tailor, Mr. Bab, whose full Assyrian name is Babajon Badalapour. Mr. Bab is a genius, and if he were a cosmetic surgeon instead of a tailor, you'd no longer recognize me, so good would I look.

My wardrobe is the fairly standard one, one blue suit, a couple of grey ones, a tuxedo, a blue blazer, a seersucker jacket, four tweedyish sports coats, the usual grey trousers and chino pants, no jeans whatsoever, white, blue, and blue-and-white striped shirts, and various neckties to lend a splash of color at an older gent's throat.

A perfect fop of respectability, as I say, except for a longstanding penchant I have for jackets. I cannot remember being without a favorite jacket. In grade school I acquired a light blue cotton jacket with dark blue knit collar, cuffs, and waistband. So much did I wear this jacket that friends came to refer to it as an Eppy jacket. In high school I had an Air Force flight jacket, with epaulets and clip pockets, that I wore through three Muscovite-like Chicago winters, vanity in those days easily prevailing over the need for warmth. In me, I have to report, vanity still prevails. I'm with Jules Renard here, who in his *Journal* noted: "It's many a day since I've felt ashamed of my vanity, or tried to correct it. Of all my faults, it's the one that amuses me most."

I went to an intensely social high school where the students were organized into perhaps forty or so clubs, each with its own jacket in the club's colors. Walking the school halls one gazed out upon billows of variously colored rayon and wool. During my years there I wore the black and yellow jacket of the Iaetas, the red and black of the Ravens, and the green and white of Alpha. These jackets were worn in class, and, if one was going steady, one's girl wore one's jacket as a public show of her affection.

I always owned a windbreaker. (Wind-cheater, the word the English use, seems to me better, as the English jumper feels a better choice than sweater.) The first windbreaker I can recall feeling a strong attachment to was a little number put out by the firm of Aquascutum; it had a rounded collar with a button flap and a plaid lining. I first saw it on a boy three or so years older than I named Jerry Dash—excellent name for a guy who himself seemed dashing. I owned the jacket first in khaki, and when that wore out, I bought a second one in blue. (Sorry to be so unsubtle on colors, but I not long ago read a poem called "Men Know Brown," the opening of which reads: "On the radio this morning: the average woman knows / 275 colors—and men know eight." Too true.)

Ten or so years ago the owner of Huntley's offered me a costly leather jacket, the last he had in stock, for half price. The rich color of Godiva's dark chocolate, it was as softly flexible as an Italian glove, and an exact fit. I wore it for a decade, until its cuffs began to unravel, and then, head turned away in sorrow, dropped it down the garbage chute.

I go about nowadays swathed—that's the verb that always comes to mind when I wear it—in a navy blue jacket of softest cashmere that I bought roughly six months ago. Lightweight yet very warm, it has a zipper front and buttons, with a placard over both, with a nice collar, perfect detailing, and no label other than "100 percent Cashmere, Dry Clean Only." Expensive though it is, I justified buying it—penetrating economist that I am—by concluding that if I wore it a thousand times, which I hope to be able to do, it will cost only a little more than 40 cents each time I wear it. A bargain, clearly. A bit long in the sleeves, it was fixed by Mr. Bab, seamlessly. Gilbert Osmond would marry a second rich American heiress to own this jacket, but, bad news Gil, no more are in stock.

The Enlivening Sins

(2001)

EVERYONE KNOWS ABOUT THE SEVEN DEADLY SINS—Pride, Envy, Gluttony, Lust, Wrath, Covetousness, Sloth—but I wonder if alongside them we ought to find a place for what I think of as Enlivening Sins. These are sins, too, but quite minor, rather sweet ones, and instead of knocking a person out of heaven, they make life on earth seem a bit more piquant, a little more heavenly even.

Gluttony, I have no doubt, will bring a person down, not to speak of doing serious damage to his or her wardrobe. But what can be wrong with an occasional brief bout of over-eating: finishing, say, a full pint of butter pecan ice cream, in the carton, while standing up in front of an open refrigerator door? Along with going before the fall, Pride is socially unpleasant; but to feel, inwardly, that one has done a bang-up job of a difficult assignment—how bad can that be? Not very, I should think.

Sloth will put a person out of the running, yet there do seem days when an afternoon nap seems highly sensible policy. When I take a nap I also remind myself that Wallace Stevens spoke of "the necessary laziness of the poet," a remark in which I find comfort and confirmation, even though, it is true, I have published only a single poem in my life.

The Enlivening Vices are much on my mind, because earlier this week I committed a splendid one. On a Monday afternoon, in the middle of the working day, I went to a movie. *Crouching Tiger, Hidden Dragon* is its name, and I paid a mere $2.50 to see it. Full of astonishing spectacle, it presented elegant Chinese women flying over buildings, fighting with swords, riding long-maned ponies through dazzling golden deserts.

Aristotle thought spectacle "the least artistic of all the parts of tragedy and the least to do with the art of poetry," but I didn't allow the old Stagirite's stricture to prevent my enjoying this flick to the max, taking time out to lapse into the briefest of naps. I regret to say that I ate only a single slice of chocolate during the movie; I should have bought a box of Mason Dots. Best of all was emerging from the movie into full sunlight, which reminded me of coming out of the innumerable Saturday afternoon movies of my boyhood.

"A poet [recall my publishing record here] always cheats his boss," an old Russian proverb has it, and it occurs to me that, as a younger man, on every job I ever had I snuck away in the afternoon at least once to go off to a movie. Often I did so out of frustration, but perhaps just as often for the sheer delicious pleasure of it. The only reason I haven't done so over the past twenty-five or so years is that I've been self-employed. One of the few things I can say against working for oneself is that some of the joy of sneaking out to a movie is lost.

I haven't made a list of the Enlivening Sins, and I'm not sure there is any need to codify them, as was done with the Deadly ones and the Commandments, though I am glad that there are only seven of the former and ten of the latter. Some enlivening sins that I have committed in recent weeks include taking a pass on an entire Sunday edition of the *New York Times*, quitting a serious but ill-written book after fifty pages, eating something called a chocolate espresso square an hour before dinner, stopping all work at mid-morning, once to listen to a full CD of Fats Waller songs, another time to one of the songs by the late Charles Trenet. Not exactly Marquis de Sade material, I realize, but one does the best one can. To be enlivening a sin must be occasional, never ending in compulsion, let alone addiction. It ought to have a fine feel of triviality to it, and affect only oneself. It ought to help get one, however briefly, out of one's regular groove, bringing no serious guilt in its wake. An enlivening sin is a deviation in the direction of mild self-indulgence. Before committing such a sin, one hears a voice within say, "Let 'er rip," but in a whisper.

The only flaw in enlivening sins is that, unlike major sins, they do not allow one to dramatize one's fall to oneself. Nor is the matter of expiation at all clear. Confession is also a problem, though there is a benign church of my imagining in which a special booth for confession of enlivening sins is perpetually set up.

"And what is your sin, my son?" I hear a priest in this new church ask.

"Forgive me, father, but I watched two college basketball games, back to back, on a Saturday afternoon."

"You must do it again, my son," the priest answers, "but not too soon. Meanwhile, for penance, sing three times the lyrics to Louis Prima's version of 'Banana Split for My Baby, A Glass of Plain Water for Me.' Go in peace."

Mr. Epstein Regrets

(2001)

I HAVE A SMALL, SLOWLY GROWING LIST OF PEOPLE who mustn't expect an invitation to lunch from me. Roger Clemens is on it; so, among others, are Donald Trump, Jack Valenti, Shirley MacLaine, Howell Raines, Jack Quinn, and Barbara Walters. Loaded with odious and silly opinions, their conversation would, I feel, seriously complicate my digestion.

I now add to this select list Anne Lamott, a writer whose name I first came across on the morning of March 29, 2001. A novelist and the author of a book called *Bird by Bird*, Miss Lamott is someone I encountered in two paragraphs toward the close of an article in the "Circuits" section of the *New York Times* by Bonnie Rothman Morris on the simultaneous spread of writing and loss of interest in elegant prose owing to the advent of quick composition via email and chat-room conversations.

Miss Lamott recently wrote a column for *Salon*, and reported that the Internet had somehow loosened her up as a writer in a way she found most agreeable. "The Internet was much more playful for me," she said. "It was like an open mike at a bookstore, much less lofty, much less elitist. You don't take yourself very seriously." And then she went on to say—and here is the reason she is going to have to get lunch on her own—"The communication is the point, rather than the beauty of the sentence. I think beautifully crafted sentences are really overrated."

Reading that last sentence I won't say that, like a drowning man, I saw my entire life pass before me, but I did see roughly forty years of it swoosh by. Those would be the forty years that I have devoted to attempting to write those "beautifully crafted sentences" that Miss Lamott so jauntily disparages.

Already lunchless, Miss Lamott is also, I believe, clueless. In his novel *The Tragic Muse*, Henry James has a character of whom he writes: "Life, for him, was a purely practical function, not a question of phrasing." Pity the man isn't around to introduce to Miss Lamott; the two might show up one Sunday married in the *New York Times*'s "Vows" section. For Henry James himself, of course, phrasing was the name of the game, if not life itself then his best method for teasing out its meaning in "the dim and tortuous labyrinths" in which we all "sit in eternal darkness." James wrote, for example, about the likelihood for happiness being less for one of his heroines, who was "inconvenienced by intelligence." That phrase, brief as it is, could not be more fully packed or absorb more truth.

Jules Renard said that only Balzac was permitted to write badly. He meant that Balzac had so much to say, and literary ambitions so large, that he alone in French literature couldn't be expected to slow down for the niceties of style. The same, I suppose, might be said for Dostoyevsky, another writer in a powerful rush; in his case, the hurry was caused by the lash of serious gambling debt. Closer to our own day, Theodore Dreiser and Alexander Solzhenitsyn, two other big-subject writers, are thought, with some justification, poor stylists. Balzac, Dostoyevsky, Dreiser, Solzhenitsyn—if our literary ambitions are less than theirs, I'd say we scribblers had better avail ourselves of as much craft as each of our sentences can bear, because, darlings, we're going to need it.

A poet achieves greatness if he can write six or seven poems that perfectly click. Click is the precise word; when I read a great poem, I hear in my mind a clicking sound, as of tiles sliding together and fitting exactly, exquisitely, forming a thought hitherto unpredictable yet, somehow, now inevitable. How many beautiful sentences does a prose writer need to compose before he or she is acknowledged a master? A hundred? Five hundred? A thousand? I may have struck off a dozen or so in my time, and when I have done so I have always known it, for—swish! goal! touchdown!—there is no other feeling like it.

Style in prose is intelligence perfectly formulated. Style is also a writer's way of seeing the world—"a question," as Proust wrote, "not of technique but of vision." And style has very little to do with the "communication" that Miss Lamott seems to think is the point of writing. The point of writing isn't communication—pandas, lions, seagulls, after all, communicate—nor is it information, of which the world already has more than a surfeit.

The point of writing is discovery. The writer discovers first for himself, by moving words around, bringing out surprising new meanings in them through arranging them in never-before-seen combinations. And if he hits upon the perfect combination, a light goes off, and the world will seem a brighter place to him and his readers. The result is a sentence called "crafted" or, when it really comes off, in Anne Lamott's phrase, "beautifully crafted."

If Miss Lamott calls, tell her I'm at lunch. Sorry to have missed her.

The Worried Well

(2001)

I WENT TO A HIGH SCHOOL with perhaps fifty different extracurricular clubs that, whatever their other shortcomings, at least let one know one's exact social standing. Status under this arrangement was as finely calibrated as any I have since encountered. Athletes, good guys, ladies' men, genial screw-offs, the quietly out of it, even the hopelessly *déclassé* each had a club of their own. I don't yearn to return to my adolescence, even though mine—luck of the draw—was an amusing one, but I have until recently suffered some confusion about what group or category I belong to today.

I'm not even sure of my social class, except to say that it's somewhere in the large and squishy middle. I'm certain that I am (pace William H. Whyte) no Organization Man; nor (pace David Reisman) inner- or other- or tradition-directed. I've never been the man in the grey flannel suit. I haven't a kitchen or bathrooms—or bankroll—big enough to qualify as one of David Brooks's Bobos. I'm too young to have been formed by the Depression, and too old to be a Baby Boomer. During the Me Decade, I lived chiefly for others. During the supposedly greedy 1980s, I managed to show a loss. With no children at home, I suppose I am an empty nester, but there's not a lot of distinction in that. As the line from the song says, "I just don't see me anywhere."

Or at least I didn't until the other day, when I first heard the phrase "the worried well." Flash: Floodlights went on everywhere, and I felt I had found my place at last. The worried well, I grasped at once, that's me and my fellow closet hypochondriacs. Except that there are so many of us worried well that I'm not sure the word hypochondriac quite applies. Where everyone is mad, after all, the word psychotic loses some of its punch. The worried well constitute those vast numbers who are, from the standpoint of health, just fine but don't believe it is going to last. And of course we are right, for the mortality rate in this country, when last checked, was still rounding off neatly at 100 percent.

What has swelled the ranks of the worried well in recent decades has been that nasty little endeavor known as health or medical journalism. I speak of those wretched jaspers whose job it is to scour each issue of the *New England Journal of Medicine* and *JAMA* (the Journal of the American Medical Association) and every National Institutes of Health report for news of fresh disease, depressing health trends, and rising rates of one or another kind of human decomposition. We, the worried well, thumbing through our daily papers or tuned in to local and national news channels, read and listen to it all, and tensely sit, waiting for the other flu to fall.

What's new, pussycat? A new strain of leukemia has been discovered, previous cholesterol numbers need to be adjusted downward, osteoporosis isn't a serious problem only for small, light-boned women. Three new miracle drugs have been developed whose side effects are just slightly more horrendous than the diseases they set out to cure. A study at Stanford finds that all allergies will be conquered by mid-century; unfortunately, another study at Penn State has found that allergies generally are on the rise. We sleep tonight, badly—medical journalism stands guard.

Bumps, blemishes, bruises slow to heal, the least deviation from perfection—worrisome all to the worried well. We go to physicians the way other people go to an IRS audit, sure that we aren't going to come out smiling. What sort of hepatitis, arthritis, meningitis lurks within our cells, bones, genes? We don't, ever, feel quite right. "When was the last time you felt really good?" a radio commercial for a local health club asks. "1950," I answer, "when I was thirteen."

We worried well, bounced around by all the conflicting medical news, have peculiar habits. We go for weeks at a time without eating red meat. We take various—and, no doubt, counteracting—vitamins. Many of us jog; others regularly go off on lengthy walks, arms swinging vigorously, looks of grim determination on our faces. Except when the endorphins kick in, we tend to seem mildly depressed. We're well, thank you for asking, but worried, very worried.

We follow the health news the way others follow the stock market. "New hope, new options for breast cancer," Tom Brokaw reports. But then Peter Jennings tells us that there is altogether too much lead in the atmosphere. New medicine is available to lower the incidence of strokes. But then, wouldn't you know it, the diabetes rate has risen nationwide. Like the Dow and the Nasdaq, up one day, down the next. We're the worried well, for whom life is hell.

Which does not mean we are ready to depart it. None of us feels, as did Noel Coward, that "life and love and fame and fortune can all be disappointing, but not dear old oblivion. Hurray for eternity!" We'd like just one more salad, please, and perhaps a cup of green tea before we go.

The Language Snob, Reinvented

(2001)

Y OUR BASIC LANGUAGE SNOB—that, friend, would be me—is never out of work. Just as he gets his wind back after railing about one or another overworked or idiotically used word, fresh misusages appear to cause him to get his knickers in a fine new twist. Everyday evidence of the inefficacy of my fulminations against the words focus and icon is available in the public, airwaves, and what is amusingly called civilized discourse. With freshly twisted knickers, then, I persevere, "boats against the current, borne back ceaselessly into the past," and so forth.

I can bear the basketball announcer Marv Albert's fulsome toupée—fulsome: "abundant to excess; offensive to normal tastes or sensibilities"—but I cannot bear his regularly misusing "differential," as in "The Lakers have wiped out a twelve-point differential in the third quarter," when what he really means is difference. A "differential" is a gear in a motor, a kind of equation, and a few other things, but never a twelve-point lead.

Sometimes your language snob lies in wait, happy to pounce when people lapse into error by turning their pretensions up just a notch. Gerald M.

Levin, CEO of AOL Time Warner, recently claimed to be "enthralled" by a new business idea, when he really meant that he was "thrilled." Decimate in place of "devastate" or "destroy" is a golden oldie in this line, misused by too many people to name. The former means reduce by a tenth, and once meant "kill one in every ten," a thing Romans were wont to do when capturing a town that put up resistance. Bryan A. Garner, in *A Dictionary of Modern American Usage*, calls decimate a "skunked term," or word now too heavily freighted with ambiguity to be used at all; even when used correctly, that is, it is likely to be taken wrongly.

Pure goofyisms are always pleasing to the language snob. A reporter in the *New York Times*'s "Vows," always good for a Sunday morning laugh, reports that, when a young woman first went out with the man she would eventually marry, her "cell phone was ringing off the hook." I'd like to meet the man who sold her that cell phone with a hook. Did he, do you suppose, sell her a wall to go with it?

Sometimes my language snobbery kicks in through pure personal pique. I don't cotton to being referred to as "guys" by youthful waiters, especially when no one at our table is under sixty and one woman is in her nineties. Used in this way, "guys," I suspect, has very unhealthy roots in political correctness. Rather than say, "Would you gentlemen [or ladies] care for dessert?" the waiter or waitress cowers behind the pseudo-friendly "guys."

The best language snobbery—which isn't snobbery at all—concerns those items that go to a concern about the deprivation of the language by lazy linguistic constructions. Take the no longer so new use of fun as an adjective, as in "fun time," "fun guy," "fun couple," "fun decade," "fun serial killer." Frank Rich, reviewing a recent biography of the choreographer Jerome Robbins, refers to the "smattering of fun gossip" in the book. Fun isn't anywhere near a good enough adjective for gossip, which can be witty, subtle, crude, amusing, or vicious. Fun is, in fact, almost never good enough in any of its new usages; its use is a sign of a refusal to search out a more distinguishing, and thereby more vivid, word.

The use of sharing is slipping out of control. I first encountered "sharing" at the National Endowment for the Arts, where people seemed always to want to share their experiences. Merely to hear them use the word made me wish I were instead at a small table in Vegas, being attacked by Don Rickles.

I don't like to be thanked for sharing, either, as I recently was for giving someone my phone number.

"Reinventing oneself" is another phrase that can use serious overhaul, with a view to being put on the list of ought-to-be endangered terms. People seem to be reinventing themselves everywhere one looks these days. Movie stars, athletes, politicians—everybody's doing it. A personal reinvention is, I gather, something akin to a makeover of the soul, usually implying a return in a new guise, always of course in improved form. Good luck.

Another word in need of the firing squad is the suffix something, which had its beginning, I believe, on the television show *Thirtysomething*. Soon after we were hearing about twenty-somethings and forty-somethings, though not yet ninety- and hundred-somethings. The sports page of the *New York Times* recently referred to Shaquille O'Neal as weighing "330-something pounds." The something-suffix is on its way to serving as the equivalent for numbers of the flying whatever, so that we shall soon have someone described as "seven-foot-something," distances between towns as 200-something miles, marriages lasting "two-decades-something." What—so to speak—ever!

Looking for King Kong

(2001)

THE PICTURE I COULDN'T GET OUT OF MY MIND from that dread-filled Tuesday morning—and still can't get out of my mind more than a week later—is the image of the second plane, turning round and flying directly into the 110-story building, setting it instantly aflame. So insane, so like a comic book, did the picture of the plane crashing into the building seem, that I quite expected to see King Kong atop the tower. I rather wished I had, so that I would know I was watching a piece of crude science fiction. No such luck.

I was stunned but not shocked, depressed but not demoralized by the events of that long day. The reason is that, completely unworked out though my personal theology is, it has always included a prominent place for evil. I happen to believe that any group of people who can talk others into giving up their lives to murder innocents comes as close to qualifying as evil as anything I know.

Still, as I watched the proceedings on Tuesday, September 11, 2001 the overwhelming fact was the innocence of those killed. That is what I couldn't shake from my mind. For years I have read in the *New York Times* about vast numbers of people being wiped out in a flood in Bangladesh, or a drought in Ethiopia, or an earthquake in Central America, and not allowed myself to dwell on the ghastliness of such events. I turned away from them as quickly as possible, not, I prefer to think, from a failure of imagination but from the possession of all too vivid—and slightly squeamish—an imagination. The killings of September 11 constituted another such event, with two exceptional facts added: that these deaths resulted from acts not of God but of men, and that in this instance it wasn't possible to turn away.

Death in its various forms—slow, quick, painful, merciful, even accidental—is not usually difficult to imagine. These deaths, though, are. Solipsistically, I see myself, a cup of coffee at my desk, my computer just booted up, ready to make an attack on the day, when I hear a shattering boom, see flame, and darkness—oblivion. I shy away from thinking about death of the kind visited upon those in the four hijacked planes, who had time for the terror to sink in.

One reads the lists of the dead and feels the defeat of so many plans and dreams. A young couple with its 2-year-old child crash in Pennsylvania, two firemen brothers are crushed in lower Manhattan, a former model who had nursed a now dead movie star husband through AIDS is used as fodder to destroy a building. All victims of a vicious political game in which they had no knowledge they were enrolled as players.

After the first day, I rationed my television watching. Among people not personally affected, depression, I noted, hit hardest those who couldn't pull themselves away from their television sets. Ceaseless contemplation of the gray rubble, empty reports from journalists ("Back to you, Tom, Peter, Dan"), clarified nothing, but only deepened despair. I wanted hard news: numbers of survivors, numbers of dead, firm facts leading to knowledge of who brought about this sorrow. I found myself taking solace from the memorial service at the National Cathedral, its dignity and beautiful music and measured speech, and was pleased to see President Bush come through admirably by speaking so well.

What I especially wanted to avoid was television interviews with people who were waiting to discover if they had lost family. I wanted them left alone. One evening I watched the man who owned the restaurant at the World Trade Center called Windows on the World and who had lost 55 members of his staff break down and weep before the already dampened microphone of Barbara Walters. Why did the man agree to be interviewed? Why does anyone who lost family and friends? The obscenity of modern television journalism was therein once more revealed, but its mysterious attraction even to the victimized remains unsolved. I clicked off the television.

"We don't have a precedent for anything like this," noted a psychiatrist at the post-traumatic stress program at Mount Sinai Hospital in New York. Nor do we have language for it. We long ago used up *carnage* and *atrocity* and *catastrophe*. The day of the crashes, television commentators gave *horrific* a good workout, and by afternoon the juju had departed that word, too. Thomas Friedman, in his column in the *New York Times*, reported that a secretary in Jordan, not having much English, had called the events of September 11 "the Big Terrible."

I don't myself have the language to put what happened into any sort of useful order or perspective, and language is my game, just about all I have and am. All I come away with is a heightened realization of the easy violability of life when it is held so cheap by enemies and my own good fortune in having thus far been spared a death devoid of natural cause or rational meaning.

A Walker Outside the City

(2001)

IN 1951, THE LITERARY CRITIC ALFRED KAZIN published a schmaltzily sentimental memoir called *Walker in the City* in which he was able to demonstrate his sensitivity and superiority to his family, his friends, and his contemporaries. I have myself become a walker outside the city, with none of the benefits of self-esteem that Kazin's walks seem to have brought. Once a boy athlete in whose mind played every sports fantasy—from the Rose Bowl to Madison Square Garden to Wimbledon, all in living color—I have been reduced to being a walker, and not all that fast a one at that.

Four or five times a week, I take the same walk, beginning somewhere between 7:00 and 7:30 a.m. I head down to Lake Michigan, thence around what is known as the landfill behind Northwestern University, and back to my apartment in Evanston. I own no pedometer, but would estimate the walk to be roughly three miles.

Although nearly impervious to nature, even I am impressed by the immensity of the lake, which some mornings is a placid, Matissely blue, some mornings menacingly choppy, and some days calm but rippley, believe it or not. A variety of birds—ranging in size from Canada geese to wrens—are aloft. Haze often blocks out the Chicago skyline to the south as I walk past the long grassy spaces set aside for soccer, lacrosse, and field hockey.

I take these walks in the belief that they are good for my health. Invigorated though I do feel at the end of them—endorphins speaking here, I'm sure—I should not be at all surprised one Tuesday morning to open the science section of the *New York Times* to discover that regular exercise, combined with the low cholesterol intake of careful eaters, hastens dementia.

Traveling in Europe, Henry James spoke of his "detested fellow pilgrims." I think of the companions I encounter along the path of my walk as my weary fellow health nuts. They grunt and glisten with sweat, some of their faces showing real pain. Lots of old flesh has been jammed into spandex, always a mistake. Joggers, bicyclists, and the occasional Rollerblader pass on the left. Every so often a real runner zips by, reminding me of how far from a serious athlete I have become. A man ten or so years older than I, the trunk of whose body is twisted and one of whose legs seems shorter than the other, has been known to pass me up.

On this path, small women show over-developed bulging calves. Young mothers jog briskly along, pushing dazed children in droshky-like conveyances. Occasionally an obese man or woman will give the path a shot. Estimating how much weight they have to walk off, I think, how hopeless! And then I remember that Evelyn Waugh was once asked how, given his rude and generally unpleasant behavior, he justified calling himself a serious Catholic. "I don't justify it," he is supposed to have replied, "but just imagine what I would be like if I weren't a Catholic." So with these people—just imagine if they didn't walk.

I do not greet many people on these morning constitutionals. An older man wearing a Cubs hat raises it to me in salute, and we sometimes exchange a quick word on the pennant race when we pass. A man walking his Airedale always says hello. Another man whose legs seem to be growing quite as short as those of his Welsh corgi keeps his own counsel under a scowling countenance. A pleasant enough looking woman walks a Weimaraner with such haunting eyes and so elegant a taupe coloring that I have formulated the rule that a woman makes a mistake to travel either with a man with a more ambitious hairdo than hers or a dog with a more impressive hide.

On my way back, I pass something called the Allen Center, run by Northwestern's Kellogg School of Management, which holds what seem like perpetual seminars for rather logy-looking middle-managers with cell phones holstered on their belts. I glimpse them through the windows of the center's dining room, packing away a heavy breakfast before having to stuff down an even heavier diet of social-science jargon about organizational behavioral strategies, or behaviors of organizational strategies, or possibly organizations and their behavioral strategies. I don't envy them. I'd rather be sweating in the sun, which at this point in my walk I usually am, when, with slightly slowed stride, I head for home.

I have until now never been good at calisthenics, or at any program of exercise that calls for regular application. As a boy and even young man, I owned light barbells and put up chinning bars, but never to any avail. These morning walks seem the exception, perhaps because they leave the mind free for what passes, at least for me, as thought. I use the time to think about problems connected with stories or essays I am writing, or to rehearse the lyrics to "Flying Down to Rio," or—ultimate luxury—to let my mind float. Very satisfying, it may even beat my bowing before the royal box after victory at Wimbledon.

Penman

(2001)

N ARTICLE IN A RECENT ISSUE of the *Women's Quarterly* bemoans the absence of the teaching of handwriting in schools, pointing out that this is especially a hardship on young boys. Handwriting apparently comes less easily for boys than it does for girls. "Boys are graphologically challenged," the article reports; a professor of special education at the University of Maryland named Steve Graham adds that boys being poorer at penmanship than girls "is one of the better established facts in the literature."

The boys in my class in the Daniel Boone School in Chicago were certainly much worse penmen than the girls. I don't remember any girls having a bad handwriting. For a girl in fifth or sixth grade to have a poor handwriting was, somehow, a judgment upon her. A girl with a wretched handwriting, during the *ancien regime* under which I grew up, was practically a slut; it was not done, unthinkable, impermissible. Being slobs and brutes, boys were also permitted to be wildly errant penmen. The highest most could hope to attain was a merely passable handwriting. Elegant penmanship might even have put in doubt one's masculinity.

Lessons in penmanship took place daily. We had workbooks, much wider than they were tall, with lines ruled like music paper. Instruction entailed making cursive letters, lower case and caps, twice or thrice the size of normal handwriting. The Palmer method was taught. I'm not entirely sure what old Palmer's method was, except endless repetition of the construction of letters from models, and then the joining and spacing of these letters. Once a woman, sent by the workbook's publisher, arrived to demonstrate how certain letters were made. She was large and zealous, and I can remember her doing the capital S over and over, singing out, with each perfect S she formed, "Swat, swat, swat [and then as she ended her stroke], swat that skeeter." Her obvious insanity brought light comic relief to the general boredom of the subject.

I don't think I had the worst handwriting in the room, but mine was close to the bottom. Mildly precocious in learning to print letters, I adopted, as a child of three or four, a grip on the pencil in which the top of my pencil slanted off to the left, causing many people to take me for a lefty. As for grip itself, it resembled nothing quite so much as the Cobra Twist, a combination half-nelson and leg lock, the *coup de grâce* hold of a handsome South American wrestler who went by the name of Cyclone Anaya.

I didn't have any difficulty with this rococo grip, but I knew my teacher would, and so, when she walked down my aisle during penmanship lessons, I changed to the conventional grip. When alone, though, I stayed with the Cobra Twist, which seemed to serve me well enough. But my writing never really attained the fluency that the Palmer method promised; try as I might, I could never quite achieve the old Palmer flow, and haven't to this day.

I admire people whose carefully measured penmanship suggests an orderly character. A deteriorating handwriting is often one of the signs of aging, yet I remember getting longhand letters in the most perfect penmanship written well into his eighties from the philosopher Sidney Hook. While still in the Soviet Union, Solzhenitsyn is said to have written his books in the most astonishingly minute yet perfectly legible handwriting, leaving no margins whatsoever on the page. This made for the smallest possible manuscripts, all the better for smuggling out of the country.

I have been working on my handwriting for better than half a century, making little alterations but with no real success. Over the years, I have changed the capital A's, G's, and S's in my script; I have added a flourish to n's that end words; I try to remind myself to cross my t's in the upper middle rather than at the very top and to make my l's, h's, and b's higher than my t's, k's, and f's. I have bought expensive fountain pens and *raffiné* inks to aid me in this effort. With ballpoint pens, I have always felt as if I were driving a car with bad tires and unreliable brakes, and, as would be the case in such a car, my handwriting was all over the road.

What can be detected in my handwriting is a certain yearning for elegance that distinctly doesn't come off. The general effect is rather like a hobo wearing an ascot. My handwriting always seems, somehow, out of uniform, even slightly unsober. Might it be that I do not take sufficient pains? Erik Satie took as much as twenty minutes to write a six-line postcard, sometimes more than half an hour to address a letter, but then he aimed at calligraphic works of art. So, in our own day, does Tom Wolfe, whose letters are not only amusing to read but pleasing to gaze upon. I, meanwhile, struggle for mere legibility. I can still read my own handwriting, but am not always certain others are able to do so. I should have swatted lots more of those flamin' skeeters.

Popcorn Palaces

(2002)

I READ JOHN PODHORETZ'S *"MULTIPLEX BLUES,"* his amusing account of the difference between the broken-down theaters of his early moviegoing days in the 1970s and the plush multiplexes and cineplexes in which the inferior flicks of today are shown, with the smug smile of the man with history on his side. The theaters with sprung seats, gum on the floors, and sad concession stands of Podhoretz's youth were earlier the dazzling movie palaces of my own boyhood.

The great difference between youthful movie going in the 1970s and in my day is that I grew up in an America that still had a unified popular culture, not then so divided as now between things produced for specific audience generations: children, youth, grown-ups. Rock 'n' roll may have been the watershed. After the advent of Elvis and following him the Beatles, the country divided between the young who wanted to stay young forever and those who thought adulthood not really so bad a deal.

Although there were childish entertainments when I was growing up in the late forties and early fifties—comic books, after-school and Saturday-morning radio shows, Disney and Lassie movies—most children partook of the same popular culture as their parents. Particularly was this so in the movies. Censorship was strict—in the movies, even married couples were allowed no closer intimacy than twin beds. Ratings were nonexistent because they were not needed.

In those days, one generally went to the movies without even inquiring about what was playing. In the era before air conditioning in private residences, one was sometimes taken by one's parents to escape steamy summer nights. Movie going was so much part of big city life that, when I was a boy, there were no fewer than seven movie theaters within walking distance of our apartment. Most of them showed double features—two full-length movies—with a cartoon or two, a newsreel, and coming attractions thrown in at no extra charge. In a child's version of a long day's journey into night, we walked into a movie theater on bright, cold Saturday afternoons at 1:00 and emerged from it into the dark at 5:30.

The largest of the movie theaters in our neighborhood was The Granada. Other grandiloquently named theaters in the Chicago of those days were The Riviera, The Oriental, The Tivoli, The Alhambra. The names were meant to suggest the promise of exotic adventure to be found within. A small, nearby theater was called The 400, and must have taken its name from Ward McAllister's socialite 400, which derived from the exact number of people who could be fitted into Mrs. Vanderbilt's ballroom in her Fifth Avenue mansion. There must once have been exactly 400 seats in the theater, which has since been broken up into four mini-theaters and is now called, rather prosaically, The Village North.

As for The Granada, perhaps only the tsar would have felt at home there. Its sumptuous lobby ended with a magnificent red carpeted staircase that led to its immense balcony. Marble was everywhere. So were enormous paintings of unidentified nobility. Ushers dressed with care as if cadets in some unknown but aristocratic regiment. The men's room was so large it gave off an echo.

The cheapest children's admission ticket I can remember was 10 cents at the small Coed Theater on Morse Avenue. Elsewhere tickets were 15 and 20 cents. Candy was a nickel—I had a serious weakness for tooth-destroying Jujyfruits—a box of popcorn cost a dime, 15 cents if one were so flush as to be able to afford extra butter. I was given 35 cents to go to the movies, and never seemed to require more.

Downtown, The Chicago and Oriental Theaters charged 50 cents, but they offered stage shows, a last carry-over from vaudeville. Alternating with the movie, there were circus acts—trained dogs, jugglers, acrobats—and a headliner, usually a popular singer. On the stage of the Chicago Theater, I heard Nat "King" Cole, Dinah Washington, the Four Aces, Johnnie Ray, and Frankie Laine, the latter singing "Mule Train."

The best age to watch movies is undoubtedly one's childhood, before either critical intelligence or cultural snobbery kicks in. I cannot remember any flicks from my early movie going days that I disliked, though I did have a mild antipathy to the overly romantic. I particularly enjoyed a lengthy sword fight, usually conducted up and down a marble staircase or near the edge of a cliff, especially one in which Errol Flynn, Douglas Fairbanks Jr., and Cornel Wilde fought Basil Rathbone, George Macready, or some other pure type of the villain. In those days, Danny Kaye's movies probably gave me more pure pleasure than any others. I have tried to rewatch them as an adult, but it's been no go. The magic they once brought is lost, gone forever, along with the astonishing popcorn palaces in which I first saw them.

Situation Comedy

(2002)

THIS MORNING, OUT FOR A WALK in wintry weather, I discovered a young student from the Northwestern School of Music struggling on the icy sidewalk while carrying a double bass. "Excuse me," said I, as our paths crossed, "but have you ever considered taking up the harmonica?" He took it, as the Victorians say, in good part. My model here was Herbert Beerbohm Tree, the actor and older half-brother of Max Beerbohm, who once came upon a mover bent almost double because of the grandfather clock he was toting on his back. "My good sir," Beerbohm Tree is supposed to have said, "wouldn't it be much more convenient to own a wristwatch?"

A phrase is needed to cover this sort of thing, preferably one in English. It would be a companion to the French phrase *esprit d'escalier*, which refers to one's regret about coming up with witty remarks or rejoinders only when it is too late to deliver them. What I have in mind is the gratuitous remark, in response to nothing but the scene in which one finds oneself. I seem to have become something of a specialist at these remarks.

Later the same day, finding myself in a large yet crowded Chicago butcher shop called Paulina Market, my package under my arm, I said to an older couple as I was leaving, "I'm getting out of here. Too many vegetarians for my taste." I'm far from sure that they got the joke. And why should they? More likely one turned to the other, asking, "Who was that maniac?"

At the supermarket, the bagger, a tall, thin kid with dreadlocks, wants to know what kind of bag I want. Instead of answering either plastic or paper, I say: "Suede." A pause; a moment of tension. Then he smiles. "Ain't heard that one yet," he says, grinning. "Not too bad."

In the restaurant, salad dishes set before us, the waiter comes round with a particularly large pepper mill. "Pepper?" he asks each of the six of us in turn, twisting the pepper on four of our salads. When he gets to me, I say, "No thanks. I don't carry pepper-mill insurance. I had a cousin who was killed by a waiter wielding a pepper mill only slightly smaller than this one." A look of disbelief is followed by a small shock—ten watts, let us say—of recognition, as the waiter realizes he is dealing with a genial but authentic screw-off.

While my material is, I hope, original, I don't seem to mind reusing it. I've hauled out the pepper-mill bit no fewer than two or three hundred times. I don't seem to mind recycling, either. A number of years ago I bought two two-volume sets of the letters of Justice Holmes—the *Holmes-Laski Letters* and the *Holmes-Pollock Letters*. The bookseller, a rather dour New Englander named Richard Barnes, asked if I would like him to wrap them for me. "That's all right, Mr. Barnes," I said, "I'll read them here." I thought I noted the slightest hint of a wisp of a smile play at the left corner of his mouth, though I could have been mistaken. Two weeks ago, I bought two dozen night-crawler worms for my turtles at a fishing equipment and bait store. The man who brought them to me asked if I wanted them in a bag. "No thanks," I said, "I'll eat them here."

I wonder if the effect of these various bits isn't to put the people on whom I use them in an *esprit d'escalier* frame of mind? Did it only later occur to the boy with the double bass to say, "No, but would you mind terribly if I smashed it over your head?" The bagger might have asked if I'd like to try one of his plastic bags over my face. The waiter might have noted that I made the same joke seven months ago, after which, near as he can recall, he spat in my entrée, the linguine and seafood dish. The fellow at the bait store might have asked if, with my worms, I preferred regular or Poupon mustard. Mr. Barnes needed only to have kept a stiff lower lip to have brought me down with a thump.

Are these remarks merely a form of showing off: Yo, look at me—clever little mother hubbard, am I not? Yet my motive, I swear, isn't to put anyone down. I fancy myself like the old lamplighter, only working a double shift, making the day a little brighter for the people on whom I try them. The bagger, in my kindly reckoning, goes home that night to tell about this nutty dude at work who asked for a suede bag (you had to be there, I'm afraid he'll have to add).

"I please myself," says Frank Cowperwood, in Theodore Dreiser's trilogy, *The Titan*. Wish I could say the same, but, alas, I am not always able to arrange it. So instead I try, as best I can, to amuse myself, and fairly often succeed. The trick, as I see it, is to continue to do so for as long as possible without getting punched out.

All the News Unfit to Read

(2002)

LOFT, ON A PLANE HEADED FOR SAN FRANCISCO, reading the early pages of the excellent biography of the Sanskrit scholar Max Muller by Nirad C. Chaudhuri, I came across the following item about life in the ducal city of Dessau in Germany, where Muller was born in 1823: "One thing which helped the peace of the town was the absence of newspapers. In his young days at Dessau Muller knew only one, which gave nothing but reports of actual events on one, or half, or even quarter of a sheet." I have long ago given up on Utopia, but this seems a sound state of affairs.

On holiday, I never read a newspaper. As a preface to going away, I call the *New York Times* business office in Chicago, and cancel my home delivery subscription for the days I shall be gone. Invariably, the polite person to whom I give these instructions asks if I would like my papers for the time I will be away to be sent to a local school. Invariably, I answer: "What! Put that poison in the hands of children? Surely you jest." Silence is generally the response.

One of the reasons for going on vacation is to get away from the daily routine, part of which for me is newspaper reading. Someone once said that each day one picks up one's newspaper in eager anticipation and puts it down in disappointment. Smart person, that Someone, for that has been my lifelong experience. I know the importance of newspapers to modern government, but my sentiments have come to resemble those of the character in Tom Stoppard's play *Night & Day* who says, "I'm with you on the free press. It's just the newspapers I can't stand."

I currently read one newspaper a day, but there was a time, living in New York, when I read three and sometimes four a day. I say read when I really mean skimmed. Still, I did this skimming compulsively. There was this thing called the news, and one wanted to stay abreast of it, not miss out on anything as significant as, say, the resignation of the minister of defense in Italy.

I now read only the *New York Times*. Since I neither read any Chicago newspaper nor watch local television news—"Triplets Found in Dumpster, more on Eye Witness News at Ten"—I am splendidly ignorant of what goes on in my own city. A serial killer could be living upstairs, the aforementioned dumpster could be in my alley, and I wouldn't know it.

After consulting the obituary pages, I read the children's sections of the *New York Times*—sports and the arts, in that order. In recent years I've been reading more business news, chiefly that having to do with media mergers and large-scale scandals and the demise of once overpriced executives. Pride may go before the fall for them, but I come after, grinning through my *Schadenfreude*.

I read the front of the paper—the adult section—in something just under the world record for the mile. Op-ed and editorials I glimpse quickly; I'd as lief read a *Times* editorial on, say, the environment as memorize the last fifty pages of recent changes in the tax code. I go through the rest of the paper, glancing at headlines, attracted mainly by the monstrous, the goofy, the egregious. I find very little that would make the Dessau news criterion of "actual events."

During my week in California, I didn't once consult a newspaper, and missed it not at all. I turned on the hotel-room television—it was the last week of the Olympics—to watch people sliding around on skis, skates, and sleds; and occasionally I clicked over to CNN, whose crawls of news squibs tend to interest me more than what the broadcasters were reading.

While on this self-imposed newspaper boycott, did I miss anything? Possibly moderately famous people I know or have heard about have died; perhaps some of the professional athletes in my city have decided to rent themselves out to teams in other cities. Arthur Miller will no doubt have received another award carrying with it a heavy cash prize. Public affairs, I assume, will have been conducted at their usual varying intensities of stupidity.

For the week that I didn't read newspapers I read instead about the immensely impressive Max Muller and also *Virgin Soil*, a novel by Turgenev that I feel I could have written myself, so familiar is its plot of the Russian intellectual going out among the people only to find they are insufficiently impressed by his idealism.

When I return to Chicago, that day's *New York Times* awaits. No sooner do I put down my suitcase and take off my coat than I find myself turning to its obit pages. No one I know has pegged out. In the sports section I learn that the White Sox have rented the services of Kenny Lofton, the excellent center fielder of the Cleveland Indians. Turning to the arts section, I wonder what new prize Arthur Miller will have won. I guess I'm home.

Sorry, Charlie

(2002)

STRUGGLING TO TELL HIS MISTRESS Louise Colet how deeply he felt about her, Flaubert exclaimed, "The language is inept." I suspect the old boy meant "insufficient," which, unfortunately, it often is. There ought, for example, to be a word that falls between "talent" and "genius"; and a word between "envy" and "admiration." The other day it occurred to me that yet another word is needed, this one to describe the relationship that falls between "acquaintance" and "friend."

Last week I learned that a man named Charles Sandusky had died. He was someone I liked a lot, but could not quite call a friend. Yet he was more than an acquaintance merely. I met Charles at the gym where we both worked out. He was a tall man with impressive wavy brown hair and a low hairline, and not all that much gray for a man in his early eighties. Under his aquiline nose lay a serious mustache, of the kind that a bandleader in the 1940s might have worn. He had courtly manners and managed to look dignified even in gym clothes. I liked him straightaway.

We first spoke to each other when we discovered ourselves side by side on two rowing machines. I told him the joke about the wealthy woman who has gone on a cruise that simulates the conditions of a Roman slave galley, with the passengers as slaves, and who asks the woman sitting next to her, "When this cruise is over, how much do you tip the whipper?" He laughed, told me a joke in return, and our acquaintanceship was underway.

In perhaps our third conversation, Charles told me that on the day of his retirement as a salesman in the cardboard-box business, he had arrived home to find his wife seated in a chair in their living room, dead, of cardiac arrest. "In the same day," he said, "I lost my job and my best friend."

His wife was central to his life. "She was the playmaker of our social life," he once told me, hinting at his current loneliness. He was very proud of her. She was a mathematics major at the University of Michigan at a time when women were not encouraged to study anything so difficult. He had a granddaughter doing graduate work in biochemistry, of whom he was also proud and in whom he felt something of his wife's scientific talent lived on.

Charles told me that, after his wife, a relationship with any other woman had proved impossible, though he had tried. He worked out five mornings a week. I don't know how he filled out the rest of his days. He watched a certain amount of sports. He watched science and nature fare on PBS. He was one of those men who take the news very seriously, seeming almost to brood over it. He thought Clinton clownish and outrageous, but also thought the unstinting degradation of him wasn't at all good for the country. He thought about the good of the country in a way that suggested disinterest of a sort that has long gone out of style.

Worrying about becoming a bore, he used often to apologize for hauling the past into our rowing-machine conversations. But he couldn't help it. "When I grew up, I not only never met but never even heard about anyone who was divorced," he would say, or, "It's impossible to make people understand what it was like during the Depression, how fragile and frightening life seemed."

On a couple of occasions, I told myself I ought to invite Charles to join me for lunch, so that we could have a longer, less interrupted conversation. But I held back. I did so out of a self-protectiveness that I suspect sets in as one grows older. Instead of plunging ahead, refusing to strangle a social impulse, forming new friendships wherever one can—in friendship, the more the merrier, right?—at a certain point one begins to consider the consequences of new friendships. Isn't one's dance card already filled with the obligations, not always met, of old friendships? One circles the wagons around oneself. In my mind, I drew a line before Charles: pals at the gym, this far and no further.

For reasons too elaborate and boring to go into here, more than a year ago I began to take my workouts elsewhere. I thought of Charles often, though I cannot say that I longed for his company. He had reached his early eighties in such good physical and mental shape that I imagined him making it smoothly to ninety. News of his death gave me a small jolt. Without claiming that his departure marks a great personal subtraction for me, the world nonetheless seemed better with him in it.

I don't exactly feel guilty about not letting my acquaintanceship with Charles deepen into a friendship; I have, alas, greater calls on my guilt. I suspect we all have such relationships, likable acquaintances who could so easily have become dear friends, and who leave one thinking both of the possibilities of life and of its limitations, too. There ought to be a better name for them.

Book Swining

(2002)

Y EFFICIENT EDITOR at Houghton Mifflin has just sent me an email informing me that finished copies of a new book I have written will come off the press on May 31, with books to be shipped to bookstores on June 6, after which I shall receive my author's shipment of—if I remember correctly—twenty copies. The physical object, the artifact, the commodity, the actual book at long last will appear. This ought to be a pleasing moment, and for the vast most part it is. But in smaller part it presents complications.

First among these is the question of to whom to give my author's copies. Some go to members of my family, some to close friends, some to those writers who have sent me copies of their own books. The risk of hurting some people's feelings by not sending them a copy is worrisome. But there is also the risk of sending copies to people who, harsh truth to tell, can live quite nicely without them. Sending a person a free book is not always an unmitigated good deed.

"You know, my dear Epstein," the late Arnaldo Momigliano, the historian of the ancient world, once told me, in his strong Piedmontese accent, "the cheapest way to acquire a book remains to buy it." I puzzled over this Zen koanish-like statement for a good bit, until I realized that what Arnaldo meant was that if you buy a book at least you don't have to read the damn thing. But if you are given a book, or even lent one, you are stuck—under an obligation to read it and comment upon it.

I know that when I give someone a copy of one of my books I feel that they are under the obligation to read it and only under a slightly lesser obligation to like it rather a lot. Writers, as perhaps you may not be aware, are swine. "I have never known a writer who was not vain and egotistical," writes the German critic Marcel Reich-Ranicki in his recent book *The Author of Himself*, "unless he was a particularly bad writer." By this standard, I turn out to be quite a good writer.

Viewing things the other way round, I am generally pleased to be sent a copy of someone else's book. True, I prefer that the book be of fewer than 400 pages—fewer than 300 pages is even better—and not on the subject of, say, the Haymarket riots, organ transplantation, or the scandal of preschool education.

I check the index of all the books I am sent for my name; also the acknowledgments for the same reason. (Did I mention that writers are swine?) Once I was sent four copies of the same book by an astonishingly prolific author and discovered, lo, the book was dedicated to me. The dedication noted my wit and wisdom, though, oddly, failed to mention my appealing humility. Although I didn't much care for the fellow, I was, momentarily, touched. Then I remembered that he was said to have written and edited more than 250 books, and thought: Being the dedicatee of one of his books was perhaps less than a thunderous big deal; I mean, it wasn't as if he had lent me twenty bucks. (Swine, I tell you, writers are utter swine.)

People given books by the author prefer them signed. I don't at all mind doing so. A signed book cannot be returned to the bookstore. Book signings are also a way of stimulating the sale of a book, of course, and if the author is someone popular enough, which usually means someone known from his or her regular appearances on television, people line up in large numbers to acquire the book with the author's signature. The other side of this is the sad story of the unknown author. I recently attended a book-signing for a former student of mine where eight people showed up, and I didn't stick around to find out how many of these actually bought the book.

I have had people I don't know send me books for my signature. There are two reasons for their doing this, I suppose: They think a signed copy somehow or other talismanic, producing magical effects; or they believe a signed first edition of a book may one day be extremely valuable. What they cannot know is that the really valuable copies of most of my books are the second editions—valuable because, alas, they don't exist.

Signed books can leave a trail. Ten or so years ago I was browsing in Powell's used bookshop in Hyde Park in Chicago and discovered, with a smile, that Saul Bellow had sold books inscribed to him by the then still living critic Irving Howe. I failed to smile when, a few years later, I discovered a signed copy of an early book of mine on the shelf of another Chicago used bookshop. The book was inscribed to a woman writer who is my contemporary: "To dear X, in friendship." To this day I wish I had bought the book, and returned it to the now much less dear X, with the amended inscription: "[Still] in friendship[?]" Swine, as I say, writers, real swine.

Khaki-Pantsman

(2002)

K HAKIS, YOU MAY NOT HAVE NOTICED, are in crisis. Sales of casual pants for men, among which khakis predominate, have fallen off. A recent article in the *Wall Street Journal* reports that they are down 11.5 percent, grossing $3.86 billion last year, while jeans have held steady, with sales of $4.94 billion. A khaki-pants man—as a traditionalist or square, I prefer the word "trousers"—I worry about this.

I should have known trouble was on the way when a student, last autumn, wrote in a composition that he had encountered a man sitting at a bar wearing white khakis. I circled the phrase, scribbling in the margin something like, "Khakis are khaki-colored; they cannot be white." When I mentioned this to the class as one of a number of small but dopey errors that had cropped up in the past week's essays, I quickly saw that the sentiment in the room was on the student's side and not mine. Everyone but I understood that khakis could be any color in the world, puce and chartreuse included.

Five pairs of khakis, all indubitably khaki-colored, currently hang in my closet. They all have pleats and turn-ups, as the English call cuffs. Although I have worn such trousers for fifty years, I have never called them khakis. (The word khaki is of Hindu derivation, meaning dusty or dust-colored, and khaki uniforms were first used by the British in India, though they were not part of regular British Army issue until the Boer

War of 1899–1902.) At various times, I have called them "wash pants" (because they could be thrown in the wash, though I now send mine to the dry cleaner), chinos (another word for khaki twill), and suntans, which is what they were called when I wore them in the US Army. They tend to be inexpensive and durable, and can be worn with anything from T-shirts to blazers and work with nearly any color in the world.

I wear khakis perhaps two-hundred-fifty days of the year, corduroys on cold winter days, and some variation of black or gray pants the rest of the time. I have done this for so long that some while ago I ran into a fellow I knew from high school, who remarked that I seemed to be wearing the same clothes now that I did back then. This wasn't meant as a put-down, just a statement of amazement. It also happens to be accurate.

I own no blue jeans. If I were Secretary of Male Haberdashery, I would outlaw jeans for men past the age of forty. Comfort-fit, wide-leg, stone-washed, parboiled, or filleted, jeans on men of middle age who aren't working construction or appearing in a cowboy movie, or who don't happen to be Robert Redford, are a grave sartorial mistake. They divest a man of seriousness. Would Justice Holmes have worn jeans? Would Thomas Mann? I prefer to believe that Colin Powell wouldn't, but I like to think that Yasser Arafat, relaxing at home, just might have an old pair around the house that would give him that Jordache look.

Khakis have changed very little in my lifetime, usually reverting to their old, solid, boring essence. They were once made with a small and utterly useless belt in the back. For a spell they were made slightly baggy; "bags" is the name by which the English used sometimes to call them. I don't believe that, during that Hieronymus Bosch period for men's clothes, the 1970s, khakis went bell-bottom; at least mine remained straight-legged. In 1999 a pants manufacturer turned out a Capri khaki pant for men, cut off at mid-calf; briefly popular, they died a well-deserved death.

Meanwhile, I worry that men's pants makers, wanting to recapture their share of the market for khakis, might let their innovative urges loose and spoil a good thing. In the *Wall Street Journal* article mention is made of one manufacturer attempting a stain-resistant version of khakis, which sounds sensible enough. But another, the company called Dockers, last year produced something called "Mobile Pants," also known as "cargo pants for grownups." These trousers have seven hidden pockets, two of them with seam zippers, allowing men to stash pagers, cell phones, for all I know a smoked fish, and perhaps a pet iguana in their pants.

I'm reminded of the late Samuel Goldwyn, he of the beautifully mangled clichés ("If I want your opinion, I'll give it to you."), who was said never to carry anything in his trouser pockets lest they lose their perfect line. I myself carry in mine a quarter pound of keys, a wallet for credit cards and driver's license, a money clip, and a small silver penknife.

Running dog of capitalism though I am, I nonetheless worry that pants manufacturers, in their attempt to find a niche in the khaki market, will get fancier and fancier. I can easily envision khakis with each leg a different color, ragged bottoms, epaulets on the pockets. "Sam," an old Milton Berle song had it, "you made the pants too long." Today it needs to be changed to, "Sam, please, I beg you, leave the pants alone."

A Cheap Night Out

(2002)

A WARM MONDAY NIGHT IN CHICAGO, and I'm feeling flush and contented, departing a parking lot with my wife, beginning our walk to the Emperor's Choice, our favorite Chinese restaurant on Wentworth Avenue. A guy in his early thirties, in jeans, a well-worn chambray work shirt, and a white hard hat, with a phone in his hand, asks, "Do you speak English?" When I tell him that I have been known to do so, he begins a long and detailed story, which I shall provide here in a much-shortened version.

He works for his father's construction company—the name is beautifully vague, like Acme or Delta Development—and he's been driving one of the company trucks, which is stalled nearby. The towing company won't take a credit card, but insists on cash, and he is twenty-seven dollars short of the sum required. Could I help him out? He promises that "Nancy," in the office, will cut me a check for the sum in the morning.

"If you are conning me," I say, "at my age I shall have to repair to the Gobi Desert, to live out my days as a hermit, forever disappointed in humankind. You wouldn't do that to an older gent, would you?"

He shows me his hands, palms turned outward, which are calloused, a cut on the left one. He offers to get someone on his phone for me to prove his bona fides. I shake him off. How much does he need? He says, eyes looking down at the pavement, the whole twenty-seven bucks. The towing company won't do business with him for less.

What the hell? Why not? I take my money clip out of my pants pocket and realize I have only twenties. If I am going to trust him for $27, why not trust him for $40? Between a twenty-seven-dollar fool and a forty-dollar fool, there is only a thirteen-dollar difference. I peel off two twenties and hand them to him. He exudes a look of extreme gratitude, says thank you, hugs my wife lightly, then hugs me.

"Did you ever see the movie *Pay It Forward*?" he asks. We haven't. He explains that in it when a person has been the recipient of a good deed, he must turn around and do a similar deed. He wants us to know that he will not forget to do so.

"Please," he says, "write down your name and address, so that I know where to have the check sent." After I do so, he asks if I would mind also writing down our phone number, so that he can have his wife call up to thank us. He wants to know what's the latest he can have her call. He shakes hands with me, and smiles. I note he seems to be missing the back teeth on the upper right side. Not a good sign, I fleetingly think.

"Thanks again," he says, "I won't forget this." And, clapping his hard hat on his head, he walks off briskly in the direction of the nearby Dan Ryan Expressway.

Surprise: His wife didn't call that evening, nor did he the day after. Now, nearly five weeks later, "Nancy" seems to have forgotten to mail the check. I have, indubitably, been conned and taken, shaken and nicely baked.

I choose, however, not to go to the Gobi Desert. For some reason, I am not as depressed about this as perhaps I ought to be. Why, I ask myself, don't I feel, in the language of my people, more of a *schmuck* than I do? Part of me admires the sheer style with which I have been taken; it entailed, after all, costuming: that hard hat, the phone, the calloused hands, the whole bit. Bringing up the movie *Pay It Forward* was a fine touch; so was the request for our phone number and the nicety of asking what was the latest that his wife could call. Our man, it suggested, was well brought up.

Forty dollars is a little more than the cost of my wife's and my Chinese dinner that evening. If the money had slipped out of my pocket, or if I had even been pickpocketed, I think I would have felt more aggrieved. Instead my wife and I were presented with a show of fairly high quality. Fewer than eighty bucks for dinner and a night's entertainment—by current standards, not all that bad.

Panhandling is becoming more and more widespread in America. Sometimes it can be menacing. Not long ago I was stopped in a supermarket parking lot by a guy with what I believe are known as felony muscles, who told me he had just got out of jail and could I let him have a buck? I forked it over without hesitation. Sometimes it can be truly affecting: men horribly crippled in motorized chairs selling newspapers for the homeless. But for the most part I shell out my dollar or two only for the really impressive and well-made cock-and-bull stories, extravagant tales of sadness recounted with flair.

"You know," I remember my father saying, "it doesn't hurt to get conned every once in a while. Keeps you sharp. Reminds you of your own fallibility." He was no dope, my father.

An Offer I Could Refuse

(2002)

A FEW WEEKS AGO a nice woman who lives in my building asked if I would be interested in teaching two morning sessions devoted to Montaigne to her book group. They would be meeting in Starved Rock, Illinois. My and my wife's expenses would be paid, and I would be given a $600 fee. The setting was quite beautiful, I was assured, and I could spend the afternoons walking in the woods with my wife.

That last point clinched it. Absolutely not, I thought. I love my wife, and I'm not going to let those mosquitoes, ticks, chiggers, poison ivy, and whole multitude of irritators have so open a shot at her. I'm not a big fan of nature. Unlike the old fight trainer Whitey Bimstein, who, asked what he thought of the country when working with a boxer at Grossinger's, said he thought it was a pretty nice place, I don't think it's such a nice place. I prefer to see it, when I have to see it at all, from out the window of a fast and comfortable car, preferably with the songs of Reynaldo Hahn on the CD player.

The combination of being in the country and partaking of adult education was an offer I had no difficulty refusing. It's not easy nowadays to have an utterly unfashionable opinion, but I wonder if my strong distaste for adult education qualifies. I can't take such stuff myself, and I don't want to dole it out—not even for a fee.

I had my first taste of adult education as an undergraduate at the University of Chicago, where, in order to arrange my schedule so that I could stay up all night and sleep late into the morning, I took a Shakespeare course in the university's downtown night division. My classmates were men and women in their forties through their seventies. Most were there not to work on an unfinished degree but for the sheer love of learning. Until then it had not occurred to me that the sheer love of learning could be a deeply disturbing thing.

This Shakespeare course taught me that one could grow older without growing smarter. Shakespeare does many things, so I shouldn't have been surprised that his plays could bring out the confident ignorance in people of all ages. My classmates were quite as clueless as I, not so much about Shakespeare as about the world. "Kids," the smarmy Art Linkletter used to say on his radio show, "say the darnedest things." But adults said things in that class even darneder. This made me sad.

The number of people signing up for adult education courses figures to rise as people live longer. Adult education is a regular feature of every so-called senior-citizen home; retirees flock to nearby universities and community colleges, ostensibly hungry for education, though perhaps hungrier still for something to do with their time.

As a quondam university teacher, I have on a few occasions been asked to give adult education courses. I can't bring myself to do it. What would be the point of my flogging away at course length to retired men and women about the majestic aesthetic virtues and wisdom of Henry James, Joseph Conrad, and Willa Cather? A lecture is one thing—it's an intellectual entertainment, a divertissement—but a full course suggests a much greater promise: a promise on which, I am fairly certain, I can't deliver.

I would, I suppose, be killing an hour or two in a long week for people who go in for adult education, but doing so would, I believe, kill more than time for me. Ignorance in the young is understandable; ignorance in the old, though also understandable, is depressing because of its hopelessness. And there is something slightly fraudulent about pretending to teach people things they are unlikely to have the time to put to use. How can you tell someone in, say, his early eighties that Henry James advises one be a person on whom nothing is lost when the likelihood is great that that person has already missed nearly everything?

Adult education is built on the premise of self-improvement—improvement right up to the moment, it would seem, of death. In his eighties, Santayana said that his physician advised him to lose fifteen pounds, evidently hoping, the philosopher noted, to have him perfectly healthy just in time for his demise. Adult education seems to operate on the same assumption.

Yet quite bright older people continue to sign up for one course after another: on philosophy, on contemporary fiction, on Zoroastrianism. I know a man, himself the author of serious books in American history, who recently took a course in the writing of Jack Kerouac. When he told me this, my first instinct was to tell him that, in a more sensible world, Kerouac ought to be taking courses from him. Shall we all end our days listening to teachers drone on about subjects we don't need to know? Will death arrive with neither a bang nor a whimper but during a short course in the politics of the Balkans?

Back on the Bus

(2003)

WFMT IS THE NAME OF A RELIGIOUS CULT in Chicago that disguises itself as a radio station. The religion is that of musical culture, classical music and opera chiefly. I happen to belong to this cult. Its announcers are careful never to mispronounce foreign names or words; the station eschews all canned commercials; a tone of seriousness pervades the proceedings, every day all day (and night) long. The station is a good reason to live in Chicago.

One morning this past summer, a WFMT announcer said that a ten-day musical tour of three great cities of Mitteleuropa—Budapest, Vienna, and Prague—was being organized over the Christmas holidays. On the tour one would hear three operas, see a ballet, and go to two concerts, the most notable of them a rehearsal performance of the famous New Year's Day concert of the Vienna Philharmonic. The cost was roughly $5,000 per person. I signed up.

I have been on only one other travel tour in my life, a 17-day Swan's cruise of the Greek Islands, Turkey, and the Dalmatian coast. Swan's was then an English-run company, which specialized in sending Oxford dons along to lecture its clients. Maurice Bowra used to do Swan's cruises; on the one I attended, John Chadwick, who was in on the discovery of the Linear B script, was a lecturer. Our fellow travelers were mainly English and

Australian, and, in the main, very winning. On this cruise, the left-wing journalist I. F. Stone was on board—the first time, you might say, that I had an actual fellow-traveler for a fellow-traveler—and each night, wearing his Magooish spectacles and a dinner jacket, he boogalooed (Magooalooed?) with his wife to the music of a small Greek band. *Charmant*!

The trade-off (to use the cant word) between traveling on a tour and traveling independently is that on a tour one sheds all worries: about luggage, reservations, meals, tickets, and the rest. For this relief from anxiety, one loses a certain sense of serendipitous adventure. On a tour, too, one abandons the luxury of waking, eating, and going about just as one damn well pleases. Alone, of course, one doesn't have to contend with one's, in Henry James's phrase, "detested fellow pilgrims," or, as I came to think of them, one's DFPs.

As for those DFPs—and there were thirty-five of us in all on this tour— my social antennae alerted me to steer clear of a number of them. Steering clear chiefly meant avoiding them at meals, and this I was for the most part able to do. Only now do I wonder if perhaps the social antennae of others advised them to steer clear of me.

We were blessed in being led by a sweet character in his late sixties, a Viennese of wide culture and great kindness and good humor, named Paul Koutny. Herr Koutny arranged superior tickets, ordered splendid meals, made things as little regimented as possible. Still, the Ken Kesey-ian question, "Are you on the bus?" had to be asked, often and insistently.

This tour also taught me about the very real limits of my cultural stamina. I had long before known that my museum stamina was fairly low— that is, one hour in a museum, any museum, and you can, as they say about major-league pitchers who are done for, put a fork in me. This tour, with six musical performances in eight days, showed me that my performing arts stamina is also fairly low.

The musical highlight of the tour was a New Year's Eve performance of Beethoven's "Ninth Symphony" played by the Vienna Symphony in the acoustically fine Wiener Konzerthaus. There we heard the greatest symphony of the greatest symphonist played under perfect conditions— musically, a 720 slam dunk. But I knew I was beginning to tire when, the following night, sitting in a plush loge seat watching *Die Fledermaus*, I thought to myself that there is perhaps nothing heavier than German light opera. And I knew I was in serious trouble in Prague when, in the same opera house in which it was first performed and the orchestra conducted by Mozart, late in the second act of *Don Giovanni*, I invoked Mozart please to hurry and kill off his miserable eponymous libertine so that I could return to my hotel to get some sleep.

Tourism of course remains tourism. No greater deception is possible than that of believing three days in Budapest, three in Vienna, and two in Prague (perhaps the most interesting city of the trio) will give one any more than a glancing sense of these cities and what is distinctive about their cultures. Tourism is, I fear, to deep knowledge what channel surfing is to Greek tragedy. In each of these three historically great cities, I felt the desire to live there for a year or more, had I the time and money to do so. I didn't, don't, and, regret to report, probably never will. So, with a smile at my DFPs, instead I got back on the bus.

The Food of My People

(2003)

I DON'T KNOW HOW SERIOUSLY to take the alarming talk about the spread of SARS, or Severe Acute Respiratory Syndrome. For now I prefer to think of it as SAMS, or Severe Acute Media Syndrome, as David Baltimore, the president of Caltech, recently called it, suggesting that its danger has been greatly pumped up by television and the press. But, either way, it is not going to keep me out of Chinese restaurants, whose business, according to various reports, has been hard hit by the SARS scare.

"The food of my people" is what I call Chinese food. When I say this, I refer to the unrelenting enthusiasm of Jews for Chinese food. An old joke has it that Jewish civilization has existed for 5,764 years and Chinese civilization for 4,701 years, which is why for more than a thousand years the Jews went hungry.

Jews make up a large, in several places a preponderant, part of the clientele of many Chinese restaurants. "How is it," the comedian Jackie Mason asks, "you see so many Jews in Chinese restaurants and you never see a Chinese in a Jewish restaurant?" The answer, obviously, is that Chinese food is so much better.

The only similarity between the two kinds of restaurants is one that is dying out: the presence of ever so slightly belligerent waiters. Innumerable are the Jewish waiter jokes ("Which of you gentlemen ordered the clean glass?" "They seem to be out of cream in the kitchen. Would you take your coffee without milk?") The old Chinese waiters somehow strove to make plain that they were above their work and that, in a more just world, you would be waiting on them. This made it incumbent upon you quickly to establish that, since we all had to live in an unjust world, you'd like to start with the Won Ton soup.

My mother, who was beautiful and highly intelligent, but less than a four-star chef, prepared the first Chinese food I ate. The dish was chop suey, itself not a genuine Chinese dish but, I'm told, an American invention. Hers was made up of large chunks of beef and vast quantities of cooked celery soaked in soy sauce and served atop rice. Nothing of the subtlety of Chinese cuisine was even hinted at in this dish.

My first official Chinese food was eaten at a neighborhood restaurant called Pekin House. Cantonese was the style of its cooking. Nothing very exotic was served: egg rolls, egg foo young, shrimp in lobster sauce, fried rice, the standard fare. So completely Jewish was its clientele that in time the restaurant's owner, a Chinese, himself began to look Jewish: He wore the same clothes as his customers, he had black-framed glasses, his very mannerisms came to seem Jewish.

In the summer of my fourteenth year, for two weeks I replaced one of the busboys at the Pekin House. After the restaurant closed, busboys could eat anything they wished from the menu, except shrimp dishes. I was a gastronomically unadventurous kid, and so I ordered the plainest provender. It may be that I am still trying to make up for that missed opportunity.

Part of the hardship of being in the peacetime Army for me was the paucity of good Chinese restaurants in Texas and Arkansas. In Little Rock, I discovered a Chinese restaurant that, in the attempt to ease its customers over the cultural bump, began all meals with a small salad instead of an egg roll and supplied its diners with white bread to sop up the gravy.

I must have been in my thirties when Chinese restaurants with Mandarin-style, soon followed by Szechuan, cooking came to Chicago. Like Bertrand Russell, who discovered sex around the same age, I couldn't get enough. Truth is, I still can't. I could eat in Chinese restaurants, good ones, four nights a week, and in merely okay ones the other three nights.

A new restaurant opened recently in our neighborhood, a joke spinning off the oldest cliché about Chinese food has it—half-Chinese, half-German. It's very good, but the problem is, an hour after you've eaten there, you're hungry for power. My only problem with Chinese food is that I find it eats too fast. Which is one of the reasons I am pleased to have learned, many moons ago, to use chopsticks. Even though I'm fairly adept, they permit me to abandon my heavy shovel method.

No other Asian food quite works for me. Thai food is too sweet, Korean too hot and too blatant; Indian food I consider mud and peppers, with curry added; Japanese food, though prettiest of all, is somehow insubstantial, with sushi, in my coarse view, being fit only for castaways. Chinese food is the only one that I look forward to eating with serious excitement.

Hot and sour soup, Singapore noodles, scallops and Chinese broccoli, Kung-pao chicken, beef and pea pods, these are some of the names of my desires. Bubonic plague, maybe; threat of earthquake, quite possibly; invasion by aliens, of course; but SARS will not keep me out of Chinese restaurants. I'd like to begin, I do believe, with the pot stickers.

No Opinion

(2003)

URING A QUESTION-AND-ANSWER PERIOD following one of his lectures, the political philosopher Michael Oakeshott was asked what he thought about England's place in the European Union. "I don't," Oakeshott replied, "see that I am required to have an opinion on that."

I found that response very helpful, for more and more things crop up on which I, too, feel having an opinion is unnecessary. Especially has this become so in the realm of popular culture. On the movie *The Matrix* and its sequel, for example, I have no need to weigh in with a penetrating, or even banal, insight. This is a subject best left to those pop culture punditi who specialize in being ten minutes ahead of the With-It Express.

In his novel *Guerrillas*, V. S. Naipaul says of a character whom he loathes that "she had a great many opinions but taken together these did not add up to a point of view." I like to think that I have by now a point of view: a reasonably settled sense of what is and isn't significant in life. Such things as *The Matrix*, the rise of rap music, the fall of the sitcom, the future of the Women's National Basketball Association, and a number of other items touching on the epiphenomena of the ephemeral do not qualify as requiring my opinion.

I'm not such an immitigable highbrow that I don't watch movies or my share of television, but I just don't feel the need to deliver finely honed opinions about them. I am content not to go beyond the subtlety of the Hollywood producer who is said to have divided all the screenplays sent him into two categories: "Piece of Crap" and "Not a Piece of Crap." Being a textured thinker, I would sometimes call upon a third category: "Not Entirely a Piece of Crap."

Other people's opinions, on popular culture, and much else, help us feel them out. Most of us search for people whose opinions are roughly congruent with our own, believing, I suppose, that anyone who doesn't share our distastes is himself distasteful. Yet congruence of opinion isn't a good test for judging character. A better test is if you think well of someone despite his opinions. More disturbing still is to encounter someone whose opinions on a great many subjects are very close to your own whom you recognize as unmistakably a creep.

Economists trained at the University of Chicago can be death on the thinness, the utter airiness, of much opinion. They make a specialty of knocking down your opinions, no matter how trivial. ("Why, exactly, would you say it's a nice day?") When last I lunched with my late cousin, the Chicago economist Sherwin Rosen, who was very good at this, he asked if he could pay his share of the lunch. "Not necessary," I said, "if you'll just give me back my assumptions."

In the political realm, of course, judging people on their opinions is trickiest of all. I know a woman who is trying to break up her dearest friend's dalliance with a man whose standard Republican politics she, the first woman, despises: How can one possibly love a man who isn't pro-choice? I don't happen to think that politics are always, or even often, a strong index of character, especially since so many people's politics don't really touch their lives. "He takes his politics from Moscow," an old put-down of fashionable left-wingers used to run, "and his cooking from Paris." For many people, political opinions are to be worn, like designer clothes, for their brand quality. But just as it wouldn't do to make a final judgment on a woman for wearing a DKNY T-shirt, neither is it smart to admire a man simply because he believes in the Invisible Hand of the market.

I imagine there must be an intellectual somewhere who has averred he could not possibly love a woman who does not hold the novels of Thomas Pynchon in high esteem. I myself have had no difficulty loving women who wanted to, and others who didn't in the least care about, saving the whale. My own preference is for people who have the independence and confidence to proclaim perfectly heterodox opinions in hostile territory. Someone at a meeting of, say, the Modern Language Association who says that he is nuts about the singing of Wayne Newton. Or a woman who announces that she thinks pro football an elegant sport.

I once read a letter that my friend Edward Shils wrote to a young contributor of his magazine, *Minerva*, in which he offered to publish an article she had sent him if she would remove the opinions in the article, which he found callow and untrue. If she felt the need of opinion in the article, he added, he would be only too glad to supply his own. That seems to me to get the notion of opinion in right perspective: as something transient, arbitrary, and shallow.

"Crudity and Falsehood copulate," wrote Paul Valéry, "and give birth to Opinion." Attend the christening, by all means, but I wouldn't send a gift.

The Attack on the Hot Dog

(2003)

THE $19 HOT DOG HAS ARRIVED. I came into this valuable news through the *Wall Street Journal*, which reports that they are gussying up hot dogs in New York and Los Angeles. The $19 dog is available at a joint called the Old Homestead. A Kobe beef frankfurter, it is "parboiled and served with Kobe beef chili, Cheshire cheese sauce, and Vidalia onions." If you're looking to cut back, you can get a mere $16 dog at the Belvedere in Beverly Hills, where the dog is made of chicken thigh meat and foie gras, served with oven-dried tomato ketchup and morel mushroom and onion relish.

Demographically, this is food, clearly, for that portion of the population of whom Barnum said one was born every minute. The promotion through upgrading of what is essentially working-class food for the palates of the wealthy has been around a long time. The lunch *spécialité de la maison* at a club I belong to is corned-beef hash with an egg on top. Cassoulet, an old French peasant dish, can be found in three-star restaurants for stratospheric prices.

Yet until now one might have thought that there would be no way to upgrade the hot dog, that "cartridge," as H. L. Mencken once called it, "made from the sweepings of the abattoir floor." Chicago, "Hog Butcher to the World," in the words of that old baloney salesman Carl Sandburg, had more and larger abattoirs than anyone else, and as a Chicagoan born and bred, I suspect that my own number of cartridges consumed has easily exceeded a thousand. The last one I bought, at a Cubs-Brewers game a couple of weeks or so ago, cost $3, which I thought high priced, but I had no choice.

Most of the hot dogs of my youth came in for around 25 cents. Fifteen cents more bought a small brown bag of fresh-cut and splendidly greasy French fries. (In those Edenic times, grease was not yet thought artery-choking but instead was considered a flavor-enhancer.) As a boy between the ages of 13 and 18, I would wolf down a hot dog at odd hours during the day or night; when my friends and I had dogs for lunch, we'd usually have two, with fries, washed down with a fine, belch-producing Pepsi-Cola.

The best hot dogs in Chicago were produced either by the Vienna or the David Berg sausage company. They were bright red, with thick skins. We ate them with yellow mustard, piccalilli, and chopped onions—never ketchup, which was considered *outré*. Ask in those days for Poupon mustard, and I could not have answered for the consequences. (Some people liked to add hot green peppers.) A properly steamed bun with poppy seeds was the finishing touch. I could go for one now, hold the peppers.

Every subject has its connoisseurship, hot dogs included. In Chicago, we never put sauerkraut on a hot dog because the kraut was felt, rightly, to compete with the flavor of the dog. The same applies to chili on a hot dog—*verboten*. Lettuce and tomatoes occasionally show up on Chicago hot dogs; so, too, mayonnaise, but one assumes such barbarities have been requested by bumpkins.

I once read that the Boston journalist George Frazier III used to bring his own hot dogs to Fenway Park, and pay the vendors the cost of the park's regular dogs to put them on the grill. A nice touch, yet here the purist would argue that hot dogs oughtn't to be grilled—again, because of the interfering taste of charcoal—but boiled, so that the rich blatant spiciness of the dogs emerges to the highest power.

The grilled sausages of my youth were Polish sausages served with French's Mustard and fried onions. I remember the powerfully tantalizing smell of them on Sunday morning visits to Maxwell Street, Chicago's oldest and most exotic flea market, which contained Gypsy fortune-tellers and black men who knew more Yiddish than a lot of Reform rabbis now under 40. I occasionally eat a Polish sausage sandwich at a ballgame, if I am in a death-defying or suicidal mood. They seemed slightly dangerous even when I was a kid; in those days we referred to them as polio sausages. Like so much that is not good for you, they are delicious.

The combination of vanity and the lust for health has reduced my intake of hot dogs radically. I may now eat fewer than 10 a year. Hot dog stands are still endemic in Chicago; not half the man I used to be, I drive by them without looking sideways.

Along with the difficulty that hot dogs present to the health-minded, along with the attack on them in the form of gentrification by dopey upscale restaurants, hot dogs now have something of an image problem. "Hot-dogging" has come to mean showing off; to be a "hot dog" is to be someone deliberately outrageous. Better, I suppose, to be a hot dog than a turkey (a hopelessly inelegant loser), but still bad enough.

The old hot dog is on its way to becoming an endangered species. What, as Lenin asked in another context, is to be done? Grab a dog for lunch, my advice is, and tell them, please, hold the foie gras.

Shine

(2003)

I HAVEN'T HAD A SHOESHINE, a professional shine, in more than a decade, maybe two. I shine my own shoes, usually once a week. Shoeshine parlors were common when I was a boy, and even a young man, in Chicago. Most barbershops also had a shoeshine man. Not always but often he was black. I stopped getting shoeshines when race relations in America became so ragged and nervous-making. The symbolism of a black man working at the feet of a white man was too heavy for me. I decided—the hell with it—to shine my own shoes.

But the other day, in San Francisco and needing a shine, I passed, on Geary Street, near the city's miniscule theater district, a small white man, with a face resembling a little that of the battling welterweight Carmen Basilio, in a blue smock seated before his three-seat shoeshine stand. I climbed up into one of the seats. He took a long last drag and prepared to toss away his cigarette, which I told him he needn't do. He replied, in a strong Italian accent, "Smoking all in the head anyway."

The shine began with his tucking the bows of my shoelaces into the tops of my shoes, so that he would not get polish on them that would rub off on my trouser cuffs. He next lit a Zippo lighter that he touched briefly to the outer sides of my shoes; this, I've subsequently learned, is to burn off any loose threads from the leather. With a toothbrush he painted the outer edges of my soles. Five or six rounds of creams and polish were applied, each followed by buffings with either soft clothes or brushes.

Several years ago, *Esquire* printed an article titled "The World's Second-Best Shoeshine." Turns out it was to be had at the airport in Cleveland, where they used an ultraviolet lamp—to precisely what purpose, I cannot now recall—on one's shoes. For the world's best shoeshine, it was, the author of the article claimed, a dead-heat tie between the shines available at Grand Central Station and at the Pierre Hotel in New York. This man on Geary Street in San Francisco should have been in the running.

Working away, he told me he was from Calabria, which he loved, though he found it impossible to earn a living there. After he asked me my age, he told me that he was seventy-two, and had attempted to retire, but after three days at home concluded it was not for him. He had four daughters, all living in northern California, and ten grandchildren.

We spoke as two men of the world, and I hope I report accurately when I say there was no condescension on either side. The shine was first-class— it lasted sixteen days. I never asked him how much it cost. When I dismounted from the chair, I handed him a $10 bill. "Grazie," he said. Had I been wearing a hat, I would have tipped it to him.

I walked off, admiring the deep brown gleam of my shoes, and pleased, not for the first time in my life, that I wasn't Gene Kelly, or I should have had to tap-dance down Geary Street all the way to Union Square, singing a lyric of doubtless astonishing banality. While perhaps less than Prozacian in its power of uplift, something there is about a fresh shoeshine that exhilarates, or at least it does me. Well-pleated pants, a colorful necktie, a good shine, and thou, and city living is paradise enow.

As a boy, I was asked to shine my father's shoes, which, unlike other small chores I was given, I didn't in the least mind. I don't recall spending much time shining my own shoes as an adolescent. Sometimes, if I were feeling flush, I might have a shoeshine in a barbershop. In the Army, shoe-shining could be nearly a full-time job. My fellow troopers, or at least the more gung-ho among them, would buy alcohol, Q-tips, and special cloths (let us not speak of the expenditure of vast quantities of spit) to achieve the highest possible sheen on their black boots and shoes. When I was a draftee in the peacetime Army, dedicated to a mediocrity of general performance, my own shines came out considerably lower than the highest wattage but were, somehow, passable.

After shining my shoes nowadays, life seems to be a touch more promising. I don't suppose anyone notices that my shoes are shined, but I, for some reason, notice when they are not. (In this, the age of the gym shoe, some men may no longer own leather shoes.) The notion of having shined shoes speaks to holding up standards, even if in a very minor way.

What really pleased me about my shoeshine in San Francisco was the craft that went into it, which, even though the task might be small, seemed to me of a high order. This Calabrian was a man supplying a service; I required that service. He knew what he was doing, and did it well. The phrase "a pleasure doing business with you," which I uttered when we parted, did not, for once, seem mere cant.

Marginalized

(2003)

I WAS READING ALONG IN A LIBRARY COPY of C. S. Lewis's book *The Four Loves*, which, to my mild chagrin, had been underlined and sidelined by various earlier readers using different markers: both fine and soft pencils and a ballpoint pen. I'm afraid that the writing of Lewis, a wise man whose style tends toward the aphoristic, encourages this activity. I am a sideliner of books myself, usually using a light pencil to do my marking. But I much prefer to do so on a virgin page, and it's more than a little distracting to have other readers underscore significant passages for me before I come to a book.

I got used to these previous readers, most of whom seemed to me percipient in their choices of passages to underscore, but then, in Lewis's chapter "Friendship," I encountered someone—a woman, I suspect—who went bonkers. Using her ballpoint pen like a dagger, she carved imprecations into the book's margins. In the few pages in which Lewis writes of the complexities of friendship between men and women, she wrote, all in capital letters, with no extra charge for the exclamation marks, "MALE CHAUVINIST!!!" On the facing page she noted "What is this bull shit?!" And atop the following page, simply, "bull shit!" She was not very happy, either, with Lewis's connection between friendship and religion, making a looping mark around the eight or nine sentences he devotes to the connection and, going off the rails completely now, providing the not quite intelligible response, "bull suck."

It occurred to me to correct her vituperations, for the taurine droppings she refers to are spelled as one word, not two. Someone else, a cooler head with an educational impulse and working in faint pencil markings, also tried to straighten her out. "He's describing what happens—not what should be," this sensible fellow advised, and a bit later he patiently instructed, "Reread all of it!" But it's too late; she's a goner—clearly beyond all hope of education or exhortation.

The temptation to write in the margins of books is not difficult to understand. It might even be construed as a compliment to the author, suggesting that what he wrote is so provocative as to require a direct response. In this wise, marginalia could be described as the print equivalent of what in the computer age goes by the name of "interactive."

Literature's most famous marginal commentator was Samuel Taylor Coleridge. Coleridge was a compulsive scribbler in the margins of books, but then he was also a compulsive talker, victim of various overmastering impulses, and the king of intellectual spillage, with endless projects abandoned, work left half-finished, genius unfulfilled. He wrote not only in books he owned but those he borrowed from friends. De Quincey remarked that "Coleridge often spoiled a book but in the course of doing so, he enriched that book with so many and so valuable notes, tossing about him, with such lavish profusion, from such a cornucopia of discursive reading, and such a fusing intellect, commentaries so many-angled and so many-coloured that I have envied many a man whose luck has placed him in the way of such injuries."

Sometimes Coleridge's marginalia were small explosions of contempt: "A very vile Poem, Mister J. Godwin, take a Brother Bard's word for it!" But more often he would inscribe little essaylets in the margins. He did this in sufficient number—8,000 or so such notes have thus far been found in more than 450 books—as to make his marginalia part of his *Collected Works*. His daughter, reading some of these notes in her father's books after his death, said that nothing brought him back, nothing so much sounded like his talk, as these particular scribblings.

I was recently told by someone who acquired one of my own early books in a used-book shop that its previous owner had expressed strong disagreement with me and had no compunction about setting it out in strong language in my margins. To write, said Stendhal, is to risk being shot in public, but he never said anything about taking the shots in the margins of one's own books. Still, I am honored to join C. S. Lewis in being among the "marginalized."

Used-book shop owners usually erase all the underlining and sidelining in books. A bookseller I know once told me that the most amusing marginal note he ever erased was one that read, "C'mon, Ortega!" Why is this funny? I do not know, but I do know that you cannot say it aloud in other than a whining voice, and I recommend using it when next you stub your toe or spill hot soup on yourself. Doing so, I find, eases the pain.

Paid Subscriber

(2003)

I AM A PAID SUBSCRIBER to *Vanity Fair, Esquire, Gentlemen's Quarterly*, and *Details*. I'm a sucker for fat, slick-paper magazines that go for a dollar or less per issue, at which price I was able to obtain all four, and *Details* even threw in a black gym bag. True, I have no use for a gym bag, but, hey, a bargain is a bargain.

Paid subscriber though I am, I begin to think that I am not the ideal reader for these magazines. After making my way through the thicket of ads from designer culture, or what I call Ralph Crapoloville, in search of a table of contents, I increasingly find in those contents less and less to read. *Vanity Fair's* special Hollywood issues, its issues on powerful corporate figures, its recent issue on the emaciated folk who constitute what remains of royalty in the world, with a wetted index finger, I pass quickly by all of these. As a scandologist, I allow my eyes to graze over the magazine's hardy perennial, lengthy articles about one or another screw-up by our own royalty, Swiss Family Kennedy, but soon graze turns to glaze, my head falls forward, and the two-pound magazine drops to the floor.

More than a decade ago, I wrote a few pieces for *GQ*, a magazine whose very title is an inaccuracy: It doesn't come out quarterly and with its very specific advice on sex techniques it's distinctly not for gentlemen. In the 1960s, when under the editorship of a man named Harold Hayes, *Esquire* was a magical magazine, crammed with brilliant and unpredictable pieces. Such was the loyalty on the part of readers built up by Hayes in its glory days, if the magazine ran an article on a subject of ostensibly little interest to you—on pinball machines, say, or the Palm Beach suit—you began it anyhow and usually stayed with it until its end.

Esquire never regained that magic, though it struggles—dare I use the word in this androgynous age—manfully to bring it back. My guess is that its editors want a magazine that they would themselves like to read, but nowadays, because of marketing interference, that isn't so easy to produce. *Esquire* stood for men's style, but when one looks at the clothes touted in its pages today, expensive *schmattes* usually worn by skinny guys with tattoos, bad haircuts, and four days' growth of beard, stylishness isn't what comes to mind. Its once famous Dubious Achievement Awards have by now themselves become dubious, its columnists strain hopelessly to be with-it, its fiction is greatly uneven, it runs dead-on-delivery celebrity profiles on its covers.

Details seems to be for that new man, the metrosexual, the man who may or not be ambisextrous, but has no problem with open vanity about his appearance. He's ready to talk skin moisturizers with you, ready to discuss hair conditioners. Articles in *Details* seem to average roughly 600 words; interviews with celebrities are often less than a page long. Graphics are such as nicely to confuse articles with advertising copy. Discussions of sex, in the body of the magazine and in the letters column, are such as to make a grown man—that would, I believe, be me—blush.

These are magazines for a post-literate world. Hope you like that phrase "post-literate world," which is one I noted in the *New York Times*, used by a woman who works for a media buying agency. It joins those other swell posties, post-modernism, post-humanism, post-toasties. Post-literate is misused here, of course, because "literate" means not literary or cultivated but simply able to read. The new readers of the men's slick magazine aren't illiterate; they just have, or are supposed by the editors to have, very short attention spans.

David Granger, the editor of *Esquire*, puts the matter accurately when he says that the movement in current-day men's magazines is in two directions: "toward the more adolescent idea of a man that the lad books

[*Maxim* and various English slicks] went after and toward a more effete idea of man." Granger sees another audience of male readers who are neither coarse nor effete. *Esquire*, presumably, is after those readers, but not, I should say, aggressively enough.

I wish someone would bring out a magazine for men that might carry the title *Sophisticated Square*. I imagine its prospectus reading:

> This is a magazine for men of all ages who, even though some of them lived through the 1960s, have never let hair grow over their ears. They have not worn—they would not dream of wearing—an earring. They believe clothes can be witty and amusing and they value the well-made. They don't mind talking about toys—cars, sports equipment, and the rest—but always with the understanding that they are finally toys merely. They need no help on personal hygiene. They prefer to think of sex as a pleasurable indoor activity but one that ought never to be discussed in any detail whatsoever. They like fine prose and believe they know it when they see it.

If some clever editor could make good on that prospectus, I'd ante up more than a dollar a month for his magazine, and he could keep the gym bag.

Quote-idian

(2003)

THE OTHER DAY I was signing a few books, after a talk I gave at a women's club in Chicago, when someone remarked on the weather, and a very nice woman cited Mark Twain as saying, "It's heaven for climate, it's hell for company." I hesitated, then remarked, "Forgive me, but Mark Twain wasn't the first to say that. J. M. Barrie was." One-upsmanship isn't really my style, and neither is correcting someone my notion of a good time.

I do, though, have a stake in that particular quotation, for, having once heard it used by Hal Holbrook, the actor and Mark Twain impersonator, I had attributed it to Twain in a *New Yorker* piece I wrote some years ago on Ambrose Bierce. A well-mannered fact-checker at the magazine called to tell me that three different dictionaries of quotations had qualified attributions of the comment to Twain, but a fourth, Bergan Evans's *Dictionary of Quotations*, claimed it was often misattributed to Twain but really first appeared in a Barrie play.

How many other quotations are misattributed to Twain? Probably, my guess is, a great many. Oscar Wilde, Winston Churchill, Dorothy Parker also must pick up credit for things they never really said. Samuel Johnson, too, is among the most quoted of writers, but his utterances are so characteristic that no one is likely to attribute to him something said by, say, Yogi Berra.

That most quoted author of all, fellow name of Anonymous, once said that you are only truly famous when someone insane imagines he is you. But I wonder if having witty or penetrating quotations you never made attributed to you doesn't also qualify.

People quote other people for all sorts of reasons. At the low end, they do so to show that they are decently well read or modestly cultivated. "Brush up your Shakespeare," the Cole Porter song from *Kiss Me Kate* has it, "start quoting him now. . . . And the women you will wow." Others use quotation to back up their arguments. How can I be wrong when a sterling dude like Cicero felt pretty much the same way? Some writers use quotations to close off further discussion: "As Hannah Arendt put it," "As Richard Rorty says," "As Harold Bloom remarked. . . ."

When I was editing a magazine, the *American Scholar*, I felt that my writers shouldn't be allowed to quote below a certain level, at least not when they expected the material quoted to carry QED authority. The three people mentioned at the end of my last paragraph, for example, would not qualify; each has said too many wrong or foolish things. My own sense is that, in prose, there ought to be a moratorium, in which one waits 50 years after an author's death before he ought to be considered quotable in an authoritative way.

Some writers appear to have written for quotation, and not alone those with an aphoristic style. Consider Alexis de Tocqueville, whom I have taken to calling "the inevitable Tocqueville," for if you write at any length on almost any subject on America you will find yourself, inevitably, quoting, usually to good effect, Tocqueville. I am about to launch out on a little book on Tocqueville, and already feel it is a great drawback that I shall not be able to quote Tocqueville on the subject of Tocqueville.

A fairly quotatious fellow myself, I write down interesting items from my reading, which I keep in small notebooks. I have more than 20 such notebooks. My entries run from the elegant to the penetrating to the historically odd: ". . . Pompey's eldest son Cnaeus, who had a short and cruel temper" is a recent entry I took from Anthony Everitt's biography of Cicero; Hobbes's phrase for laughter, "sudden glory," is another. These notebooks have become too numerous to serve as a filing system. Yet I cannot resist copying out items I find of genuine interest, including, sometimes, one writer quoting another: "The spirit, says Aristotle, ages like the body," wrote Montaigne, himself one of the great quoters.

I have a weakness for quoting Paul Valéry, the French thinker and poet, who said so many smart things usually seasoned with a nice tang of paradox. "Everything changes but the avant-garde" is a characteristic Valéryism, as is "The future isn't what it used to be." Sometimes people one generally doesn't care for say dazzling things, and so one quotes them with a touch of regret. "What are the three saddest words in the English language?" Gore Vidal asked, then answered, "Joyce Carol Oates." Whenever I quote that I generally follow it up with Henry James's remark that the two most beautiful words in the English language are "summer afternoon." An Arab proverb runs: "When your son becomes a man, make him your brother." Lovely, and in my case it turns out to have been perfectly and pleasingly true. But why couldn't it have been a Jewish proverb? Quoters, alas, cannot always be choosers.

Let Old Acquaintance
Be Forgot

(2004)

I RECENTLY RECEIVED AN INVITATION to my fiftieth-year high school reunion, and am impressed with how little interested I am in attending it. For many people, their adolescence was an awkward, painful, really hellacious time. Mine, on the contrary, was so pleasing that I sometimes think that I peaked in my seventeenth year. Nearly every day I went to high school the way aging brides go to their weddings: filled with feelings of contentment, success, and anticipation. Yet I have decided to take a pass on this, my fiftieth reunion. I feel, somehow, that it is best I not return, as the announcer for *The Lone Ranger* radio show had it, "to those thrilling days of yesteryear."

In some ways, a fiftieth class reunion ought to be easier than a tenth or a twenty-fifth. At these earlier reunions, all the cards have not yet been dealt. One can appear still to have a good shot at mastering life; one can brag a bit about one's children's extraordinary accomplishments, one's own bright future. One can try to make the case that one has become a much deeper person than the rather shallow character everyone remembers roaming the halls of high school.

I attended a thirtieth-year class reunion, to which I had looked forward. My reigning memory is of a very noisy band that seemed, for much of the evening, to be playing a hideous rendition of "New York, New York"—and this in Chicago—with the bandleader singing the words at a decibel level slightly above that of the response of a man who has just been pushed off a cliff. I recall regretting that I hadn't been financially more successful than I was, so that I might give the band a couple of grand to pack up its instruments and depart the hall instanter.

Thirty years out, too, I could see the ravages that time had begun to make on my old classmates. More than a few heartbreaking toupees were on display. A number of people seemed to have widened considerably, as if someone had fooled with their horizontal buttons. Outcroppings of gray and even some white hair were showing forth. We were, as a class, not 50 years old, so there were not then a great many people taken out of the game by death. Lots of divorces, though; and a few people had had bouts with cancer to report.

What I noticed more than anything was that most people were not much different than they had been at eighteen—they were their old selves, only, somehow, more so. The vain were vainer; the funny, funnier, the dopey, dopier; the slightly crazed now well along to madness. The most impressive success in the room was a man, a peripheral figure when in high school, who owned a national chain of sporting-goods stores. Two class clowns, apparently having gotten serious, turned out to be physicians. Some, prominent when kids, didn't show up at all, leaving one to wonder if the defeats dealt them by life were too obvious to be displayed at a reunion. Twenty more years have now surreptitiously slipped by. Things cannot have gotten better for most of my classmates.

I have, I think, an inkling of what it would be like to see them all assembled in their aged state. Several weeks ago, while giving a talk in Chicago, I noticed a face in the audience from high school days. "My God," I thought, "who put the white hair and white mustache on Dick Karlov?" Take my reaction and multiply it by a few hundred: That's what it would be like to attend my reunion.

"For a few seconds I did not understand why it was that I had difficulty in recognizing the master of the house and the guests and why everyone in the room appeared to have put on a disguise—in most cases a powdered wig—which changed him completely," Proust, in his great novel, has his agent Marcel observe. Marcel goes on to remark that, in his mind, the men at this party were not old men, but were "young men in an advanced state of withering." Too true. "Time," Marcel remarks, "which changes human beings does not alter the image we have of them. Indeed nothing is more painful than the contrast between the mutability of people and the fixity of memory, when it is borne in upon us that what has been preserved with so much freshness in our memory can no longer possess any trace of that quality in life. . . ."

I can face the fact that we all grow older, but I prefer to face it only one or two persons at a time. A large room filled with people in this condition is more than I can handle. That is why I shan't be attending my fiftieth-year class reunion.

If the announcement of the reunion had asked for a reason for not attending, I would have replied: "See Proust, *Time Regained*, pp. 957–1157, passim. C. Scott-Moncrieff, Terence Kilmartin and Andreas Mayor translation. Random House. Best wishes, J. E."

It's Only a Movie

(2004)

L AST SATURDAY I SAW A MOVIE so inept, so stupid, so generally and particularly wrong that I felt justified in not having paid much attention to movies over the past decade or so, but it also gave the peculiar kind of pleasure that only a genuinely bad movie can sometimes give. The movie is called *Mona Lisa Smile*, and is about Wellesley College in the early 1950s, and stars Julia Roberts. Dorothy Parker is supposed to have said of Katharine Hepburn—wrongly, it turns out—that, as an actress, "she ran the whole gamut of emotions from A to B." Roberts takes things all the way to C. She does Happy, Angry, and Sad, but nothing beyond or between. *Mona Lisa Smile*, in its unsubtlety, is perfect for her.

For a bad movie to give pleasure it must be dead-on wrong in an impressive way. *The Best of Everything* (1959), which was about three beautiful young women who come to New York to work in publishing, was such a movie. A detail I recall, nearly 45 years later, is Hope Lange, a lowly secretary at a publishing firm, reading unsolicited manuscripts, putting a piece of paper in her manual typewriter and tapping out, "This novel shows careful delineation of character." Bang, next thing you know she has become senior editor, a job she has taken away from the menacing Joan Crawford.

Mona Lisa Smile is about the pressures of conformity at Wellesley in the 1950s. I found this premise highly amusing, since some of the most impressively nonconformist women I know went to Wellesley during those years: the classicist Mary Lefkowitz, the writer Diane Ravitch, the columnist Judith Martin (also known as "Miss Manners"). Well-made art makes the unpredictable seem plausible. In this flick everything is predictable and implausible. It also has the added charm of ahistoricism, such as using "rip-off" more than a decade before its time and referring to an academic department chairman (in 1953) as "chair." Discovering historical *faux pas* in movies is a fine indoor sport. "Hey, Caesar, check it out."

I watched *Mona Lisa Smile* on DVD. I watch most movies on VCR or DVD these days, even though a 14-theater cineplex is three blocks from my apartment. I feel no urgency about seeing any movie, and make it a special point to neglect the big movies that are being most talked about at the moment. I waited three years before seeing *Schindler's List*; I plan never to see *Titanic*; and a horde of wild Jews, prodded on by Roman soldiers, couldn't drag me to *The Passion of the Christ*.

I retain a mild addiction to movie-watching, one getting milder all the time. At *chez* Epstein we try to find a watchable flick every Saturday night, which we view with popcorn, Granny Smith apples, and a beer. I say "watchable" as opposed, say, to great or to nauseating. My expectations have been greatly lowered. I don't hold out much hope for movies, though I am still pleased, as happens every so often, to be surprised at an artful flick.

When I am surprised, it is by small movies. I recently saw a swell Canadian movie called *Owning Mahowny*, about a mid-level bank manager with a high-level gambling problem. It didn't change my life, you understand, but neither did I feel I had been taken when it was over. I find myself watching more and more foreign films, including lots of Chinese ones, and older French movies that I missed the first time around. I've even come to like subtitles, which help concentrate the wandering mind.

The bigger the budget, bank on it, the worse the movie. The more talked-about the movie, the more disappointing it turns out to be. In the late '60s and through the 1970s, when Pauline Kael was the colossus astride the *New Yorker*, movies became topic number one. Wherever you went, people wanted to know if you saw this or that movie, or read this or the other critic on it. Not to have an opinion on the latest flick felt like leaving home without some necessary piece of clothing.

I suspect it's better that movies are no longer at the center of conversation or of the culture. (Not that I know what has replaced them.) Movies are merely movies, and no great fuss ought to be made over them. The people who make movies are generally not even close to intelligent. When movies are really excellent, such as *Casablanca*, they are so almost by accident.

When my granddaughter was four years old, she sat on my lap and we watched *The Fox and the Hound*. During a scene in which the fox is being gently ejected from the home of an old woman who had cared for him when he was injured, I exclaimed, too insistently perhaps, about the sadness of what we were watching. "Grandpa," my granddaughter said, without turning her head, "it's only a movie." The kid got it dead-on right.

Jacques Barzun:
An Appreciation

(2012)

I FIRST MET JACQUES BARZUN in the autumn of 1974. I had just been named editor of the *American Scholar*, the quarterly magazine published by Phi Beta Kappa, and he had long been on its editorial board and was among its leading contributors. He seemed to embody the best of the magazine in its intellectual aspirations and cultural standard. He had earlier told me, by letter, that he was planning to leave the editorial board, and the prospect so alarmed me that I made a special trip from Chicago to New York to try to dissuade him from doing so.

We met at the Columbia Faculty Club. He was as I imagined him from author's photographs on his books, tall, with excellent posture, handsome, elegant in an understated way. He was born in France, to a family whose intellectual connections extended to friendships with the poet and art critic Guillame Appollinaire, the composer Edgar Varese, and the novelist and biographer Stefan Zweig. Jacques came to this country at age 13, had thoroughly Americanized himself, yet had never quite altogether lost the aura of a bred-in-the-bone superior old-world culture. He was cosmopolitan in an elegant way that intellectuals rarely are.

Perhaps pleased at my full-court-press attempt to keep him on the *American Scholar*'s editorial board, Jacques fairly quickly agreed to do so. We then settled down to talk about the magazine and, more interesting, about the contemporary university. Regarding the latter, his outlook was dour. A young colleague of his passed our table, about whom Jacques remarked that his greatest accomplishment seemed to be his beard. I told him that George Balanchine had said that in his father's generation beards were still authentic; all beards grown since were fakes. We were, he now understood, on the same side of things.

I was very pleased to be on his side. No intellectual reputation seemed quite so strong, so impeccable, so splendid as Jacques Barzun's. He wrote in a flawless and magisterial manner on a vast array of subjects: Darwin, Marx, Wagner, Berlioz, William James, French verse, English prose composition, university teaching, detective fiction, the state of intellectual life, and finally, published when he was 93, his magnum opus, *From Dawn to Decadence: 500 Years of Western Cultural Life, 1500 to the Present*. None of this writing seemed motivated by his desire to advance his career; all of it derived from genuine intellectual passion.

Although Jacques Barzun's professional life was lived almost entirely at Columbia University—where he was himself a student from undergraduate days through acquiring his PhD, and where he later served as provost and university professor—he never seemed entirely, or even chiefly, an academic. There was nothing academic about his prose, his person, his point of view. He and Lionel Trilling, with whom he taught the great-books course at Columbia, always seemed para-academics. Theirs was the metropolitan spirit, urban and urbane, suave and sophisticated in the best senses of those words. Jacques was for many years a literary adviser to the firm of Charles Scribner's Sons. W. H. Auden was his friend. His first wife was a Lowell. He was very much in and of the world.

I cannot claim to have been a close friend of Jacques Barzun, though he would occasionally send me a note about something I had written. His approval meant a great deal to me. He lived to 104, and his death scarcely comes as a surprise. Chiefly it is a reminder that a great model of the life of the mind has departed the planet. Not many such models left, if any.

Fighting Poverty

(2014)

WITH ALL THE TALK currently being bruited about the 50th anniversary of the war on poverty, I am reminded that for a year, between 1964 and 1965, I was the director of the anti-poverty program of Pulaski County, Arkansas, which Included Little Rock, the adjoining city of North Little Rock and the surrounding rural area. I was then 27 years old, appropriately left-wing, and confident that society could be greatly improved with the help of large infusions of money and the serious thinking of people like myself.

My only qualification for directing a local anti-poverty program was that a few months before I had been approached for the job I had published an article in *Harper's* magazine about urban renewal. The article was roughly 6,000 words, and my total knowledge of the subject was perhaps 8,000 words. Based on that article, I was, for four or five months, one of the leading housing experts in America.

Nobody at the time was much of an expert on poverty. The main book on the subject was Michael Harrington's *The Other America: Poverty in the United States* (1962). Harrington's book was less a study than an exhortation; its argument was that in a society so affluent as ours, poverty was an egregious sin.

The population of Pulaski County was roughly a quarter of a million. I had on my staff a secretary and three assistants who had the title of "field workers." Two field workers were young black men, the third was an older (than I or they) and remarkable woman named Ruth Arnold, whose model of a good society was an integrated one, which was—and remains—mine.

The way money in the anti-poverty program worked was that the local community put up 10% of the sum they asked of the federal government; the 10% could also be "in kind." This meant that one could charge off office space, desks and chairs, and stationery and anything else to count toward the 10%. My salary as director was $10,000.

One of the first things I did was attempt to work out a map illustrating Pulaski County's "pockets of poverty." Little Rock and North Little Rock had blocks and blocks of shotgun houses—a straight shot from the front door to the back—still without indoor plumbing. I remember remarking to a female black schoolteacher, with the heavy irony available to the ignorant, that shabby as these houses were, almost all of them had television sets. "Please don't knock those television sets," she said, "They give these children the only chance they will ever have to hear decent English."

Some of the programs Washington wanted us to administer were fairly exotic. A number of others were merely silly. I remember one called "Foster Grandparents," in which the elderly would be paid to baby-sit the children of officially poor mothers who could then go off to work. Rubbing up against human nature, the program failed to recognize that the elderly do not necessarily long for the company of the very young, or vice versa.

Many of the shotgun houses I visited were inhabited by black single mothers with multiple kids. I attempted to explain all the good things the anti-poverty program would do for them and their families. I also gave talks about poverty to middle-class women's groups, informing them that there were children in Harlem who had never seen an orange. The women's eyes teared up. I spoke in black churches, quoting arid statistics on poverty to which men in the audience would chant, "Tell it, brother."

Around this time the civil-rights movement was well under way. I used to hang out with members of SNCC, the acronym for the Student Non-Violent Coordinating Committee. I taught the SNCC people how they might apply for federal funds to get out the black vote.

I had genuine regard for those SNCC members who were not merely doing left-wing tourism but were in the movement full-time. Many had participated in protest marches in Alabama, Louisiana and Mississippi, and paid for it by having local police billy clubs smashed over their heads and being attacked by German shepherds.

I spent some time with one of the leaders of the Little Rock SNCC organization, a man named Bill Hansen, who had put in time in some of the worst jails in the South. We once had lunch together in a dingy restaurant in the black district. I picked up the check. Hansen put three quarters on the table for a tip. "You know, Bill," I said, "Trotsky never tipped." He picked up the quarters.

As anti-poverty program director, I decided to set up fundamental programs: Head Start, the preschool program for poor kids; legal aid; and birth-control counseling. I left Little Rock and the anti-poverty program before they were put into effect.

Not long before I decided to return home to Chicago, I received a phone call from a young woman at SNCC inviting me to join a mass protest at the Arkansas capitol building. I told her that if I were to do so my usefulness as a government representative would be at an end. "You're either with us or against us. You decide," she said, and hung up.

For a while after I left Little Rock for Chicago I kept in touch by phone with Ruth Arnold, who told me that things were fizzling out with the local anti-poverty program. Middle-class children were now increasingly going to preschool, which effectively wiped out any true head-start that poor children might have obtained. The poor used legal aid, not to sue the city and the school board, as political-minded anti-poverty workers had hoped, but mainly to sue one another: for divorce, debt collection, paternity. As for birth control counseling, who knew or could know for years to come what its effects would be.

I've not been back to Little Rock for decades, but my guess is that little has changed for the poor since my days as director of the anti-poverty program there. The poverty in Pulaski County, make no mistake, was and is real. Only the ways of dealing with it remain in the realm of fantasy.

Mel Lasky

(2004)

I N HIS POEM "ESTHÉTIQUE DU MAL," Wallace Stevens speaks of "the lunatic of one idea." Melvin J. Lasky might be thought such a person. He had the energy of a lunatic, and, though widely read and interested in everything, he could nonetheless be described a "one idea" man.

That idea, however, was the most significant political idea of the 20th century: Anti-totalitarianism was its name—and far from being the idea of a lunatic, it was absolutely crucial to any claim of political integrity in what now appears, in sheer number of people murdered for political reasons, the cruelest of all centuries in history. Melvin Lasky, who died on May 19, 2004 at age 84, devoted his life to the anti-totalitarian idea and contributed heavily, on the intellectual front, to the defeat of communism in his lifetime.

Born in the Bronx in 1920, Mel Lasky grew up in an intensely political milieu. He went to City College, and was of the generation there of Irving Howe, Daniel Bell, Irving Kristol, and other young men who cut their Marxistical distinctions finer than they cut the belly lox at Katz's old Lower East Side restaurant. Unlike these others, Lasky longed for Europe, and would soon become one of those mid-Atlantic men: Americans most at home in Europe, and Europeans most at home in America. After serving in World War II, he stayed on in Germany to edit the magazine *Der Monat*, to which he brought such continental writers as Arthur Koestler, Raymond Aron, Bertrand Russell, and Ignazio Silone. The Swiss writer François Bondy wrote of Mel's German editorship that "a young American gave several generations of Europeans not only a literary platform but something like a common intellectual homeland."

Mel Lasky acquired wider fame as the second American editor of *Encounter* (the first was Irving Kristol). He edited it with panache, and, while drawing on the best English writers, enriched it with his many continental connections. He was editor when it was revealed that *Encounter* was partly financed, through splendidly labyrinthine ways, by the Central Intelligence Agency, which caused a great intellectual scandal in its day. Not everyone was scandalized; and I myself have long viewed the CIA's helping to underwrite this perhaps best of 20th-century magazines as one of its solidest achievements.

I knew Mel Lasky through Edward Shils, who was an occasional contributor and full-time though usually ignored adviser to Mel during his *Encounter* days. In a letter, Edward described Mel to me as "awful, remarkable, and admirable." The "awful" referred to Mel's more flamboyant side; he had the dramatizing imagination of a boy who grew up on revolutionary fantasies. He frequently availed himself of such Trotskyist phrases as "hoist on his own petard" (I like the phrase better with "petard" replaced by "foulard"), "crossing polemical swords," and "it is no accident that," even inserting them into other people's articles. He was also a nearly nonstop talker, even at transcontinental telephone rates, but the talk was high quality and when directed at me I enjoyed it.

Mel was small, wiry, bald, and wore a Lenin-like goatee. At one point during the 1970s, he added long thick sideburns, causing Shils to say to him, "Now, Melvin, you can be either Lenin or Brahms, but I will not permit you to be both simultaneously." More likely, Mel thought himself the 20th-century Alexander Herzen, a man inspired by the socialist impulse but very wise about all the ways that utopian dreams go astray. Lasky's most ambitious book is *Utopia and Revolution*.

"A Farewell to Utopia" is the title that Mel gave to an essay I sent to him about my own mildly radical youth. I had published earlier pieces in *Encounter* in response to his red ballpoint scrawled notes asking me for contributions. Because *Encounter* was often in financial trouble, the checks for payment were frequently very late arriving. Because this particular essay had been commissioned as part of a book, for which I received a good fee, I instructed Mel that he need not pay me for it out of *Encounter* funds. Naturally, a check arrived straightaway. Perfect Mel. "Melvin is like a dog who knows seven languages," Edward Shils used to say about him, "and obeys in none."

Although he published a number of books, Mel Lasky was foremost an editor, a man who finds things for other people to write. Like all superior editors, he had an instinctual sense, in the realm of intellectual life, of the fashionable and the enduring and the right balance between the two. *Encounter* always had a firm line on totalitarian communism, but, owing to the breadth of Mel's interests, there was generally a great deal else in the magazine for curious readers. He was himself such a reader, and a compulsive clipper of articles from journals and papers around the world. One of the changes he made over his predecessor's *Encounter* was to add little boxes of material from the world press, so that the magazine's pages sometimes seemed the intellectual equivalent of a collage.

When financial troubles finally drove *Encounter* under, Mel Lasky was, for the first time in his adult life, without a magazine. You have to imagine Roy Rogers without his horse, Frank Sinatra without a microphone, Rita Hayworth in flats. Unthinkable, really.

Mel lived his last years in Berlin, where he wrote the first of a projected three-volume study on *The Language of Journalism*. He continued clipping stray articles, and his last scrawled note to me contained a clipping from the English press on goofy new usage, which he thought I might enjoy. He asked that I send him some news, by which of course he meant gossip about intellectual life in America. I sent him what little I had, and told him how much I missed *Encounter*, which I did and still do. The magazine was passionate, turbulent, overflowing with items of oddity and interest, done with genuine flair—like Melvin J. Lasky himself.

"Won't You Join Me?"

(2004)

AS I STEPPED OUT INTO THE STREET after a performance of the Chicago Symphony Orchestra the other evening, it occurred to me that there have been three distinct changes in the urban landscape over the past quarter century: the end of indoor smoking at all but a small number of public places, forcing smokers out of doors; the pervasiveness of cell phones, indoors and out; and the presence of begging on heavily trafficked big-city streets.

As a former semi-pro smoker—a two-pack-a-day man, now 26 years off the weed—I find I don't miss the smell of tobacco in the atmosphere, though I don't like the hounding of cigarette smokers, who may be the last pariah group in America. I used to mock people with cell phones, thinking them jittery jerks who couldn't bear the least repose, even in their cars. But of course I have long since acquired such a gadget myself; and all I can say in my own defense is that I leave it in my pocket and only two people know its number.

Of these three changes in the urban landscape, the one I shall probably never get used to is the omnipresence of beggars, among whom I include those people who sell "homeless" newspapers. (The one in Chicago is called *Street Wise*.) Begging is probably the world's second oldest profession. Every civilization must have had its beggars, but it is only relatively recently in America that begging has become so evident.

When I was a kid, most begging was confined to one or the other of Chicago's two skid rows. Beggars were utterly defeated men, bedraggled, often toothless, asking for a dime or a quarter, ostensibly for a cup of coffee, more likely to be used for a shot of rotgut. Begging was rare enough for comedians to make jokes about it. Henny Youngman used to tell about the bum who asked him for fifty cents for a cup of coffee. "I said to him, 'But coffee's only a quarter.' 'Ah,' he replied, 'won't you join me?'" Such jokes are no longer told, and we certainly no longer use the word "bum."

The presence of so many beggars on the streets is a sad reminder that, even in our opulent country, lots of people can't make a go of things. In my neighborhood, some of the same beggars have been around for at least a decade. Begging has become not a fall-back but a full-time job. Many of them are black men and women, but some are white; and quite a few of both races are fairly young. An occasional beggar will be faintly menacing, but most are not; a couple of them are even cheerful. I blame the number of beggars in America not on capitalism, but on the great human lottery, which awards less skill, little power of forming good habits, and simple bad luck to a small but, it now seems, not insignificant number of people in every society.

A man I know who sells *Street Wise* tells me that he needs $25 a day to make his nut, or expenses. These include breakfast and lunch—I believe he gets dinner at one of the local soup kitchens—and money for doing his laundry, and a few bucks for a place to sleep. *Street Wise* costs $1, and twenty-five cents of each copy sold goes back to the publisher. In his 70s, he schleps all his possessions around with him in plastic bags and sits, while selling his paper, in a beach chair.

I cough up roughly four or five bucks a week to local beggars, plus odd amounts of change to the zonked-out, half-mad people who appear from time to time along the streets I travel. I give this small sum out of a goofy array of motives, none of them very elevated. If I can help someone make his $25 nut a little quicker, why not? The fear of feeling myself closed-hearted may be a stronger motive. Lowest of all is the superstitious dread of bringing the furies down upon myself by not giving, which could shut off my own good fortune in making an easy living.

The presence of beggars is a very great drag on the spirit. Going about the business of a lucky life, I am brought up by confronting a man or woman who so obviously eats dreary food, works in miserable weather, and sleeps in conditions under which I could probably not sleep at all. Mine is a merely normal, not an overactive, conscience. But the sight of people begging gets to it.

I don't know what Sweden and Norway do with their beggars; I recall encountering beggars in Amsterdam, but nowhere so many as in big American cities, where the problem doesn't seem likely soon to go away. For the most selfish of reasons, I wish it would. Beggars are too much in my and everyone else's face, underscoring and italicizing the essential unfairness of life. In my American utopia, they wouldn't beg but carry a coffee and thumb pump cell phones on which they call their brokers, like, you might say, the rest of us beggars.

They Said I Was Low-Tech...

(2004)

YESTERDAY, TO AVOID THE LONG LINES, I used the recently installed automated system and checked myself out of my local supermarket: two pints of Häagen-Dazs frozen coffee yogurt, three rolls of white necessary paper, a package of six Bays English muffins, a small bag of vine-ripened tomatoes. Following instructions, I used my preferred customers card, I scanned each item, I paid in cash, I took my change. After bagging my groceries, I moved on out, smartly. One small step for man, I felt, one large step for Joseph Epstein.

I'm always pleased when I am able to avail myself of the most recent bit of new technology that life throws up nowadays. It makes me feel I'm still in the game. I have a number of friends, contemporaries, who dropped out some while ago, most at the stage of home computers, which they decided they didn't really need. Why did they need email when the phone was at hand; word-processing when a typewriter had served them so well over the years; Google when they lived so close to a library? Who needs it, they exclaimed?

I fear that they do—that we all do. I think that something more is at stake than the greater efficiency that technological change sometimes brings about. Not, to be sure, that all of it is absolutely required; I, for one, don't need a remote at my bedside to put the lights on in the bathroom should I wake in the middle of the night. I feel telephone technology generally is vastly overdone, and I've never met a telephone menu I didn't dislike. But a lot of these gadgets have made life easier, a tad happier, a bit better. Bring 'em on, I say.

Some of us are selectively stymied by the fresh advents of the new high tech. I felt myself a wizard of my old VCR, then made a mistake and bought a higher quality, more complex one—with a voice that uttered instructions—that left me baffled. I have friends, a couple, retired physicians, who have a highly complex arrangement of multiple computers, yet have concluded that they cannot handle the relatively simple mechanics of ATMs. When I asked the wife what they do to obtain cash, she said that each month they just take out a stack of money—the amount was not specified—and put it in a drawer, and use it as their own personal ATM.

Many people are born with a natural curiosity about how things work. I, alas, wasn't. My curiosity has always been restricted to how human beings work, not that I have been all that successful in satisfying it. I was not a boy who could make model planes; left alone with an X-acto blade, I would probably have greeted the digital age with many fewer digits. Nor could I lose myself in the intricacies of Lincoln Logs, an Erector Set, or test tubes and chemicals. When science became at all intricate, when it left the state of simple wonder, my mind departed the room. Several decades later, it has yet to return.

Yet I take great pride in being able to do simple tasks around our apartment. A few years ago, I changed all our bedroom and bathroom doorknobs. I discovered I have an eye for hanging pictures true. I've learned to replace batteries in my and my wife's wrist-watches, saving four or five bucks each time by being able to do so. I can handle very minor plumbing jobs. I have learned how to replace halogen bulbs. None of this qualifies me for being on a first-name basis with the crowd down at Home Depot, but I derive small but genuine satisfaction from doing such tasks.

Where I do often run into trouble is remembering from one season to another how to make minor adjustments on modestly high-tech equipment. At daylight savings time, I can be counted on to forget how to change the digital clock in my car. Adding software to my computer is always an adventure, one that not infrequently ends up in frustrated anger—"I sense rage," as the shrinks say—at my own ignorance.

"Man rides machine," wrote Emerson, who never had to ride any machine more complicated than a train. I doubt he would have felt the same if his car had broken down on a major thoroughfare owing to an electrical failure; or if he'd been rendered unable to write a sermon because his computer had gone down. The prig Thoreau, seeing us frustrated by technology, would probably have said, as it seemed to please him so much to say, "I told you so."

You won't find me plugged into an iPod or checking into the Mayo Clinic for the first cell-phone implant, but should you see me using the computer check-in at O'Hare or doing some other mildly high-tech operation you might note a certain smugness in my manner. Come a bit closer and you might hear me lightly singing, "I ain't nothin' but a houndog. They said I was low-tech, but that was just a lie."

Letter from Bedlam

(2004)

THIS MORNING, out for my regular constitutional, I was called Adolf and accused of being a Nazi by a man with long orangish hair carrying a purse. I saw him coming down the block, and I nodded to him, for he had turned up some months ago at a book promotion talk I gave at a nearby Borders. During the question-and-answer session, as part of an otherwise less than clear general statement, he'd quoted Emerson—almost always, in my experience, a sign of nuttiness to come.

But now, beyond mere quaint nuttiness, the man was screaming at me. "We don't need people like you in this country," he yelled. "Get out of the United States—now!" He was missing several lower teeth. Reasoning with him was not among the responses available to me. I voted with my feet, walking, actually trotting, away, leaving him cursing me on the otherwise quiet street. I walked on, unnerved.

Five mornings previous, out again for my walk, I ran into a homeless woman I have occasionally met in the neighborhood. Usually I find her, with three suitcases, sitting in her blue raincoat on the side-entrance steps to the library, waiting for it to open. One day, as I held the door to the library for her, she revealed that she knew who I was. In the calmest of cultivated voices, she told me that she had read my stories and essays, and that she was honored to meet me. Clean in her person, she, too, was missing lots of teeth, uppers and lowers.

When I saw her last week, with her luggage and her raincoat, she told me, in her habitually calm voice, that she was very worried, because she knew a great wrong had been committed and she felt that she had to do something about it. When I asked her what the wrong was, she mentioned the death, roughly nine months earlier, of a local newspaper columnist, who was found in his car in his carbon-dioxide filled garage, apparently a suicide. She didn't think it was a suicide. She thought that powerful interests in the trucking industry, which the columnist had been attacking, had murdered him. Knowing this, she couldn't, she said, stand by and do nothing about it. I implored her that nothing was precisely what she must do about it, though my advice didn't get through. Crumpling a twenty in my pocket, I offered to buy her breakfast, which she politely turned down. We parted on good terms.

Another neighborhood character, an older man who sits selling a homeless paper in front of a local supermarket I patronize, used to engage me in conversation on a wide variety of topics. "What do you know about Nietzsche?" he once asked. Every so often he would drop a resounding name; he once mentioned having met, in a hotel in St. Louis, Casey Stengel (clang). We had these brief, pleasant interchanges for a number of years.

Then suddenly I noted him turn away when I passed. After a few weeks of this, I asked him if I had done anything to offend him. "You know that conversation we had in the library?" he said. (We had had no conversation in the library.) "I know you reported every word of it to the police." And then he went off into a tirade about the local police being out to get him. We haven't spoken since.

Reading these paragraphs you will think I live in Bedlam. I don't, but there are in town two halfway houses for the undangerously mad. Some walk along muttering to themselves; others, drugged to the gunnels, silently trudge the streets through the day. Somehow one notices them more during the quiet hours. They all were—many may still well be— other people's children.

Who knows how many came into life with the wretched luck of bad brain chemistries and other disastrous mental jigeroos? Some blew their minds on drugs. Many others may have been battered by life itself into their various paranoias, hallucinatory states, ungodly mental dishevel-ments. For all, the price of a reasonably tranquil life proved exorbitant.

What purpose can insanity serve, either for those afflicted with it or in the grand scheme? The mad were once considered saintly, in touch with higher things, but surely no longer. One would like to think that there exists a segment of the happy mad, who hallucinate only lovely things, but I doubt it.

When a maniac is yelling in my face, as the orange-haired man did yesterday, I am made to realize the unexplained terror life can hold and the great good luck of all of us who, for now, are on the right side of the divide between the mad and the sane.

I, who believe in the existence of evil, who do not consider a just world in the realm of possibility, who grow more and more impressed with the mysteries of life, nonetheless find madness a deep affront to my rational-ity. Is this because the mad remind me that the notion that the world is itself a rational place might just be the greatest hallucination of all?

Tailor-Made

(2004)

I WAS IN NORDSTROM, buying a black blazer. My salesman was a genial man in his forties, bald and plumpish, carefully turned-out. Good at what he did, not pushing in any way, he smoothly played along with my desire to be taken as a man of the world. Our transaction complete, he gave me his business card, suggesting I ask for him when next I came in.

The name on the card was the same as that of a Jewish family that used to make and sell ice cream in Chicago. Was he, I asked, of that family?

"No," he said. "My grandfather was a tailor and so was my father. And if I could have had my way, so would I have been."

"Really," I said, marveling at the notion that today, in the early 21st century, a middle-class American would want to be a tailor.

"Did you know that a good tailor can make a salary in the six figures?" he said. "We have tailor-made ties in this store that go for more than $200 a shot.

"I remember, as a young boy, watching my grandfather at his bench making neckties," he continued. "I was fascinated. I wanted him to teach me how to do it. But he wouldn't. He and my father both discouraged me from becoming a tailor."

"Sounded too immigrant-like, too old world, to them?" I asked. "Exactly," he said. "They would have felt great failures in life if their grandson and son had become a tailor. It's too late for me to learn how to do it now."

An aura of dolor clung to our conversation. It's one thing not to know what one wants to do in life; another to know what one wants to do but not have the talent to do it; but a third, sadder thing, is to know precisely what one wants to do and never be permitted to discover if one can do it. Wanting to work at the useful craft of his ancestors, my salesman was prevented from doing so by the very American aspirations of his family.

These same aspirations probably explain why it seems so difficult to hold on to a family business for three generations. An exception is a younger friend of mine, who, along with his brothers, is among the third generation in his family to run a number of restaurants in Chicago. He recently sent me a half-joking email announcing that his restaurant received an award for having the best tap beer in Chicago. I consider that award more significant than many poetry prizes given out over the past year, because the beer doubtless gave more pleasure than the poems, and I say this as a reader of poetry who is not an enthusiastic beer drinker.

This man also happens to have been a student of mine. He wrote a very solid paper on Joseph Conrad for a master's degree. He could have been a respectable academic, but my guess is that he is more content and providing more happiness running an excellent restaurant.

I know a man, the son of Greek immigrants, who sells produce west of the Loop, who once told me that he shall always honor my friend Edward Shils because he discouraged him from going to school to become a dental technician and encouraged him to remain in the business of selling fruits and vegetables.

Yet the pull (ostensibly) to improve one's status is always there, turning out to be a goad, often, to dissatisfaction. Perhaps it all started with John Adams, who, in a famous letter to his wife Abigail, wrote: "I must study politics and war that my sons may have the liberty to study mathematics and philosophy . . . geography, natural history, naval architecture, commerce, and agriculture, in order to give their children a right to study painting, poetry, music, architecture, statuary, tapestry, and porcelain." Put in more contemporary terms, this might read: "I worked at dry cleaning in order that my son could have the liberty to study sociology in order that his son could have the right to undergo a sex-change operation."

I search the long roll of my friends and acquaintances and discover that scarcely any of them actually makes anything. They write and teach and go to court and attempt to reduce pain and gamble on markets and shuffle paper generally. I, too, am a paper shuffler; the only difference is that the papers I shuffle have my own words on them.

Before I went to college, my father, who was himself a salesman, told me, an indifferent high-school student, that he would pay for my college education, but he thought I would make a fine salesman and my college years might just be a waste of time. I often wonder what my life would have been like if I had listened to him. I wonder, too, what would have happened if my father had said that, given my high-school record, he would not permit me to go to college. The only way I could have got him to change his mind would have been to reply, "That's okay, Dad, I really want to be a tailor anyway."

Sublime Competence

(2004)

A MAN AFTER MY OWN HEART, Peter Kramer of Hillsborough, North Carolina, recently wrote a letter to the *New York Times Book Review* questioning the novelist Philip Roth for describing George W. Bush as "a man unfit to run a hardware store." Mr. Kramer's point is that Roth could not have chosen a poorer comparison, and in his letter he remarks that his own local hardware-store owner, a fellow named Wesley Woods, is one of the most trusted and helpful men in the community and that perhaps it wouldn't be a bad idea if he, Mr. Woods, ran for president.

I had the same thought when I read Roth's misguided statement: Nowhere is competence more on display in America than in our hardware stores. What most of us bring to these stores is our vast ignorance about the small mending tasks that life puts before us and that we, left to our own devices, could easily turn into catastrophes, possibly even felonies. Almost always this ignorance is met at the hardware store with patient good sense and magisterial know-how.

Roth's ignorance on this point suggests that he himself doesn't go in much for home repair. His comparison reminds me of a telephone conversation I once had with the economist Thomas Sowell, in the middle of which I told a joke about a plane in trouble whose pilot has to call on a single passenger to jump out without a parachute so the plane can be landed safely. The captain, over the loudspeaker, remarks that he and the crew have decided to ask that person to jump who is of the least importance to society. At which point, the punch line goes, a disc jockey and a used-car dealer get up in the middle of the aisle and start fighting.

Complete silence from Professor Sowell. When I asked him why he didn't like the joke, he replied, "I should have preferred it if the punch line were 'at which point a psychotherapist and the curator of a contemporary art museum got up in the middle of the aisle and started fighting.'" In this same Sowellian vein, I should have preferred Philip Roth to say that George W. Bush hadn't the competence of a university English teacher or a political pundit.

Competence is a quality I much esteem. I reject the phrase "merely competent," considering it either an oxymoron or possibly an ironic witticism, like "merely dazzlingly beautiful" or "merely a genius." My own pocket definition of competence is quiet mastery.

Encountering incompetence in quotidian dealings—when, say, one has to call a repairman back three times to get one's refrigerator fixed properly, or a physician has badly misdiagnosed an illness or injury with serious consequences—inevitably gives me those terrible decline-and-fall feelings that lend life an unpiquant air of hopelessness.

I have known a few admirable people who seem omnicompetent. Whether the job is prose composition or building bookshelves, playing guitar or putting up preserves, they see what has to be done and calmly do it. Admiration in my case is also close to envy. I envy them because I don't have lots of competence myself.

When I lived in the South I came across a number of people immensely competent at things I wouldn't even attempt, lest I maim myself. I knew men who could tune their own cars, do their own electrical work; in one instance, I knew a man who, on weekends, was building his own house, from, as they say (certainly I'm not entitled to say it), scratch.

As no one confidently thinks him- or herself brilliant or beautiful, I wonder if many people are deservedly confident of their competence. Lots of people—consultants, psychoanalysts, pollsters—have to put up a strong show of confidence in their competence if only because it is the basis on which they get paid. A deeply hesitant brain surgeon would be greatly nervous-making. Nor do you want a plumber who tells you he's never had much luck fixing toilets like yours.

When one runs into real competence, the world seems a fine place. After making a few hopeless calls recently to obtain two mildly obscure classical music CDs—one of the piano music of Reynaldo Hahn, the other of Judeo-Baroque music sung by the Boston Camerata—I found a man named Eduardo, at Tower Records, who not only knew the music I wanted but was able to supply me with the phone number of the producing company of the Reynaldo Hahn recording because his store didn't stock their products. Ah, I was in the secure embrace of competence.

Eduardo ought to join with Wesley Woods of Hillsborough, North Carolina, to form a ticket for the 2008 presidential election. I can't of course speak for Philip Roth, but they'd have my vote.

Do Go Changin'

(2005)

CONSERVATIVES COME IN MANY STRIPES and various hues. There are the paleoconservatives (the guys who want to get the cars off the streets but haven't yet found an efficient way to deal with the horse manure once they've done so) and the neoconservatives (those former liberals famously mugged by reality and now, Leo Strauss volumes in hand, intent on world domination) and the economic conservatives (whose belief in free markets is as absolute as the belief of the rest of us in gravity) and the libertarians (whose motto is "let 'er rip").

My own conservatism is one of temperament: I get a kick out of tradition and am usually made edgy by too-rapid change. I don't go as far here as Evelyn Waugh, another conservative of temperament. Waugh once claimed that he was not going to vote Tory because the party had been in office for eight years and hadn't set back the clock a single minute.

The reason I bring this up is that, for a man of conservative temperament, I find myself having a strange reaction to radical change in my own neighborhood. A vast amount of new building, most of it residential, is popping up all around me. A conservative of my kind should be saddened by it; as an aesthetic snob—none of the buildings is particularly handsome—I should also be smugly appalled. I find I'm neither. I like what is going on, and am eager for more of the same.

My neighborhood is downtown Evanston, just outside Chicago, on whose edge I have been living for the past 15 years. A 26-story building has gone up across the street from me. Another building that will take up the better part of a full city block is now under construction less than two blocks away. Smaller buildings—of five or six stories—have been put up nearby. Almost all these buildings are condominiums—the entire neighborhood, like much of urban America, has gone condo-maniacal.

Most of the new owners are younger people. In the building across the street lived a high-scoring guard from the Chicago Bulls (before he was traded). Four or so blocks to the north, a second-year quarterback of the Chicago Bears is said to have bought two apartments and combined them into one.

The prices for these various apartments range from $385,000 to $1.3 million. Couples seem to be the principal buyers: a man and a woman each earning in the low six figures, with perhaps a bit of help from one or the other set of parents. The overall effect is to give the neighborhood a greater feel of vibrancy, more restaurants, more people on the streets, more action generally.

When I was a boy this same neighborhood was dominated by blue-rinse dowagers. The town was then by law as dry as these women—it's still the headquarters of the Women's Christian Temperance Union—which condemned it to dreary restaurants, many of them tea rooms, where you could get chicken-salad sandwiches and a demoralizing little peach cobbler.

In those good/bad old days, people came from the west and farther north to shop in Evanston, which had a number of shops, including a small branch of Marshall Field's. But the building of a large mall a few miles to the west soon left Evanston bereft of most of its useful stores, and fast food joints catering to the Northwestern students began to dominate. The best measure for the quality of a town is the number of blocks of good shops it contains—New York and London win hands-down here—but until recently Evanston couldn't even put together a single block of interesting shops. Soon after the new building began, though, a Peet's coffee-and-tea shop, a Whole Foods supermarket, and a cineplex moved in. With all the building going on, with the continuing influx of young, mildly opulent people, there is hope more will follow.

I hear lots of grumbling about the changing local scene. Parking, already a problem for local merchants and people who come to shop, will presumably become an even greater problem. One of the builders seems to specialize in odd colored balconies—copperish brown, bright red—which much offends the Ruskinians among us.

The entire scene has what a temperamental conservative might call the nauseatingly depressing smell of progress. Yet far from feeling nauseated or depressed, I feel enlivened by the spectacle. Might it be that, unbeknownst even to myself, I have undergone a subtle conversion from a conservative of temperament to a free-market man? (The famous invisible hand of the market has not yet tapped me, awake or in my dreams.) I wish I knew what's going on. All I do know is that, walking in my neighborhood, I now hear myself mutter, the reverse of the "Burn, baby, burn" mantra of the 1960s rioters, a new little mantra of my own: "Build, baby, build."

The Postman Won't Even Ring Once

(2005)

"FRED IS DEAD," read the note my wife left on the small table in our front hall on which we leave each other messages when one or the other of us has gone out. Fred was Fred Austin, our mailman for the better part of the past fifteen years. Three days before I had put a twenty in his hand, as I do every year, instructing him to have a Christmas lunch on me. It's a small enough show of gratitude for many services. "The pleasure's all mine," he said, and then his attention was distracted by a woman entering the lobby asking if he could take care of her mail over the Christmas holiday, while she was off to visit her son.

This was the last I'd heard from Fred. I saw him one more time: in his coffin at a memorial service at Faith Temple Church of God in Christ on Dewey Avenue in Evanston.

He had missed two days of work without calling in, most uncharacteristic behavior. He was a bachelor. No one answered the phone at his apartment. The local postmaster, worried, found a way to enter his apartment, where Fred was found dead of a heart attack. He was fifty-one.

Fred played high-school and small-college football at Ripon College in Wisconsin. He was perhaps 6'1", weighed roughly 220. Like a number of black men I know, he had blood-pressure problems, and more than once he dropped 40 or 50 pounds for health reasons.

Late one Sunday I was filling my gas tank at a local station, when a black Ford Expedition—the largest of the SUVs, I believe, next to the thoroughly egregious Hummer—pulled up, a large man with a black Malcolm X hat got out, and, lo, it was Fred, whose great smile drained all the menace out of the car and the hat both. "Can't you get a bigger car than that, Fred?" I asked. "As soon as they make one," he replied, "I promise that I will."

Much of my conversation with Fred was about sports, that *lingua franca* in which American men of otherwise ostensibly discrepant interests find ways to speak to each other. He knew a lot about sports. At Evanston Township High School he played with Emery Morehead, who went on to play tight end for the Chicago Bears. Through his Morehead connection, Fred would go to Bears training-camp sessions and had no trouble getting tickets for regular-season games.

He was a man of strong, but with me never disruptive, opinions. We agreed that contemporary professional athletes were the physical equivalent of lottery winners; they were, that is, damn lucky: all that money, all that attention. ("Know the toughest thing in the NBA?" Fred once asked me. "Not smiling when you kiss your wife goodbye before going on a road trip.") With only a few exceptions—Walter Payton, Andre Dawson, Cal Ripken Jr. are three I recall—was Fred willing to allow that professional athletes of recent years were other than loutish and hopelessly selfish.

We didn't talk much politics. I assumed he voted Democratic, though, such was his naturally critical bent, my guess is that he could not have been easy on politicians of his own party. "A lot of pressure on the kid," was his one remark about Barack Obama, then a new black senator from Illinois. He agreed with me that it would be interesting to see what attempts Jesse Jackson makes to coopt him. I told him that at one time I would have voted for Colin Powell for president on either party ticket. He didn't respond. He wasn't crazy about Condoleezza Rice, whom he thought the type of the good student, teacher's pet division.

Fred would always honk at me when he passed in his mail-truck. One of his favorite bits, when he would find me in a neighborhood restaurant to which he was delivering mail, or when I was walking with a friend, would be to say in a loud voice, "Excuse me, sir, but aren't you George

Steinbrenner [or Jerry Reinsdorf, or the agent Scott Boras]? You look awfully familiar."

As a mailman, Fred was up on what was happening in the neighborhood. When a new shop or restaurant was going to open, he was the one who first brought the information to the rest of us. His cheerfulness was almost permanent; and it made it difficult to be grumpy in his presence. After his death, a neighbor wrote to the local paper about how good Fred was at his job, adding that even the simplest meeting with him made her happy.

I read the obituary pages of the *New York Times*, and every week there are two or three people who, if I hadn't myself known them firsthand, were friends or colleagues or editors or friends of friends of mine. But I found I could not shake off Fred's death—can't quite shake it off yet. A replacement for him hasn't yet been found. Whoever the person is, things won't be quite the same. Nobody's ever going to call me Mr. Steinbrenner again.

A Secret Vice

(2005)

I N THE EARLY TWENTIETH-CENTURY medical encyclopedias, the article "The Secret Vice" was about onanism. Inevitably accompanying the article was a photograph of a practitioner, a young man, poor fellow, who looked to be in the moral equivalent of advanced leprosy.

I have a secret vice of my own to report, and this is listening to talk-radio shows devoted to sports. I practice this vice only in my car, when alone, and until now nobody knew about it. Why, I have often asked myself, do I degrade myself in this way? For my own intellectual health, I've got to stop, and stop soon.

In the console of my car are CDs of Dvorak string quartets, Mitsuko Uchida's sublime rendition of Schubert piano music, Sarah Vaughan singing old standards, and Joel Grey doing the subtler show tunes. This ought to be sufficient to keep me from the tedium of city traffic. Not so, it turns out.

Instead I prefer to hear argumentative men gas away on the exploits of other large and sometimes bulky men hitting, kicking, and stuffing balls of various shapes and sizes over different shaped fields and courts. I, who during the evening might be reading a biography of Dante (Alighieri, not Culpepper), in my car listen to the thin iconoclasm and even thinner commonsense observations of ex-jocks and newspaper sportswriters.

Chicago has two stations devoted to sports talk. Some of the men employed by these stations come on as very moral and perpetually ticked off; others are worldly and calmly cynical; everyone is terribly knowing.

Part of the attraction is what I believe the feminists would call "masculinist." One of the shows I listen to advertises itself as America's last corner bar. It has three so-called hosts: a pugnacious Irishman, a not especially brainy Jewish guy, and a retired Green Bay Packers defensive lineman. All are happily overweight. They eat unhealthily and are pleased about it; for them women are purely sexual objects, except wives, who are figures of mild terror that exist to raise one's children and be outfoxed.

For your sports-talk show man, host or audience, life is largely lived in front of the television set, watching two, three games a night, and uncounted ones on lost weekends. No war on terror is going on, the state of the economy is a matter of little concern, gay marriage is a subject good chiefly for raw jokes. The only questions worth pondering are how corrupt are college sports, was Notre Dame right to fire its football coach, and was Sammy Sosa on steroids the years he hit more than 60 homers.

Much of the content of sports-talk radio is about old, obviously unsettleable arguments: Who are the five all-time best quarterbacks in the NFL? How does Barry Bonds's record stack up against Babe Ruth's? Are all basketball games really won on defense? Gruff opinionation usually wins the day: "Whaddya mean you'd rather have Peyton Manning than Brett Favre in the red zone late in the fourth quarter in a playoff game? Look at the numbers, for God's sake." Ephemeral scandals and trades, potential and real, fill the day's chitchat. The same few bones are gnawed continuously.

Occasionally I learn a little something. When the White Sox traded a power-hitting outfielder named Carlos Lee, I wondered why. On one of these shows I learned that, though Lee hit more than 30 home runs and batted around .300, and had an error-free year in left field, he also hit 50 points lower with men in scoring position, and more than 100 points lower with two outs with men in scoring position, and the reason he fielded as well as he did is that he played a short left field and the balls that sailed over his head did not count as errors.

These shows are all the radio equivalent of interactive—they allow the audience to put in its rusty two cents through call-ins, emails, faxes. I've never called in or sent an email myself. Even though I've wasted a vast portion of my life watching games, I find I have no strikingly original insight into any of them. I could, I suppose, call in politely to point out that the word "fortuitous" doesn't mean fortunate. Somehow, though, I feel my pedantry would not be well received.

My mind would be so much better engaged listening to serious music. Shoot the Schubert to me, Hubert, should be my byword, or Hit me with more Dvorak, Jack. Yet I listen to the trivia-meisters of sports-talk radio instead. All I can do is admit to the vice, and, in the manner of Alcoholics Anonymous, hope, now that my vice isn't secret any more, that I've taken a first step toward recovery.

Orchidacious

(2005)

RCHIDS LOOK TO BECOME MY NEXT OBSESSION. I do not,
I think, qualify as a truly obsessive personality, but I do like to
have an obsession going from time to time. For a while I was
obsessed with finding the perfect fountain pen, which I believe I've now
found. Books were a more enduring obsession, lasting decades: I wanted
to own and read all the good books. That, too, is well behind me, and all I
care about now is having a few well-written books around the house that
I haven't yet read.

As an obsession, orchids, though, are very different, coming out of
nowhere. A city man, an apartment dweller, I have never kept a garden,
nor do I desire to do so now. I have never taken a course in botany, and
the pistil and the stamen exhaust my knowledge on the subject. If a
grandchild were to ask me to explain photosynthesis, "Kid," I'd have to
say, "lemme get back to you on this one."

My interest in orchids began roughly a year or so ago, when a friend, in
commemoration of his wife's death, sent my wife and me and a few other
of his friends a grand double-orchid plant, species *Phalaenopsis*, whose
large but delicate white flowers, sitting in the middle of our dining-room
table, lasted nearly four months. Looking at them refreshed my spirit;
and when they finally withered, I felt a genuine subtraction.

Not long after, at our local farmers' market, an orchid grower set up a stand. I began buying orchids from him, at $25 for a six-inch pot, usually keeping three or four such pots in the apartment. When the farmers' market closed in the autumn, I discovered that Home Depot, in its gardening department, carries a good supply of orchids, and I now buy them there ($20 for a six-inch pot). Standing in the checkout line, holding my single potted orchid, behind two guys with eighty-pound sacks of concrete, and in front of a guy with a heavy cart filled with insulation, I feel like Oscar Wilde, freshly arrived in America, posing with a long lily in his hand.

I mention prices because orchids were once thought to be a luxury available only to the very rich. Anthony West, the natural son of H. G. Wells and Rebecca West, and a man with a keen interest in orchids, reports that in the 1880s and '90s, keeping and growing orchids was the sport of the very rich in England: "The mark of arrival, beyond having a town house and country place, a shoot in Scotland, or a string of race horses, was having an orchid house—and having in it something from the heart of Brazil, or darkest New Guinea, or upper Burma, that they hadn't got at Chatsworth, or in the Rothschilds' orchid house at Tring Park." This is but another instance of how those of us who are mere members of the *schleppoisie* can now enjoy pleasures once available only to the very rich.

The actor Raymond Burr is said to have been mad about orchids, and so is the historian John Hope Franklin, who grows them. Rex Stout's detective Nero Wolfe was another orchidizer, and for him the more exotic the species the better. Hercule Poirot used sometimes to wear a small orchid of subtle color in the lapel of his exquisitely tailored suits.

Part of the attraction of orchids is their color. When it comes to orchids, my vocabulary isn't subtle enough to register the astonishing range of their colors. I have a plant now with no fewer than eleven blooms and three more in bud, all in what I call a washed yellow, turning to lightest green, faintly pink in the middle, with extraordinary brown markings that, close up, resemble Chinese hieroglyphs.

The exoticism of these flowers supplies another part of their pleasure for me. With them in my apartment I feel I have a butterfly collection, on loan for as long as they live, which is usually roughly three months. But it is a butterfly collection not pinned to velvet but instead shown in perfect stop-action, or, if you prefer, *tableau vivant*. There are some 30,000 species of orchid that grow wild around the world, and, if Vladimir Nabokov were alive, he could tell me whether there are more or fewer species of butterfly. After he did, I would tell him that the nice thing about the orchids is that at least one doesn't have to run around in shorts with a net to capture them.

We couldn't keep flowers in our apartment until the decease of our highly civilized cat, Isabelle, whose only flaw was to treat all flowers as her personal salad bar. I don't plan ever to grow orchids—mine is an obsession with clear limits—but I do like to acquire them with as many buds as possible, allowing myself to believe that my careful watering—three ice cubes in their terra cotta pots every other morning—is what causes them to bloom and flourish. So please, in the future, do not send small plaques, tall trophies, or jeroboams of champagne. Orchids will do nicely.

Switch & Rebate

(2005)

I'VE READ THAT SOMETHING LIKE 80 PERCENT of the people eligible for rebates on purchases of new appliances, computers, even automobiles, faced with the irritating paperwork involved in collecting the money, adapt what are supposed to have been W. C. Fields's death-bed words and say, "On second thought, screw 'em," and walk away in defeat. Not me. I'm determined they aren't going to cheat me. I think of myself as neither a running dog nor a jackal of capitalism, but a fox out to get all the system has to offer. As such I'm not about to let its trickier practitioners pull the wool over my toes, not in this life, buddy boy, they won't.

"*Du calme*," Old Fox, I say to myself, pen poised above the formidable not-yet-filled-out rebate papers before me, "*du calme*." This is the advice for survival the physician in Brussels gives to Joseph Conrad's main man Marlow before he plunges into the heart of darkness that was the Belgian Congo.

I now plunge into my rebate-coupon paperwork. I carefully check the box next to the name of my new computer printer on which I'm applying for my rebate. I print in my name and address with a steady hand and an impressive clarity in which I take much delight. Not to seem uncooperative or otherwise a cold or remote person, I check Yes in the boxes that will allow the company to send me further information about other of their products, and even agree to sharing "customer information with the sellers where you purchased the product." Hey, I want them to know that I'm a sharing, caring kind of guy, but at the same time would like to find a way to establish that I'm not someone to be trifled with.

At first the mail-in rebate checklist seems straightforward enough. They want the rebate coupon-form filled out. Already done: check. They want the original receipt for my purchase or a copy of it. I've got it right here on my desk: check. They want the original UPC and serial number of the product, which I've already cut off the box: check. They want, for some reason, my mother's maiden name, which banks sometimes ask for, too. No problem. I write in "Abrams." Check yet again.

Things are going fairly smoothly, but then I am brought up a bit when they want to know the name of the first boy my mother went out with in high school. I'd heard these guys can play rough. Only this time the Fox happens to be ready for them. I recall my mother telling me that the first boy she went out with at John Marshall High School on the west side of Chicago in 1925, when she was 15, was Sidney Silverman (alliteration here is a great aid to memory), who later in life made a bundle in used auto parts. He bought her a wrist corsage and took her to a dance at the Palmer House. I hear trumpets sound dimly but triumphantly in the background as I print out Sidney's full name.

The next item on the list asks for dental X-rays and a small sample of hairs from my head to be placed in a Ziploc bag. I pull out a few of my ever-sparser hairs and insert them in a plastic bag, and make a note to call in the morning Dr. Primack's hygienist Pat, who just acquired a bichon frise pup named Myron, about whose health I must remember to inquire. I'm not sure about the dental X-rays, but I assume that they want the hairs to check out my DNA, for rebates have by now been in business long enough to attract scam artists and maybe they want to make sure I'm not one of them. Okay. I can live with that.

Things start to get sticky with the next item, which asks for a liver biopsy, which really seems to me pushing it. It's less than clear whether they want the actual tissue or a report on a biopsy. I'm assuming the report. In any case, I'm in luck, for I have had such a procedure within the past three months. I make another note to check with Jim Rosenberg, my gastroenterologist, in the morning. But why, exactly, do you suppose they want a liver biopsy? I have no notion but feel fortunate that they didn't ask for a lung or kidney biopsy. These guys play hardball.

As I read the final item, a dark cloud forms before my eyes. I fight off fainting. They ask for my foreskin—I mean, my actual flamin' foreskin—though there are no instructions about how to package it. (For women, an asterisk footnote says, they will accept a maidenhead.) I was circumcised 68 years ago. Could I, I wonder, fake it, slip a fresh one, sort of antiqued up, by them? But where would I get it? For the first time in my entire life I regret not knowing a mohel. Maybe . . . or maybe. . . . And then, maybe. . . . Crumpling up the almost-filled-out rebate coupon in my hand, I hear the plaintive voice of W. C. Fields, "On second thought, screw 'em," and now the Old Fox, too, retires in defeat.

Early Riser

(2002)

TALKING TO A FRIEND NOT LONG AGO, I paraphrased a remark of Einstein's: "Only a monomaniac gets anything done." "No," replied my friend, "only people who get up at five a.m. get anything done." I happen to be both a monomaniac and a five o'clock riser, so why, I wonder, do I continue to feel so slothful? Before attempting to answer, let me say that though I'm not someone who bounds out of bed like a wide receiver breaking from a Notre Dame huddle, I do look forward to getting up early. I like the darkness, I like the silence, I like the company I encounter at that hour—which is to say, I enjoy the hour or so of solitude. And as a grateful pessimist, I like the fact that I have made it—still alive!—through another night.

I also immensely like my morning regimen. I turn on the stove under the tea kettle, fill the tea ball (alternating Assam Extra Fancy one morning with Irish Breakfast the next), and await the whistle of the kettle while I make out a list of the day's errands, meetings, and responsibilities. Then I sit on a high stool at the kitchen counter and read, more often than not from some thickish book having to do with something I have promised to write. I sip tea, I take notes on my reading, I await the sunrise.

Sometimes I am accompanied by music from WFMT, Chicago's last remaining and splendid classical-music station, though I turn it off if the music becomes too dramatic, thereby interfering with my reading and my sense of a day's calm beginning (not much Beethoven, no Wagner, and scant Richard Strauss permitted at this early hour). I hope no one will think me nauseatingly sensitive if I add that I used to be joined by a striped cat, now dead, named Isabelle, who, after I fed her, sat beside my book, always on my left, demanding no attention, content to be nearby and to look elegant. During baseball season I turn on an AM station at 5:13 to get the previous night's scores and, while I'm at it, the weather. No phone rings; I generally do not turn on my computer, allowing email, and hence the outside world, to invade my morning. For the same reason, I wait until 6:30 or so to go to the door for the *New York Times,* in which I turn first to the obituaries to see who has been taken out of the game. I could still be sleeping—a pleasure I do not slight—but I really am happier awake.

I am happier awake because I am a man who has long been on a schedule. What put me on this schedule I do not know, but on it I have been for most of my adult life. I waste money, food, energy, and doubtless much else, all fairly lightheartedly, but I do have a bad conscience about wasting time. Not that I don't waste plenty of time, too, gassing away on the phone with friends, looking for excuses to take me away from my work, indulging in magazine-reading binges, taking long lunches. But wasting time abed I cannot do. If I sleep as late as seven o'clock, even on a weekend, I feel the day is lost.

As for this unwritten schedule, I'm not, please believe me, madly intent on achievement, keen to produce fifty books before I die or determined to earn 20 percent more this year—every year—than last. I'm not in competition with anyone, living or dead. My schedule is entirely self-imposed. It calls for my getting something useful done every day, and useful, for me, means writing two or three or—if the planets are in perfect alignment— four or five decent pages. When I read years ago that Thomas Mann, a prodigious—and famously slow—worker, settled for a page a day, this *petit* Chicago *bourgeois* was much impressed by that *haute* Baltic German one. Of course a page a day, knocking off only on Sundays, means a respectable-sized book a year.

I began getting up early not because of conscience or because of the intrinsic pleasures that doing so has subsequently come to give but because, as a man then in my middle twenties, married, with a house full of children, dogs, cats, and other livestock, and working at a full-time job, I found that was the only time I could get any writing done. So I began waking up at 5:00 a.m. After splashing cool water on my face and revving myself up with coffee and cigarettes (in those days not yet considered death in the afternoon), I staggered over to my old Royal Standard and began tapping away.

Getting up at five wasn't all that easy at first. On cold Chicago mornings I kept my psychic furnace stoked with guilt. Having struggled to get up, and having then accomplished little, left me feeling stupid to a very high power. I would tell myself that I hadn't hauled my carcass out of bed to write one wretched and ill-made paragraph: Concentrate, type, form words into sentences, remember that sentences make paragraphs and paragraphs pages—keep things moving, kid. Self-scolding in those days worked well for me. No longer, I fear; nowadays I have only shame to spur me on.

Up to the age of twenty-five or so, I was susceptible to neither. From my late adolescence through my early twenties my weekend *modus operandi* was to come in at around five in the morning and sleep heavily till three or so in the afternoon. Dreams when I was young seemed richer, less complicated; they were more about the future than the past, about promise rather than loss. One quarter at the University of Chicago when I had only morning classes, I stayed up nights and slept days all week long, which worked out beautifully, providing lots of time to get schoolwork done along with reading of my own and ample goofing off. When young, I could bounce back quickly after a poor night's sleep or a full night's revels; the elastic wasn't yet worn out. Now I feel I almost need to go into training just to get a decent day's work done.

"Beddy-bye," W. H. Auden used to say to his hosts at 9:30 p.m., or to his guests when he was the host, for he was a 6:00 a.m. riser and required a full night's sleep for a full day's wrestle with language at his cigarette-ash-laden and untidy desk. Auden never wrote at night, believing, as he told his friend Orlan Fox, that "only the 'Hitlers of the world' work at night; no honest artist does." Not quite true. The novelist John O'Hara claimed later in life that he got to work only after the last television show was over. Balzac worked through many a night, nicely wired by vast quantities of coffee.

Edmund Wilson, on the other hand, according to his daughter's testimony, used to stay up late at night drinking and then trudge off to bed with a full tumbler of Scotch, but most mornings he showed up at his desk ready for a full caseload of literary judgments.

By 9:30 p.m. put a fork in me, I'm done. I try to be in bed by ten. Sometimes, I'm told, the forms that matchmaking services ask their clients to fill out include a question about whether they are morning or night persons—a sensible query. Fortunately, my wife is on roughly the same timetable as I, sleeping only an hour or so later most mornings. The mornings after nights that we stay out late feel like a punishment—that damn elastic again.

I used to joke that as I grew older, the minutes, hours, days, weeks, months, continued to feel as long as ever; it was only the decades that passed more quickly. But now the days have begun to seem shorter. FedEx, email, Internet downloading, and much else are supposed to be saving us vast quantities of time. I think they've only heightened expectations for a faster response. With all these marvelous conveniences added, the load somehow seems heavier. Where once people fell behind in their correspondence, now they can't keep up with their email, while still owing letters.

Living the good life as a member of the so-called enlightened classes (or are we by now the masses?) entails some form of working out, careful shopping and cooking, keeping up with high and popular culture through watching the right movies, listening to the right music, reading the right books, traveling to the right places. Let us not speak of the relatively new expectations regarding fatherhood and motherhood, wifehood and husbandhood. Anyone who attempts to do everything on the list in a thorough way had better block out another few hours a week for visits with a therapist. One of the chief reasons that I—quite possibly along with you—feel slothful is that our greatly sped-up life, with all its new conveniences, has raised my expectations, has led me to think that I ought to be turning out much more work than I do, has left me to feel at the end of so many days that I ought to have done better.

But at 5:00 a.m., waiting for the kettle to boil, contemplating the book before me, with thoughts floating lazily in my head, it gives serious—I only wish I could say abiding—pleasure to know that I still have three or so hours before having to get, even in my mildly engaged way, into the

fray. One of the reasons that nineteenth-century writers and intellectuals and scientists seem to have gotten so much done—monstrous oeuvres
of novels, poems, diaries; thousands of letters; scientific exploration and
widely varied experimentation in two or three fields—is that they didn't
have all the conveniences we do. For "conveniences," of course, one might
read "distractions." Many of those people must have felt as if they were
living their lives at 5:00 a.m. all day long. Lucky them.

Fred

(2004)

FREDERICK MORGAN, for fifty years the editor of the *Hudson Review* and an accomplished poet who died on February 20th in Manhattan at the age of eighty-one, was a serious and substantial and immensely attractive man. He also had a smile in his voice, an upper-class version of a New York accent—"Jee-o, hi," he would greet me over the phone, "it's Fred Morgan"—and a wonderful laugh it always pleased me to be able to evoke.

I first met Fred Morgan in 1970, and I began writing for him not long afterward. The *Hudson Review* paid much lower rates than other magazines; it even had a policy, before the onset of computer printing, of charging contributors for changes on galley proofs, which meant that, theoretically, one could actually lose money writing for it. Yet it always delighted me to find my prose in its pages. Sydney Smith, listing his motives for writing to Lord Jeffrey, editor of the *Edinburgh Review*, included, along with the jollity of punishing folly and making money, "the love of you." I myself felt something of this last-named motive in writing for Fred.

Fred was rich, though he displayed few obvious outward signs—no ritz, no glitz—of his family's wealth. I once met his mother, a gracious woman then in her eighties, who resembled nothing so much as one of those upper-class women in the Helen Hokinson cartoons. As a young man, Fred had the luxury of deciding to become richer through dull work or to devote himself to his love, which was literature. He sensibly chose the latter, and he never, in my presence, expressed the least doubt about the rightness of the decision.

The first time I met Fred was in his magazine's old office on 55th Street. He had just brought in a milkshake and a turkey sandwich, which he ate, as we talked, with what seemed to me serious pleasure. On our second meeting he took me to lunch at Giovanni's, a restaurant his father used to patronize, where everything tasted wonderful and a quiet but pleasing fuss was made over Fred and his wife, Paula Deitz.

Fred Morgan had the ability to concentrate on the moment and enjoy it to the maximum, but, like so many people with genuine *joie de vivre*, behind it lay deep sadness. Fred buried three of his children. He was too manly to talk about, or even hint at, the effect of these horrific events in his life. Paula, whom he married in 1969 and who currently edits the *Hudson Review*, was a great find for him, and his adoration of her never seemed, when I was with them, less than complete.

I spent an afternoon in Fred's company once at his summer home on the ocean at Blue Hill, Maine, driving there in a rented white Lincoln Town-car. I recall saying to Fred that "White Lincoln at Blue Hill" sounded like a Wallace Stevens poem, and then remembered that he was old enough to know Stevens, whom he had convinced to contribute to his magazine. He had also gone to St. Elizabeths Hospital in Washington, DC, to see Ezra Pound, from whom he acquired a contribution for the magazine. He once told me of a visit to his apartment from T. S. Eliot, who sat on the sofa, seeming shy and holding hands the entire time with his second wife Valerie.

Fred Morgan was a man of the age of the quarterlies. When he and two Princeton classmates—Joseph Bennett and William Arrowsmith—began the *Hudson Review* in 1948, the quarterly literary magazine was a thriving and, in its own quiet way, powerful literary institution. Editors of the quarterlies—John Crowe Ransom at *Kenyon Review*, Allen Tate at *Sewanee Review*, Philip Rahv and William Phillips at *Partisan Review*, Karl Shapiro at *Prairie Schooner*—were great figures. Fred Morgan, though younger than all these men, was their peer.

In some ways he was superior to them in editing a magazine that was astonishingly free from literary and intellectual and political fashion.

Although I knew Fred for more than thirty years, he died without my knowing his politics. Many professors wrote for the *Hudson Review*, but, through the skill of Fred's editing, it always seemed more a metropolitan than academic magazine. I knew many of the things he loved in the realm of art, but even more, I knew that he had very little tolerance for nonsense and cant. Because he wasn't afraid to act on this low tolerance through his magazine, he was never a prize-winning poet, a member of the American Academy of Arts and Letters, or an establishment figure. One of the specialties of the *Hudson Review* in the 1960s and 1970s was the deflation of the second- and third-rate in literature, film, and theater. Marvin Mudrick (on literature), Vernon Young (on chiefly European film), and John Simon (on theater) wrote in nearly every issue, three tough guys guarding the gates against the tawdry and pretentious.

Although quarterly magazines retain their usefulness as places to publish a thoughtful essay, a well-made longer poem, or a short story that is not freakish but quietly situated in everyday life, quarterlies themselves no longer seem central to the hum and rhythm of contemporary intellectual life. In the age of email, fax, FedEx, and omnipresent cell phones, it sometimes seems as if the only fit periodical would be an hourly.

I never spoke with Fred, a quarterly man to the bone, about this, but my guess is that he would have made a persuasive case for the literary and intellectual quarterly—as a place to be more reflective and to impose the old standards, a tent from which to watch the ever-more speedily passing caravans and hear the ever-more loudly barking dogs, and, with ample space and leisurely deadlines provided, make a scrupulous attempt to understand what is really going on in the world of intellect and culture. That, after all, is what Fred Morgan did for all his adult life, and did it, over a longer haul, better than anyone else.

No Joke

(2005)

As is its relentless wont, the *New York Times* has brought me bad news, but not just bad news about the world, its standard fare, but about my own life. In a recent Sunday Styles section, the newspaper announced that jokes, formal jokes, with a beginning-middle-and-end structure, are out. "It's a matter of faith among professional comics," the paper reports, "that jokes—the kind that involve a narrative set-up, some ridiculous details and a punch line—have been displaced by observational humor and one-liners." The older kind of jokes now don't cut it, in other words, aren't even yesterday.

Reading this, I felt like a man with a store full of hula-hoops, simulated mother of pearl Zippo lighters, and bolo ties. I have a repertoire of perhaps four hundred jokes that are, if the *Times* is correct, no longer in demand, possibly even in bad taste. Perhaps I should add that I also have the accents to go with these jokes.

I love a well-told joke, which I consider an oral version of a good short story. I once asked students at the beginning of a creative writing course to write out a joke for me. The result was dismal, the jokes dreary, which didn't bode well for the class.

As for how I came into possession of my large stock of jokes, the answer is that when you tell a joke you tend to get a joke told back to you. Having a small reputation as joke teller, I find people with a nice sense of *quid pro quo* often have a joke ready for me. A woman who works at a nearby bakery last week stopped me, one of her sourdough breads in my hand, to report: "Joe, my brother is going with a beautiful and intelligent homeless woman." I looked at her quizzically. Then she continued: "And the best thing about it, he says, is that at the end of the evening he can drop her off anywhere."

Already you will have seen the problem with the old-fashioned jokes: political correctness, that enemy of wit, paradox, and the clear-eyed observation of human oddity. Freud had it that jokes were essentially a form of aggression. People who subscribe to political correctness would agree. For them there are no good jokes—and they, like Freud, aren't kidding.

The great preponderance of jokes are about Irishmen, Scotsmen, Poles, blacks, and above all Jews. Nuns, priests, rabbis, dumb blondes, Texans, golfers, and elderly people with undiminished sexual longings also figure in heavily. The homeless woman joke above is of course in wretched taste, but what could be more useless than a joke in good taste?

As other people cannot remember jokes, I find it difficult to forget them. The first off-color (not quite blue, closer to aquamarine) joke I ever heard had the punchline, "Rectum, hell, it almost killed him." I walk the streets with lots of punchlines in my head: "Comfortable I don't know— I make a nice living." "Oy, was I thirsty!" "Whaddya mean Heaven. I'm a buffalo in Montana." "If she dies, she dies." "Last night, and then again this morning." "Who listens?" "If you had a brother, would he like noodles?" "Women of Frampol, I beseech you, move a little."

To avert being shunned by the politically correct, I could, I suppose, fall back on my better quality animal jokes, some of which feature dogs who have spied on the KGB, grizzly bears from whom Chicago policemen are able to wring false confessions, and parrots who know the full liturgies for Rosh Hashanah and Yom Kippur. I also don't mind a joke in which someone is strangling a parrot or threatening to exile him to the freezer for excessive use of profanity, but I recognize that such jokes could easily land me in difficulty with the animal-rights people.

The *New York Times* also blames the Internet for helping to kill jokes. Too many are now whirring around in cyberspace, instead of passing from person to person, as they were meant to have done. In contradistinction to Mae West's law about not being able to get too much of a good thing, opening up an email that begins "Have you heard these?" and is followed by 11 flatly told jokes, ten of which one has indeed heard, can take the smile out of Christmas morning.

I have been in the same room with joke-bores, and it is no *dejeuner sur l'herbe*. I hope I have not myself become one. I have, as I say, four hundred or so jokes in my repertoire. If you've heard any of them before, please don't stop me.

The Big Picture

(2005)

SOME OF US LOOK AT THE BIG PICTURE and some of us, unfortunately, do not. I have myself only recently begun to look at the big picture. And by big picture I mean a picture 42" diagonally across. In plainer words, I just purchased a new large-screen plasma television set, and the size and perfection of it both appall and thrill me. I am appalled at my weakness for such a bit of unnecessary luxury and thrilled by the delight I'm finding in it.

I had a standard size (27") television set for, roughly, twelve years, and it hummed along without once needing to be repaired. It wasn't the television set but I who was beginning to break down. The last year or so I discovered that, in my adagio (I hope) foxtrot to the grave, I did not see things on it as clearly as I used to do. Three-point shots, close calls at second base, small boxes showing the inning or quarter or time left on the shot clock were no longer quite visible to me without a proper squint or, sometimes, having to rise out of my chair and walk right up to the television set to find out how or where, precisely, things stood.

I probably would have suffered along in this way until my old television set broke down, but then a month or so ago the mail brought a check for rather larger royalties than I expected for one of my recent books. I use the word "royalties," but until recent years I used to designate these checks, such were their negligible amounts, as "peasantries." I determined a portion of this check ought to be spent in an entirely self-indulgent way. A plasma television set seemed to fill the bill nicely.

I bought a Sony high-definition set, with its various bells and whistles. If one is going to hell, then I say let's go first-class, so I added HBO and Turner Classic Movies to my cable package and a DVR that allows me to record ballgames and movies and shows without requiring tape.

You might think it obvious beyond all reckoning when I report my pleasure in this new television set. But when I also report that I am an intellectual, University of Chicago bred, you will understand why it is not obvious at all. Intellectuals are trained to loathe television, seeing in it the seeds of violence in children, the vast dumbing down of American culture, and the ruination of political and public life generally. When it is not purely evil, television, the catechism here holds, is a thorough waste of time.

I have never seen a television set in the living room of an apartment or house in Hyde Park, the neighborhood of the University of Chicago. My old television set sat in our living room but in a large dark cabinet, with the stereo system on shelves below; its doors were often closed when it wasn't in use. My new television set, too large to hide, dominates the room. Stepping into my living room, I gaze at this piece of gleaming machinery, which goes with none of the surrounding furniture, and feel as if someone has by mistake parked a Ferrari there.

My general pattern is to be haughtily contemptuous of creature comforts and then, once I acquire them, grow accustomed to them with an unseemly haste. Had I been born much earlier, I'm sure to have made an utterly persuasive case against indoor plumbing. What do I need it for, I would no doubt have asked, as I have since asked about multiple other conveniences, all afterwards acquired and enjoyed with uncomplicated pleasure. I am a moral puritan, saved only by his hypocrisy.

"Things are in the saddle and ride mankind," said Emerson. Easy for old Waldo to say. He never saw, in high definition, Aaron Rowand, the center-fielder of the Chicago White Sox, loping back to catch a long fly ball at the warning track in center, or was ever able to reheat his morning tea to perfection in a microwave, or tapped a Macintosh X Tiger program to bring up the new Dashboard feature that yields a five-day weather forecast, all of the previous night's baseball scores, the listings at local movie theaters, an account on the progress of one's stocks, and many more such items. If things ride man, very well, I say toss a saddle over me.

I watch some news on television, and doubtless too much sports, and always hope a good older movie will turn up. I usually sit there with a magazine in hand or a book of lesser intellectual density than any of those written by Johann Gottlieb Fichte. *Seinfeld* was the last show I looked forward to. But now, if my new television turns me into even more of a couch potato than I already am, so be it. If I am to live out the rest of my days as a couch potato, this television set will at least allow me to do so *au gratin*.

Trend Stopping

(2005)

THE OTHER DAY, ON C-SPAN, I saw Bernard-Henri Lévy, the French intellectual, giving a talk plugging one of his books at a Barnes & Noble. Monsieur Lévy is a man with a vivid face, including a nose that doesn't disappoint, high coloring, and a small mouth worth watching. Yet I soon found my mind wandering from his heavily French-accented pronunciamentos about the state of the world. Instead I concentrated on his white shirt, worn under a black blazer, the top three buttons of which were unbuttoned down the front as were the cuffs of his shirt, which flapped loosely from under his jacket sleeves. Why this *déshabille*? Was Monsieur Lévy late getting to his talk and unable to finish dressing? But then not long after, I saw a photograph of him in a back issue of *Vanity Fair*, and, lo, there they were, the same three unbuttoned buttons down the front of his shirt, the same flapping cuffs.

Clearly, this was a look that the Frenchman was going for, a fashion statement. But as a fashion statement, what did it say: I am dashing, madcap, unconventional, I suppose. Whether other men on the continent are similarly unbuttoned these days, I do not know. But the other night I saw a version of the great Cary Grant-Rosalind Russell flick *His Girl Friday* introduced by the director and film historian Peter Bogdanovich, and damned if his shirt front and cuffs weren't similarly unbuttoned. "Peter, Peter, Peter," I hear Cary Grant saying. "Button up, my boy, button up."

Is a trend beginning: the unbuttoned male? Will it catch on? Will all men now have to go around with flapping shirt cuffs and *pupik*-plunging shirt fronts? Will shirt makers soon dispense with buttons on cuffs altogether? Is there no way to stop it?

Fred Astaire wore beautiful clothes as well and wittily as any man in the twentieth century. Billy Wilder claimed to have a recurring dream in which he asked Astaire where he bought his clothes, and, just as he was about to tell him, Wilder woke, ticked off at missing out yet again. But at one point Astaire began to wear a necktie at his waist in place of a belt. A bad move from an otherwise flawlessly elegant man: bad because it was too calculated and artificial, and finally silly.

I recently mentioned this to a friend now in his nineties, who told me that for a brief spell he, too, wore a necktie in place of a belt. He did so, he added, because his deceased wife, taking her lead from the great dancer, had asked him to do it. "God," I said, "you must have loved her." Fortunately, the necktie as a belt substitute business did not catch on; it was the only production of Fred Astaire's, that, so to say, didn't have legs.

A number of people who love the movies agree that the last splurge of swell American flicks came in the 1970s, with the rise of the directors Martin Scorsese, Robert Altman, Bob Rafelson, and others. But one of the problems with these movies is that the clothes, especially the men's clothes then trendy—the long-collared shirts, the bell-bottomed trousers, the long sideburns (every man his own Elvis), the Afros and Jewfros and dopey helmets of hair worn over the ears—make so many of these films seem like goofy costume dramas. Perhaps through the magic of redigitalization, the clothes of the actors in these movies can be changed and the movies made freshly watchable.

I was sitting at Wrigley Field earlier this summer with a friend who is a physician, a hematologist. Looking at the tattooed back of a perfectly middle-class girl sitting in front of us, my friend said that if he were thirty years younger he would devote all his efforts to finding an effective way to remove all the tattoos that people in their twenties today are now having done. When these people get to fifty, my friend is confident, they are going to be looking around desperately for ways to remove their tattoos.

Tattooing by the middle-class young is a trend whose sense I haven't come close to plumbing. The pain, the expense, the permanence—why would anyone put himself through this torture for such an aesthetically displeasing result? Because of the power, the only and immensely unsatisfactory answer is, of trendiness. Can a trend, once begun, be stopped? No one has ever found a way, short of embarrassing the trend-setters before things get out of hand.

I don't know if Monsieur Lévy is a trend-setter or not. He may well have picked up the way he wears his shirts from a now aging Alain Delon or some other Parisian more elegant than he. But I think he ought to be told, straightaway, to knock it off. Perhaps one man in the last fifty years looked good with the front of his shirt unbuttoned, and his name is Harry Belafonte. As for those flappy cuffs, one can only hope that Monsieur Lévy pours enough soup—preferably hot, rich, red soup—on them to prove to him that he needs to button up, and now.

Santayana's Chair

(2005)

I HAVE BEEN READING, with immense pleasure, the first four volumes of *The Letters of George Santayana* in the handsome edition published by the Massachusetts Institute of Technology Press. I read them with my first cup of tea before breakfast, usually in short takes, between ten and twenty pages at a go. They give my day a bit of tone, elevating me just a touch above the torrent of mundanities that are to follow.

The letters thus far published are from 1868 to 1932—Santayana's birth and death dates are 1863 and 1952—and four more volumes are planned. Santayana's prose was richly aphoristic and as elegantly cadenced as his name. He was one of those sensible people who, to save time, became extremely smart when young. The level and ratio per page of amusing, often profound observations is impressively high. On a fellowship studying in Germany, he notes the utter incapacity of Germans for boredom, which to me explains a lot.

No one was more happily detached than Santayana. At 48, he had finally come into enough money to flee, with unalloyed delight, his job in the philosophy department at Harvard. He lived out his days alone ("I find solitude the best company."), in various temporary quarters in Europe ("To me, it seems a dreadful indignity to have a soul controlled by geography."). A victim of what he called "the contemplative disease," he wished to observe the world and as clearly as possible, which, he understood, is finally not all that clearly. "My philosophy," he wrote, "has always been that disillusion is the only safe foundation for happiness."

Reading along one morning, I came across the following passage in a letter to Santayana's wealthy Harvard classmate, Charles Augustus Strong, who allowed him a room and the use of his apartment when in Paris: "I have bought an arm chair—blue and grey striped velour, walnut frame, warranted genuine Directoire [made, that is, between 1795 and 1800]—which suits me very well for writing (although most people would find it too low). It doesn't jar with the other furniture, I think, but it can always be relegated to the *petit-salon* if you think it *de trop*."

Sometime in the middle 1960s I had written a review of a number of reissues of Santayana's books for the *New Republic*. Not long after, I received a letter from Austria, on chambray-blue stationery, from a man with a Dutch-sounding name. He announced that he was one of Santayana's last students at Harvard and was in possession of an armchair that once belonged to his professor and wondered if I might like to have it.

I wrote back to say that I would be honored to have Santayana's armchair, and that I hoped that my correspondent would allow me to pay whatever shipping charges were entailed in sending it to Chicago. Not only would he allow me to pay for shipping, he revealed, but he also wanted $800 as the purchase price for the chair. At the time eight hundred dollars was rather a big ticket, at least for me, and then doubt crept in: How could I know the chair really belonged to Santayana? Maybe this man sold lots of Santayana—and perhaps not a few Henry Adams and Mark Twain—armchairs to culture-gullible Americans.

Thanks to the MIT edition of Santayana's letters, I now know that my correspondent, a man named Andrew Joseph Onderdonk who was a Wall Street lawyer and expert in international law, was offering me the real goods. With World War I about to break out, Santayana, hoping to lighten the load of the small number of his possessions in Strong's Paris apartment, wrote to Strong, "Onderdonk writes that he will be glad to relieve me of the chair."

Santayana writes to Strong that Onderdonk is among those former students who, after a few years "in the world," seem "to have no intellectual interests or clearness left." He notes that his mother is "a Viennese Jewess of sixty, very flirtatious and friendly but a good soul." A sister is mentioned. Onderdonk visits Santayana from time to time in Paris. Elsewhere he writes that Onderdonk has grown "so fat that he can't open his eyes." Yet Onderdonk wrote Santayana's will, and was, briefly, his literary executor.

Whether Onderdonk, like Santayana, remained a bachelor I do not know. Considering that he was a Jew, his shoring up in Vienna seems an odd fact. One assumes that he didn't remain there during the Nazi era. Where, through that period, did he store Santayana's chair? Having graduated Harvard in 1910, he must have been in his late seventies when he offered to sell me the chair. Was he broke? By 1966 what condition was the chair in? And where is it now?

But for $800 (plus shipping) and a want of faith in my fellow man, I could be sitting in George Santayana's armchair, and writing, I somehow feel, much better than I do now.

The Artist Athlete

(2013)

THE OTHER DAY, reading a little book called *Reflections and Shadows* by Saul Steinberg, the *New Yorker* cartoonist and artist, I came across an interesting passage about the connection between baseball and art. An immigrant born in Romania, Steinberg was not brought up on baseball as a kid, but he was charmed by the game when he came to it as an adult. In the passage, Steinberg writes "Baseball is a philosophical, psychological sport, based, like life, on courage and fear—think of chess and bullfighting. The players have to have extraordinary ability, ready reflexes, and above all an inventive spirit, a creativity that might be called poetic and which puts the sports champion close to the artist."

Is this so? Are great athletes like artists? How high a quotient of truth is there to Steinberg's observation?

Sufficiently high, it occurs to me, to justify some of my own interest in watching athletes perform. Like lots of sports fans, I am interested in competition, in watching people operate under pressure, in witnessing acts of physical fearlessness I myself could never undertake. But what pleases me above all is watching athletics when it rises—which it doesn't do that often—to the level of artistry.

Artists are defined by their unique visions, their mastery over the materials they work with, their *sprezzatura*, or ability to hide the effort that goes into their work. Some athletes have had splendid careers based on grit and determination and endless hard work. Hustlers and fighters, they grind it out. Pete Rose was such an athlete in baseball; the late Carmen Basilio, who was briefly welterweight and middleweight champion of the world, exemplified the gritty boxer; football has too many such figures— sturdy linebackers, three-yards-and-a-cloud-of-dust fullbacks, burly interior linemen; basketball used to have players known as hatchet men—Jim Loscutoff of the Boston Celtics and Bill Laimbeer of the Detroit Pistons come to mind—who were in the game to bang and bruise and slow down the other teams' stars; tennis had dinkers and defensive players, such as Bobby Riggs and Harold Solomon. These athletes, and many more like them, sometimes rise to genuine distinction, but they are not artist athletes, who comprise a different, more elevated category altogether.

The artist athlete never seems to have to gut it out. However hard he may work to have it come about, he makes everything seem to flow naturally. Consider Joe DiMaggio gliding over to catch difficult fly balls to center; everyone else raced, DiMaggio glided. Or Ted Williams, with his long, looping swing and his apparently beyond perfect eyesight, effortlessly whacking balls for clutch hits. (When a pitcher complained of a call while Williams was in the batter's box, an umpire is supposed to have said "Mr. Williams will let you know when you throw a strike.")

Artist athletes seem to have been imbued with perfect bodies for their sports. Oscar Robertson was not only 6'5" but had a backside of a width aptly designed for blocking out and rebounding. The reliever Randy Johnson was 6'10" which, with the added height the pitching mound gave him, lent his delivery more than an extra dollop of terror as he bore down on batters. Martina Navratilova had a left arm absolutely masculine in its musculature: the better to smash aces down the center, granddaughter.

Like superior visual artists, artist athletes see more than do normal people. In a glance, they take in the entire field, court, or ring, and instantly note developing defenses and possibilities for winning responses. One thinks of the San Francisco 49ers quarterback Joe Montana, with monster opposing linemen closing in on him, out of the corner of his eye finding that free wide-receiver jutting past the cornerback and in the clear for a nanosecond, just long enough for Montana to hit him with a perfect pass. Or Michael Jordan bringing the ball downcourt and seeing that slight opening in the defense that allows him to slash to the basket.

Athletic intelligence, of a kind never mentioned by the psychologist Howard Gardner, the John H. and Elisabeth A. Hobbs Professor of Cognition and Education at Harvard and a specialist in formulating various types of intelligence, is one of the world's minor mysteries. Artist athletes, not otherwise in any way necessarily smart about the world, tend to be possessed of superior intelligence while at their game. It's difficult to remember Julius Erving, Oscar Robertson, or Bob Cousy ever committing a turnover. Or Derek Jeter ever throwing to the wrong base. Or Tom Brady not in utter command during a final two-minute drive for a winning score. Cubs fans used to say that Ryne Sandberg, the team's great second baseman, never seemed to dive for a ball. Such was Sandberg's anticipation and quickness that in fact he never had to.

The number of artist athletes is small at any time. They pop up without pattern. Sugar Ray Robinson was such an athlete, and so was Muhammad Ali. Gordie Howe and Wayne Gretzky were hockey's artist athletes. I can think of only three artist athletes at work currently: Tom Brady, Derek Jeter, and Roger Federer.

Roger Federer might just be the Picasso, the Rembrandt, the Michelangelo of athletes. In a game sometimes dominated by power, he prefers prowess, though he has the command of power when he needs it. He does things on the tennis court that the human body is not supposed to be able to do. His footwork astonishes; the angles at which he strikes balls for winners, even when on the run, is unmatched. His unforced errors are few, his temperament such that he rarely defeats himself. Like no other tennis player, he can "build" a point: in four or five strokes he can work his opponent into a corner so that he is set up for one of Federer's down-the-line or cross-court or impossibly angled winners. Federer's perfection sometimes makes him seem para-human.

Exempted from certain physical laws, endowed with an ability to penetrate their opponents' weaknesses, gifted with a mental balance that prevents them from making self-defeating mistakes, artist athletes, during the years given to them to compete, are, if not minor deities, surely favored by the gods. From our couches, we watch them in awe, freshly impressed with the range of human possibility.

Fat Moe, Hot Doug,
and Big Herm

(2005)

THE SIGN, IN RED LETTERS ON A YELLOW AWNING, reading "Moe's Maxwell Street Polish" caught my eye as I drove past. I remember the smell of those Polish sausages, and especially of the onions, grilling on a winter's day on Maxwell Street, the old peddler's open-air market in the Chicago of my boyhood. Polio Sausage, we used jokingly to call it, for it seemed slightly dangerous—not to mention *trayf*, or unkosher, to the highest power—even to my boyhood gang of semi-ruffians, all of us Jewish, none from Kosher-keeping homes. I made a mental note to return to the restaurant, whose proper name is Fat Moe's.

The Polish sausages and onions on the grill at Fat Moe's did not, regrettably, give off that same stirring smell. The place is what the English call a take-away: You order at one of two windows and take your sandwiches off in brown bags. Fat Moe himself was not on the premises, I was told by a man who called himself Thin Moe. When I inquired just how fat Fat Moe was, he reported, disappointingly to me, only that he was losing weight. I hate to see a man shed his sobriquet through diet.

My friend and I took our sandwiches to a nearby park, where we ate them seated on a bench, the wind at our backs. The sandwiches were good, though not memorable, and the French fries notably greasy, for which, as a connoisseur of Chicago grub, I never deduct points. The paper napkins, as is always the case at such joints, were small and of course too few. Proudly I report that I left no mustard on the red sweater I was wearing, though I cannot vouch for my lips, chin, and cheeks. Pity that Manet wasn't there to paint us.

Fast food doesn't quite define the kind of food served at Fat Moe's, though they serve it up quickly enough. Junk food doesn't feel right, either. Certainly it doesn't qualify as comfort food: not in our time of cholesterol terror. Male food is the way I think of it: It is for men who like coarse blatant flavors, juicy, spicy, rich, greasy, and sloppy. Men are brutes, information I continually press upon my granddaughter, and if she could have seen her grandfather attack Fat Moe's Polish sausage sandwich the point would have required no further repetition.

I limit myself severely in my visits to joints like Fat Moe's, going to them perhaps once a month. Not long ago I discovered another, in an out-of-the-way Chicago neighborhood, called Hot Doug's. Doug, a man who looks to be in his late thirties, is a sausage specialist who likes to name his sandwiches after his friends ("The Paul Kelly. Bratwurst soaked in beer—sort of like Paul."), Chicago athletes, and entertainers ("The Don Rickles. Thuringer: Beef, pork, and garlic—you'll like it, you hockey puck."). The crowd at Doug's is very Chicagoan: of good cheer, unpretentious, and tending toward the heavyset. Chicago is a city where they don't hold it against a fellow if he happens to be twenty or thirty (all right, make that forty or fifty) pounds overweight. I modestly had a Shawon Dunston ("Chicken sausage, zesty Italian style") and an order of excellent fries. On Fridays and Saturdays the *spécialité de la maison* at Hot Doug's is fries cooked in duck fat. I have yet to sample these, never having felt sufficiently suicidal.

I don't go much anymore to Big Herm's, which a witty friend calls L'Hermitage. I've always found the atmosphere rather glum. Not too many guys under 250 are there; most of them are munching on Italian beef-sausage combo sandwiches, sweet peppers added. The clientele has the look of a waiting room for depressed former National Football League interior linemen, now in therapy.

Big Herm at one point sold the joint, then moved in next door, putting up a sign that read "The Original Herm's," which seemed far from fair play, even in the Chicago sandwich wars. Driving by the other day, I noted that only one Herm's is left, calling itself "Herm's Place." Whether this is owned by the original or unoriginal Herm is a mystery I am prepared to leave unsolved.

The greater mystery is why I continue to yearn for such food—I, who do not weigh 130 pounds. That it continues to exist is attractive to me in itself. I'm also pleased to know that people are still eating outside the laws of the health police. In my own neighborhood, just a block or so away, Al's, which advertises itself as "#1 Italian Beef,"—an accolade given it by *Chicago Magazine*—is about to move in. A few blocks away there is Merle's, a Texas-style barbeque joint, specializing in ribs.

Even if I do not eat this food regularly, I like the notion that it is still there, well within my reach should the desire for it hit me. I once heard a chubby female comedian describe herself as a bulimic, but without the throwing up part. I guess I'm a glutton, but without the eating part.

Out of Business

(2006)

ELLOW NAME OF PRUFROCK used to measure his life in coffee spoons, but I am beginning to measure mine in favorite old restaurants that go out of business. Another such establishment, The Berghoff in Chicago, bit the dust a couple of weeks ago. It had been in existence for 107 years, and now the 70-year-old grandson of the founder is closing it down.

I like a restaurant with a definite article before its name. The Berghoff was the definite article in the other sense, too. It may have been the last restaurant in town with professional waiters. These days most waiters are passing through, killing time between jobs. "Actor, oh actor," a silly joke has it, "there's a fly in my soup."

The Berghoff dates from an era when the German presence in Chicago seemed greater than it has for a long time. When I was growing up, a few beer gardens were still around, also a Germania club, and a restaurant called The Red Lion where, in the late 1960s, the editor of the *Atlantic Monthly Press*, Peter Davison, took me to dinner to inform me that I had lost out in the running for the job of biographer of Walter Lippmann. Since I hadn't known I was in the running, the news was less than shocking, and the food was great.

The first restaurant whose closing I took as a personal loss was Miller's, a steakhouse on Western Avenue, owned by a man in the air-conditioning and heating business, who had the Midas touch. He used to bet combinations of 13 (the 6 and the 7 horses, or the 4 and the 9 horses) on the daily double every day, and he seemed to win there, too. He also bought the prize steer at each year's stock-yard show, when Chicago still had a stockyard. The steaks, the ribs, the baked potatoes, the cole slaw, everything at Miller's was done to perfection. An air of success pervaded the place. I remember the maître d' once announcing over the loudspeaker that someone in the parking lot had left the lights on in his eight-year-old Dodge Dart, and saying to my dinner companion that no one would have the nerve to leave the restaurant and thereby acknowledge he had arrived in such a dull car.

I don't know what became of Joe Stein's, located first on Roosevelt and then on Sheridan Road, whose specialty was Rumanian strip steak and large platters of French fries, with pickled tomatoes and chopped liver served on serious rye bread for starters. They had tired, flat-footed Jewish waiters who had wandered out of Jewish waiter jokes to work there.

When I was a student at the University of Chicago, I ate at the Tropical Hut in Hyde Park every chance I got. A woman there greeted you at the door, asking, "How many in your part-tee?" If you staggered in alone with a knife at your back, she would still ask, "And how many in your part-tee?" The Tropical Hut was one of the few restaurants in the city of Chicago in the 1940s and '50s where one could take a black friend or business acquaintance to dine without having to worry about his or her being seated. I once saw Joe Louis in the place. He was eating a ham steak in a pineapple sauce, and seemed to be enjoying it immensely.

Ashkenaz, a large deli on Morse Avenue, half a block west of the El, was noted for its soups. It was crowded at all hours. Signed glossy 8 x 10s of secondary show-business celebrities were on the walls. I remember one of the comedian Shecky Greene, who grew up in the neighborhood. He must have dined out a great deal, for lots of restaurants had a signed Shecky Greene 8 x 10 glossy. Ashkenaz named sandwiches after show business celebrities. I remember a sandwich called the Lou Breese, after the band leader at the Chicago Theater. I'd rather have had a sandwich named after me than an honorary doctorate from Oxford.

Was the food in all these restaurants as good as I remember? Probably best that I am unable to find out. Everyone ought to have a long-defunct restaurant about which he can fantasize.

My friend Edward Shils used to recount stories to me of his own favorite restaurant, Strulevitz's on Roosevelt Road. He would describe Homeric meals that, in the 1930s, cost 65 cents. Mr. Strulevitz was always on the premises, his wife and sister-in-law cooking in the kitchen. They must have worked an 80-hour week. Edward kept a menu from the place, documentary evidence of its existence.

When Mr. Strulevitz died, his nephew Howard took over. The quality of the food did not drop off. He, too, worked the seven-day week, no rest, no holidays. Then Howard bought a white Lincoln, and took his family off on a brief vacation. He apparently hadn't realized that such things as vacations existed. He enjoyed himself so much it ruined him. He never reopened the restaurant. Talking about it, Edward gave off the faint suggestion that he'd remained faintly hungry ever since.

Plagiary, It's Crawling All Over Me

(2006)

I F IMITATION IS THE SINCEREST FORM OF FLATTERY, what is plagiarism? The least sincere form? A genuine crime? Or merely the work of someone with less-than-complete mastery of quotation marks who is in too great a hurry to come up with words and ideas of his own?

Over many decades of scribbling, I have on a few occasions been told that some writer, even less original than I, had lifted a phrase or an idea of mine without attribution. I generally took this as a mild compliment. Now, though, at long last, someone has plagiarized me, straight out and without doubt. The theft is from an article of mine about Max Beerbohm, the English comic writer.

The man did it from a great distance—from India, in fact, in a publication calling itself "India's Number One English Hindi news source"; the name of the plagiarist is being withheld to protect the guilty. I learned about it from an email sent to me by a generous reader.

Here is the plagiary:

- **JE:** "Beerbohm was primarily and always an ironist, a comedian, an amused observer standing on the sidelines with a smile and a glass of wine in his hand. G. K. Chesterton said of him that 'he does not indulge in the base idolatry of believing in himself.'"

- **TP** (Tasteful Plagiarist): "Beerbohm was primarily and always an ironist, a comedian, an amused observer standing on the sidelines with a smile and a glass of wine in his hand. G. K. Chesterton rightly observed of him that 'he does not indulge in the base idolatry of believing in himself.'"

In 30 years of teaching university students I never encountered a case of plagiarism, or even one that I suspected. Teachers I've known who have caught students in this sad act report that the capture gives one an odd sense of power. The power derives from the authority that resides behind the word "gotcha." This is followed by that awful moment—a veritable sadist's Mardi Gras—when one calls the student into one's office and points out the odd coincidence that he seems to have written about existentialism in precisely the same words Jean-Paul Sartre used 52 years earlier.

In recent years, of course, plagiarisms have been claimed of a number of authors themselves famous enough to be plagiarized from. The historians Stephen Ambrose and Doris Kearns Goodwin were both caught in the act. The Harvard law professor Laurence Tribe has been accused of the crime. The novelist Jerzy Kosinski, a man who in some ways specialized in deceit, deposited chunks of writing from Polish sources into his books without attribution. Some years ago there was talk of plagiarism in Martin Luther King Jr.'s doctoral dissertation. Schadenfreudians are usually much pleased by the exposure of plagiarism in relatively high places; to discover that the mighty have not fallen so much as cheated on their way up excites many who have never attempted the climb.

I have myself always been terrified of plagiarism—of being accused of it, that is. Every writer is a thief, though some of us are more clever than others at disguising our robberies. The reason writers are such slow readers is that we are ceaselessly searching for things we can steal and then pass off as our own: a natty bit of syntax, a seamless transition, a metaphor or simile that jumps to its target like an arrow shot from an aluminum crossbow.

In my own case, I have written a few books built to a great extent on other writers' books. Where the blurry line between a paraphrase and a lift is drawn—not always so clear when composing such books—has always been worrisome to me. True, I've never said directly that man is a political animal, or that those who cannot remember the past are condemned to repeat it. Still, I worry that I may somewhere have crossed that blurry line.

In the realm of plagiarism, my view is, better a lender than a borrower be. (You can quote me on that.) The man who reported the plagiarism to me noted that he wrote to the plagiarist about it but had no response. At first I thought I might write to him myself, remarking that I much enjoyed his piece on Max Beerbohm and wondering where he found that perfectly apposite G. K. Chesterton quotation. Or I could directly accuse him, in my best high moral dudgeon, of stealing my words and then close by writing—no attribution here to Rudyard Kipling, of course—"Gunga Din, I'm a better man than you." Or I could turn the case over, on a contingency basis, to a hungry young Indian lawyer, and watch him fight it out in the courts of Bombay or Calcutta, which is likely to produce a story that would make *Bleak House* look like *Goodnight Moon*.

The Perils of Prolificacy

(2006)

I SEEM TO HAVE WRITTEN ANOTHER BOOK, my eighteenth. I'm gratified that the ecologists haven't thus far come after me for destroying so many trees. The most ambiguous compliment a writer can receive is to be told that he or she is prolific. I fear that I may be getting prolific, if I'm not already there. "Oh, him again" is how prolific writers suspect their new books are greeted. "Basta!" they fear, is another common response to their latest creation.

Writing a book is often compared to having a child. At quick glance, the analogy seems cogent enough: Both entail, in a rough sense, conception, gestation, and birth. Having a child is obviously much the tougher assignment. What having a book and having a child do have in common is the unresolved question of why anyone who goes through it once would want to go through it again.

One of the two chief ways of writing a book is to read everything available on the subject, talk with all the people who might be helpful, do such legwork as is required—and then, after however long this requires, sit down and begin writing. The other way, my way, is to start writing the book and do the research as you go along. I don't think my way is better; in fact, the first way sounds to me much more sensible. My problem is that I don't have the organizational power to do all the necessary groundwork and then keep everything in good order until I need it.

One difficulty with my way is that, less than half way out to sea, you begin to feel that writing this book is a serious mistake. You tell yourself you really don't know diddly about the subject, you certainly haven't anything interesting (let alone original) to say, and you wish you hadn't already spent the publisher's advance. Only a devotion to craft combined with a grudging unwillingness to return the money to the publisher has, in the case of a number of my books, kept me at my oars, hoping eventually to sight land. Fortunately for me, land has always turned up, even if the destination isn't quite where I had imagined it would be when I first set out.

The chief feeling I have upon completing a book is that it is a pity the book is finished because I'm only now ready to write a fine book on this subject. Some writers are more patient than others; I am among the others. George Santayana worked no fewer than 45 years (not continuously, let me add) on *The Last Puritan*, his only novel, which turned out to be an unlikely bestseller and a Book of the Month Club selection, which not so secretly delighted him.

I enjoy revising my books, eliminating repetitions, correcting errors of fact and grammar, tightening things up, battening things down. I reread and rework each chapter as I write it, sometimes several times. But until the book is completed I never go back and reread all the chapters that I've written to see if what I've done thus far hangs together. I'm too frightened lest I discover that it doesn't. If every sentence is well made, if each paragraph works, I tell myself, then things can't be in entirely wretched shape. Still, there are mornings when I have to ask, what, exactly, is the story here? Why, apart from the hope of lucre and a bit of temporary fame, am I writing this book? These can sometimes be exceedingly touchy questions.

I feel less than triumphant when I've completed a book. To revert to the cliché childbirth analogy, neither do I feel anything like post-partum depression. I feel instead a calm pleasure in having finished a task I've set myself. Although I've had some commercial and critical success with my books, I've never written a book at whose completion I felt that, like a gymnast making a perfect landing, I've nailed it, a perfect ten. Only a year or more later, when for one reason or another I might open the book and find a passage that pleases me, do I say to myself, "Not bad, not bad at all. I wasn't stupid when I wrote that. How come I'm so stupid today?"

I wish I had a better way of celebrating the completion of a book. Pop open a jeroboam of champagne, buy a vicuna coat, book a flight to Paris. Usually I don't even treat myself to a Snickers bar. The best I seem able to come up with is to fritter away the next few days, putting in order the books and notes accumulated in composing the recently finished book, answering email, allowing myself some desultory reading.

I do have a sense of qualified freedom. This usually means the freedom to start thinking in a more concentrated way about my next book. I've neglected to mention that my recently completed book is about Alexis de Tocqueville. My next book is to be about Fred Astaire. Perhaps I ought to combine the two and call it *Dancing in Democracy*. Give it a dust-jacket with a golden retriever on the cover and it could be a big seller.

A Plague of Phones

(2006)

THE FIRST CELL PHONE JOKE I EVER HEARD was in fact about car phones. Sophie Ginsberg calls her friend Sylvia Glick from her Mercedes to tell her that she has just acquired a car phone and what a marvelous convenience it is! To keep up with her friend, Sylvia persuades her husband to provide her with a car phone. Once it's installed, she calls her friend Sophie, car phone to car phone. "Sophie," Sylvia says, "it's me and I'm calling you in your Mercedes from the car phone in my Mercedes." "Excuse me, Sylvia," Sophie replies, "can't talk now. My other phone's ringing."

The joke is of course about keeping up with those Jewish Joneses, the Ginsbergs, and about the silly conspicuous consumption required to do so. I found the joke a lot funnier before I recently acquired my own second cell phone.

I bought my first cell phone many years ago chiefly for security reasons, when my wife was traveling to visit her ailing mother a hundred or so miles away, and I worried about her car breaking down en route. I keep my own new cell phone for roughly the same reason as well as for calls, mostly made to my wife. Only two people know my cell phone numbers, and I have never done business on either phone. I used to mock people I saw talking on their car/cell phones, thinking them incapable of the least repose, even in the sanctum of their cars. As a two-cell phone man myself, I've now forfeited my mocking rights.

Phones have long since come out of the cars and are everywhere part of the urban landscape. In my neighborhood, it seems almost unusual to find a person, especially a younger person, who does not have either a smart phone or a cup of coffee in hand as he or she walks along the street.

People talking to themselves used to be fairly common in Manhattan, but the assumption was always that those doing so were a little—sometimes much more than a little—nuts. Now lots of people walk the street talking not actually to themselves but to other, unseen parties, and generally much louder than your standard maniac talks to himself. Maniacs, in my experience, tend to mutter; cell phone talkers to be stentorian. Perhaps because cell phones are so small people feel they have to make up for the size of the instrument by shouting into it.

I don't think I'll ever get used to looking at someone alone talking loudly as he ambles down the street, especially when he is doing so into a headset, with no phone in sight. I'm often amazed at the subjects on which people talk in public on their cell phones—many of them very private subjects. I've not yet heard a woman breaking up with a lover, though I have heard a man tell someone off at a high level of vituperation while waiting for a stoplight to change. Once, on Michigan Avenue in Chicago, I heard a young woman say into her cell phone, "Yes, Mother, I'm calling you from the top of the Ferris wheel at Navy Pier. I can see the entire city from here." I wanted to call out: "Madam, your daughter is a liar. She's here on the street carrying a Gap bag."

All this loose talk over cell phones can be irritating, even infuriating. On a bus ride between San Francisco and Santa Rosa, I witnessed the driver ask a passenger to leave the bus because the loudness of his cell phone conversations was bugging her and everyone else on the bus. We all felt like applauding.

Everyone, I suspect, has had a moment when he wished he could grab the cell phone from a boisterous talker and smash it on the sidewalk. A friend of mine named Ann Poole told me about sitting on a commuter train from her suburb into Chicago, in front of a young woman who made no fewer than ten cell phone calls to friends, explaining in great detail why she was changing the restaurant in which she was giving a lunch party that Saturday. Many of the people she called weren't in, so, in a loud and irritating voice, she left elaborate instructions on voice mail about the change in plan along with the reasons for the change. "Hi, this is Amy Hemstead [I'm making up the name], and I thought I'd let you know that I've changed the location of Saturday's lunch from the Zodiac Café to Phil Stefani's. We're still meeting at noon...." And then she babbled on a bit more as my friend Ann, who fervently believes that trains are for reading not phoning, seethed in a quiet but genuine rage.

"Did you do anything about it?" I asked.

"I said nothing," she replied, "but when I got to work, I called Stefani's and, using dear Amy's name, I cancelled her reservation for Saturday."

Devastating, and delightful, I'd say, and richly deserved.

Perchance to Dream

(2006)

AT LUNCH THE OTHER DAY, someone asked me what I thought about *The Charlie Rose Show*. I answered that I didn't think anything about it, because by the time it comes on in Chicago I'm usually waking up for the first time. I appear to be entering the stage in life where sleep is topic number one for me and my contemporaries. "Getting much," the rude phrase from my youth, has come to take on a whole new meaning—"much" nowadays referring to sleep, sound, solid, restful sleep.

"How did you sleep?" I recall once asking a friend when we were fellow houseguests. "Splendidly," he said. "I didn't make a single error." I must be making lots of them, for I seem to sleep well perhaps one night out of seven; and splendid means getting up only once or twice without any goofy dreams disturbing my sleep.

Lots of articles on sleep deprivation, insomnia, and other bedtime maladies are popping up in the press, which suggests that sleep problems may be fairly widespread. The *New York Times's* health writer, Calamity (as she's known) Jane Brody has recently written two such articles. Television stories about the troublesome side effects of sleeping pills—Ambien and others—are getting lots of play, though no one has yet written the advertising line about sleeping pills to match the gem turned out by the genius copywriter for Cialis, the sex stimulant pill. Perhaps the line might be: If sleep persists for more than eight hours, be sure to see a physician.

I try to be in bed by 10:30 p.m. and up not later than 5:30 a.m. That makes me, on good nights, a seven-hour-a-night man. Yet fewer and fewer are the nights when I get those seven hours uninterrupted. Part of this is physiological, having to do with aging bladders, a subject upon which I prefer not to dwell. But part of it is mental.

I don't usually have a tough time getting to sleep. I've found that cello music, played adagio, provides an excellent inducement to sleep. A few years ago I acquired an excellent CD called *Lullaby, Sweet Dreams for Children of All Ages*, in which the cellist Julian Lloyd Webber, accompanied by various pianists, plays Brahms and other lullabies with such sweet soporific titles as "Gentle Dreams," "Shepherd's Lullaby," and "Slumber Song."

Even better than the cello for sleep is listening to a radio broadcast, at low volume, of Chicago Cubs games played on the West Coast. No one, in bed in a dark room, could hope to make it beyond half an inning listening to the assemblage of platitudes and commonplaces of the Cubs' two serenely dull radio announcers. Fortunately, I was clever enough to put in my nuptial agreement that I be permitted to listen to West Coast games in bed for the rest of my life.

I read before falling asleep. I'm selective here: Nothing dark or tricky is permitted bedside; my current fare is Tolstoy's *Childhood, Boyhood, and Youth*. The dopey cliché about "curling up in bed with a good book" has never applied to me. I can't read in bed for more than half an hour. Nor, when I wake in the middle of the night, do I ever return to my book.

No, once awakened, I try my best to lull myself back to sleep. Often I revert to scenes of my boyhood to do the job. I imagine myself playing tennis at Indian Boundary Park with my friend Bob Swenson, and all my serves go in. I picture a charming Yorkshire terrier named Max romping along the beach. I attempt to disengage my mind, let it wander where it will, and call it back only when it threatens to go into the troublesome territory of night fears or anxiety.

A chief worry one encounters on sleepless nights is that one's lack of sleep will ruin the next day. Suddenly one can't sleep because one is nervous about not sleeping. A good way to combat this, though I'm not always able to achieve it, is to attempt actually to enjoy one's insomniacal nights. On occasion, at 2:37 or 3:18 a.m. (thank you, digital clock), I can calmly sort out quotidian complications, seek solutions for problems in things I'm writing, or instead just lie there counting not sheep but my blessings.

My night life, it occurs to me, may now be more interesting than the life I live during the day. Certainly it is more unpredictable. As I turn off my bed lamp, I never know how long I shall be able to sleep without interruption. My dreams, meanwhile, get wilder and wilder. Last night I was playing a deep leftfield in a night softball game on an unlit field. The night before the dead wife of a much older and now also dead friend turned up and flirted with me. Last week I lost my then-aged father at Heathrow.

Give me, I don't say, a break, but just a little more sleep would be nice.

Spandexless

(2006)

I HAD MY FIRST BICYCLE when I was eleven, and it was a disappointment. Schwinn seemed the only bike worth having in those days. My father, for some reason, surprised me by bringing home an off-brand bike called a SunRacer. Red and white, it had nothing wrong with it, but it wasn't a Schwinn. I soon removed its fenders, chainguard, and kickstand, and bent its handlebars downward. But there wasn't much else I could do to add to its glamour. Had I had a Schwinn, who can say, today I might be president of the World Bank, artistic director of the Orchestre de Paris, chairman of Disney.

I rode that bike everywhere. I don't remember having to lock it up, unlike nowadays when I lock up my current bike even when parking it in our garage. (I recently read somewhere that the use of the word "nowadays" suggests a reactionary, for nowadays are always understood to be much worse than thenadays. Something to it, I fear.) At fifteen, the age one could then get a driver's license in Chicago, my friends and I, putting away childish things, abandoned our bikes for cars and the wondrous freedom they gave to roam the city.

Bikes for adults didn't come into play until the exercise craze hit. I owned a green Raleigh racer in the late 1960s. In the early '80s at a police auction I acquired a three-speed Huffy. I used sometimes to ride it to the university where I taught; pipeless and suede-patchless, a bike was the only professorial accoutrement I had. Then, a decade or so later, I bought a standard, handlebars-straight-up, three-speed green Slipstream bike, which I used for a while, then forgot about. A young man in our building has recently gone into the bike-repair business, and so, summer coming on, feeling the need for a bit of exercise, and bored with longish walks, I had him clean up my long unused Slipstream, which now I take out for a spin three or four times a week.

By a spin I mean nothing marathon but four or five miles. I don't suit up for these little excursions but wear whatever I happen to have on. I'd as soon put on Spandex shorts for a bike ride as give the Charles Eliot Norton Lectures in a Speedo. I eschew a helmet because I look too goofy in one, and nowadays (there's that word again) have just enough vanity left to wish to look merely ungoofy. I do use a clip around my right ankle to prevent my trousers from getting caught in the chain.

I find myself looking forward to these rides, which I do not take at any set time of the day but when the mood strikes. I am a bit tentative on my bike; the thought of a serious fall never quite deserts me. I haven't yet worked up the courage to ride "no-hands," but then maybe one needs a living mother to do so ("Look, Ma, no hands!"). As kids we specialized in trick riding, including riding while seated backwards. The toughest trick of all—accomplished only by my friend Norm Brodsky—was to drive oneself on one's own handlebars, facing forward. I was with a boy named Ronny Harris who, attempting it, ended up with a concussion and several facial lacerations.

My current bike ride always follows the same route. At the beginning it goes slightly downhill, which provides a slight thrill. The return is of course slightly uphill, which leaves me having to work a bit, ending up breathing more heavily, which gives the impression of a workout. I ride through a nearby park, then alongside Lake Michigan. Joggers, young parents pushing their children in the new troika prams, Asians with pastel umbrellas out for walks, are on the same path. I go at a medium pace, every so often pumping hard to build up a bit of speed off which I let the bike glide.

My exercise does not include the element of progress. I do not anticipate going for longer and longer rides, getting in better and better shape. I am merely trying not to fall too quickly into even worse shape. I ride my bike less for reasons of health than for the delight in pedaling along, noting the lake in its many moods and differing colors, and taking in the views. One somehow sees more on a bicycle than in a car or even while walking.

For all the pleasures bike-riding gives, I do have a single regret. Many years ago, I met a man who, having read an essay of mine on juggling, asked if I would like to learn to ride a unicycle, which he would be pleased to teach me to do. I would love to ride a unicycle, I told him. He gave me his business card, but, for some reason, I never got around to calling him. I have long since lost his card, and now, alas, it is too late. If there is a heaven, and if I am permitted entry, you will not fail to notice me there: I shall be the fellow without the helmet juggling while tooling around on a unicycle, grinning.

$129 on the Dotted Line

(2006)

A FRIEND TOLD ME HE DISCOVERED ON EBAY that someone is selling my signature, asking the odd price of $129. The signature itself appears on a plain postcard containing a stamp with a picture of Rachel Carson. Not an eBayista myself, I have no way of knowing if the seller ever got anywhere near the sum asked. I do know that, at some point in the past, doubtless out of the usual scribbler's mad vanity, I must have agreed to sign an otherwise empty postcard for him or her.

The possibility that one's signature might be, even if only in someone's delusory mind, worth anything at all is amusing to contemplate. I wonder if this means that henceforth, when paying bills by check, I can notify the party I am paying that the reason my check is for $129 less than the actual bill is that the signature on the check is itself worth $129? Why do I feel this might not sail?

I have never understood the mania about autographs. The other day the *New York Times* ran a longish piece about a man whose specialty is collecting the autographs of secondary basketball stars from the past. People with more elevated tastes collect Founding Fathers or great poets. Selling autographs of the historically famous is a business. For myself, I cannot think of a single autograph that would thrill me. The same goes for original documents. The only original document I would care to own, now that I think of it, is the Ten Commandments, written in the hand of the Author.

Something talismanic, or magical, is thought to inhere in the autograph of a celebrated person. How else to explain the scandal of well-known athletes—some retired, some not—signing balls and other athletic goods for $10 and $20 and more a shot! They should be ashamed. After a fortunate and usually financially rewarding life playing games, they should be grateful that anyone would want their signatures and pleased to provide them gratis.

But the magical allure of the autograph is not restricted to Mencken's dear old Booboisie. The other day, on Chicago's classical music station, WFMT, I heard an otherwise sophisticated announcer say that Shostakovich signed one of his album covers for him and it remains one of his, the announcer's, most treasured possessions.

When I was a kid of 11 or 12, two friends of my father's ran a boxing gym in downtown Chicago; I would sometimes drop in when in the neighborhood. The two most famous fighters training there during those years were Tony Zale, then middleweight champion, and an excellent welterweight named Johnny Bratton. I had 8"x10" glossy photographs of both, but it wouldn't have occurred to me to ask either man to autograph his picture; besides, whenever I saw them, their hands were always taped.

Around the time of grammar-school graduation at the Daniel Boone School, we all bought autograph books: small leather zip-around folders with colored paper inside on which friends signed their names. We used these books to write vacuous things to one another, some sentimental, some comic. "To a fine athlete and a great guy, Your friend, Marty Summerfield" is an example I remember from mine, maybe because it was Marty who was the finer athlete and greater guy. The smiley face had not yet been invented, but girls dotting the i's in their names with hearts was not uncommon. *Autres temps, même moeurs.* I lost the book decades ago. A pity, for I could have used it, when in the doldrums, to remind myself of how fine an athlete and great a guy I once was.

I am about to set off on a small tour to flog (a word I love, except for its faint suggestion of a dead horse in the background) a new book, on copies of which I shall be asked to sign my name. I shall do so delightedly, for I remain immensely pleased—not to say slightly astonished—at the notion of someone willing to pay cash money for my scribblings. Doing these signings has shown me the dissimilarity of my handwriting from day to day. As some people have what is known as bad-hair days, I seem to suffer bad handwriting days, when my writing is wriggly, shaky, looking as if it might have come right out of the Alzheimer's ward.

The copy of my signature on sale for $129, I notice from the picture shown of it on eBay, has clear enough letters but tends to slant slightly upward toward the end of my last name. Perhaps in the future I should charge for my signature based on the quality of that day's handwriting. If you care to inquire further about acquiring my signature, don't hesitate to write to me. Don't be surprised, though, if you get back a letter that reads "dictated but not signed by Joseph Epstein." At these prices, I really can't afford to be signing my own correspondence.

Cleaning Up My Act

(2006)

ROUGHLY THREE MONTHS AGO, I resolved to stop swearing. Not that I used profanity relentlessly, but I had begun to notice that I was availing myself of it more and more—and doing so in situations where I used to be more restrained: among what used to be called mixed company.

Lots of women have now taken to swearing. The right to use profanity is, I suppose, one of the—some would say highly dubious—benefits of women's liberation. "When I was young," Tom Lehrer has said, "there were so many words you couldn't use in the presence of a girl. Now you can use them all, but you better not call her a girl." Too true.

I decided to banish profanity from my conversation because it began to seem indecorous, especially in a man who is a grandfather. A clue that it was time to cease was when I began to part words in the middle with the F-word: as in unf—believable. Besides, I don't want my deathbed words to include profanity.

Precocious in small vices, I learned swearing at an all-boys camp in Eagle River, Wisconsin, to which I was sent when I was eight years old. I never swore around my parents, of course, or around girls. Most of my bad language, as swearing used to be called, was done on various athletic fields, in locker rooms, and around pals.

My use of profanity increased in high school, where swearing and cigarette-smoking were taken as early, if obviously bogus, evidence of manhood. Hard to imagine going without swearing in the US Army; apart perhaps only from seminaries, any all-male environment is fertile ground for profanity. (Men are brutes, in case you didn't notice.) Certain of my basic-training sergeants taught me that swearing could be put to comic purposes; they seemed to specialize in inserting profanity into sentences that also included the words "behooves" and "mandatory," and to do so with a rhythmical nicety that always delighted.

Swearing can be wittily, even artfully, done, as my sergeants of those days regularly demonstrated. When I was in high school, I worked briefly for a fat man who swore chiefly from behind the wheel of his car, where much profanity gets uttered even by otherwise mild-mannered people. Once, when a man about to pass on his left honked at him, he quickly rolled down his window to riposte, "Blow it out your duffelbag, farthead."

I've never been complimented on the artfulness of my profanity. But if it wasn't artful, I do like to think it was at least mildly discriminating. I never liked and very rarely used the dysphemism for anus (itself a sufficiently ugly word); I steered clear of all the slang words for female private parts, though not of the many more in use for male parts. Never in earnest have I attached the prefix mother to the F-word. I should have liked to have invented a new swear word, but failed to do so.

I do, though, believe I hold the record for using the F-word more times in a single piece in the London *Times Literary Supplement* than any other contributor. The occasion was my review of the first volume of J. E. Lighter's *Historical Dictionary of American Slang*, which stopped at the letter G and contained no fewer than twelve pages on the F-word. What is it about the need so many Americans have for this word, so that it has four not-quite-adequate substitutes: effing, friggin', freakin', and flamin'? Perhaps it's the word's rhythm that makes it so fine an emphasizer.

I wrote the foreword for the new *Yale Dictionary of Quotations*, where quotations using the F-word and other profanities have been permitted entry. (As they also have in the most recent edition of the *Oxford Dictionary of Quotations*.) The reason behind allowing this is, such have been the changes in the tone and temper of contemporary culture, that not permitting them would constitute prudery, and so it probably would.

Still, when I edited the *American Scholar*, I refused to allow profanity in its pages. Not much was offered, but when I struck profane words from manuscripts I instructed the authors to take comfort by telling them how unusual they were to find themselves censored so late in the twentieth century.

As for curbing my own use of profanity in speech, it has been largely successful, with only very occasional slippages. I no longer use profanity, but the problem is that, like old Jimmy Carter walking around with lust in his heart, I still cannot stop thinking in profanity. I'm like the old European immigrant who forces himself to speak only English but still dreams in his native language.

Don't Call Me Ishmael

(2007)

T HE MAGAZINE *EDGE*, on its tenth anniversary, recently asked a number of scientists and thinkers what they found in the world or in their particular lines of interest to be optimistic about. I'm pleased to say that I was not asked. I am of course not a scientist, but I might, just possibly, have passed for a thinker. A certain portentousness, sententiousness, general pomposity goes with being a thinker. Nobody has ever called me a thinker, and I'd like to keep it that way.

I have on a few occasions been called a National Treasure, which I much resented. You never want to be known as a National Treasure. Walter Cronkite is a National Treasure, so is Studs Terkel. Russell Baker may be a National Treasure. Poor Bill Moyers seems to have been born a National Treasure. The actress Helen Hayes was a National Treasure. A National Treasure is someone you can count on to say predictably uninteresting things while giving off the blurry aura of wisdom.

I don't think I've ever been called a humorist, which is fine by me. A humorist, poor fellow, is under the pressure of being relentlessly, and therefore drearily, funny. Much better to be sometimes witty, or even faintly amusing, than to be a humorist. The late Art Buchwald was a humorist, which perhaps explains why I never found him in the least funny. Andy Rooney ditto. No one has ever called me a humorist, and, again, I am grateful.

I'm afraid that I've been called Professor thousands of times. True, I taught at a university for thirty years, but at least I did so without any advanced degrees. Besides, professors don't even look like professors anymore, and I look nothing like what they nowadays do look like. They wear backpacks and Nike gym shoes and baseball caps turned backwards. I prefer to think of a professor as the man who plays the piano in a bordello. The reason I never liked being called Professor is that it is synonymous with academic, a word that over the past forty years has become synonymous with ridiculous.

Because of my past university connection, I've also often been called Doctor, which causes me to giggle, at least inwardly. Sometimes I'll say that I have no doctorate, other times I just let people "doctor" me. A time or two when people have called me Doctor Epstein on the phone, I have instructed them to read two chapters of Henry James and get right into bed, adding that I'd be right over.

I have also been called a "man of letters." This once seemed a great honorific, but today there is something musty about the term, something that suggests less an endangered than a vanished species. I don't believe I have ever been called America's "last man of letters"; Edmund Wilson was always called that, and how it must have galled (if not bored the pajamas off) him to have heard it so often.

An Intellectual is another thing I've been called on various occasions, though never, I'm pleased to say, a Public Intellectual, a perfectly empty phrase. Intellectual is another of those words that has gone from approbative to pejorative in recent decades. An intellectual is someone who lives on, off, and through ideas, and used to be unconnected with institutions. Now an intellectual is someone who offers his opinions on talk shows and writes op-ed pieces; hence the adjective "public." Intellectuals have come to be known for not having a genuine stake in things, for being usually wrong in politics, for being distanced from reality, for being without responsibility. Not a good thing to be called, an intellectual.

In the good-bad old days of *Time* magazine, under the then famous Timestyle, where concision was important, a person was usually designated by a single word, thus: socialist Thomas, philosopher Dewey, editor Luce. Had I been born twenty or so years earlier, I might have appeared in *Time* as "essayist Epstein."

The reason I am uncomfortable about being identified as thinker, national treasure, humorist, professor, doctor, intellectual, or essayist is that none of them feels to me a good fit. I'm not a renaissance man either, and certainly no polymath; I'm not sure I even qualify as a unimath.

I prefer to think of myself as just plain Bill, the guy in the torch song, who's not the type at all. "Only my tailor fits me correctly," Samuel Johnson is supposed to have said when people wished to label him as this or that. Given Johnson's reputation as a notably sloppy dresser, it may well have been that even his tailor got him wrong. I, on the other hand, don't even have a tailor.

Memory Laine

(2007)

EVERY GENERATION IN AMERICA grows up with its own singer or singing group. Elvis is perhaps the most notable example. All sorts of men and women now in their early and middle sixties still vibrate to his hit songs of the late fifties and early sixties. For those who came a bit after, it was The Beatles and then the Rolling Stones, who Tom Wolfe once described as like The Beatles "only more lower-class deformed." Just before my time, especially for the girls known as bobbysoxers, it was Frank Sinatra. The singer of my own generation—kids who came of age during the late 1940s and early '50s—was a man named Frankie Laine, who died a couple of months ago at the age of 93.

As a singer, Frankie Laine was a dramatizer; his songs all told stories. Most of these stories took place out of doors, with geese and mules and devils and whips cracking all over the joint. Laine was a belter, always singing at the top of his voice. Nobody slept while he was on. He made way for other dramatizing belters, among them Johnnie Ray and Tom Jones. Not a brilliant tradition, let us agree.

"Cry of the Wild Goose" was the title of one of Laine's greatest hits, in which he sang, "I must go where the wild goose goes"—wherever that was. It is Frankie Laine who sings in the background of Mel Brooks's *Blazing Saddles*. He had twenty-one gold records, for such singles as "Jezebel," "I Believe," "Jealousy," "High Noon," and "That's My Desire," every one of them sung with the throttle out, the pedal all the way down.

Laine was born in 1913, *né* Francesco Paolo LoVecchio, the son of a barber. (The crooner Perry Como had himself been a barber before he caught on as a singer.) He chose the stage name Laine after Lane Technical High School, where he had gone in Chicago. He started out as a marathon dancer—not an easy way to make a living—and then turned to singing with jazz bands. But only when he turned the volume up and got out of doors did he strike the gong of commercial success.

I first heard Frankie Laine in the early 1950s, when he was nearly 40. This was before the age of television, so in those days one frequently listened to singers without any notion of their looks, unless there had been articles about them in *Life* magazine. In Frankie Laine's case, given his songs, one always imagined him singing with mountains in the background, storm clouds above, horses cantering off in the distance. If John Wayne had sung, he would have sung like Frankie Laine. Asked to describe him before I saw him, I'd have said that he had rugged good looks.

When I did get to see Frankie Laine in the flesh—as I did onstage at the Chicago Theater when I was 15—he looked, far from a hero in a cowboy flick, more like the guy who ran the general store, or the bartender who ducked under the bar at the first hint of gunplay. He was a widebody, heavyset; not fat, but not especially trim either. He wore a toupee, and had an impressive nose. The aura he gave off was completely urban: He was one of those Italians who could have been taken for Jewish, or the other way round: a Jewalian, an Italiew. He had briefly worked as a car salesman, and a car salesman is what he most resembled, at a Buick dealership, I'd say. He may possibly have eaten a wild goose, but the likelihood of his ever having seen one alive seemed remote.

In later years, Laine grew a beard and took to wearing cowboy hats, which at least brought him a bit more in sync with his hit songs. But what was there in this unsubtle singer, who roared away about the still wild west and women tormenting him, that caught the attention of so many city boys? (I don't think Laine was a big item with young women.) A few of his songs could be danced to, but most, as the old disc jockeys used to say, were strictly "for our listening pleasure." In what, quite, I now wonder, did the pleasure reside?

Was there something in urban boys of that day that wanted to sight wild geese, crack whips over the heads of mule trains, and have our lives destroyed by Jezebels? Were these our secret desires? They were never mine. My own notion of roughing it, then as now, is poor room service; I prefer a woman who, far from tormenting me, is punctual. What the true attraction of Frankie Laine was will evidently have to remain a mystery, to be solved perhaps only after I learn where, exactly, those damn wild geese went.

Excellent Choice

(2007)

MANY YEARS AGO I gave the Mencken Day lecture at the Enoch Pratt Free Library in Baltimore. After my lecture, a man in his late seventies, possibly early eighties, came up to tell me that he knew H. L. Mencken. He then drew out of a battered briefcase a small light brown frame, in which, tapped out on an old-fashioned typewriter, was a letter from Mencken himself. The letter went something like this:

> Dear Phil,
>
> I want to thank you for being so good a bartender all these years at the Rennert Hotel. You have always done your job with tact and craft, and I admire a man who brings these qualities to his work, no matter what a man's job is.
>
> Sincerely,
> Henry Louis Mencken

I thought about that letter the other night at a restaurant called the Chicago Firehouse, lodged in a converted firehouse built in 1905, in the city's south Loop neighborhood. I had not been to the restaurant before. The rooms were decorated in a calm and understated way, and there wasn't any of that din that contemporary restaurants seem to feel gives customers a go-go feeling of success. The people already seated seemed serious feeders, not there for status or other non-gustatory purposes.

Once seated, my wife and I and the couple we were with felt the air-conditioning too high and the music too loud. After our waitress, a tall woman, heavyset, blonde, in small glasses and wearing a white jacket, took our drink orders, I asked if she could do something about the air-conditioning and the music. She said she would, and straightaway did. A promising start.

My wife ordered a glass of Riesling, and when the waitress brought our drinks, she poured a small amount of the Riesling for my wife to taste and also, in a second glass, a small amount of another wine, a combination of Riesling, Gewurstraminer, Muscat, and Chardonnay, that she thought my wife might like even more. Which, it turned out, she did, a lot. We were, obviously, in the hands of someone who knew her business.

Before we ordered our dinners, this waitress answered such questions as we had with a no-nonsense precision and authority. Presently our dishes were gently slid before us. Our waitress returned to our table once to ask if everything was as we wished; and a second time to refill my wife's wine glass. She and I exchanged brief stories about wine snobbery. She set down menus for dessert, on which we all passed, but we did have coffee, over which we lingered. When she left the check, I, grateful for the professional quality of her service, tipped her 25 percent. If I'd been Mencken, I would have returned home to write this woman a letter of the kind he wrote to Phil, the bartender at the Rennert.

Two days later, I met a friend for lunch at another restaurant. I was five minutes late, and when I asked the maitre d' if my friend had arrived, he said, "Yes, and he anxiously awaits your presence." What crap, I thought to myself, and by the way, chum, he "eagerly," not "anxiously," awaits me. If you can't tell the truth, at least get your usage right.

The waiter, a young man with spiky hair and rather a sad, wispy beard, reporting the special dishes of the day to us, paused to cite one of them as "my own favorite." I saw my friend's jaw muscles tighten. After the waiter left, he said, "I can't tell you how much I hate that 'my own favorite' stuff." "Be grateful," I said, "that he didn't tell us that we made excellent choices or ordered very intelligently." Four or five times, this waiter broke into our conversation to ask if everything was okay. Which it was until he broke in to ask.

Today most waiters, middle and upper-middle class young hoping to be actors or screenwriters or Bill Gates, are merely passing through. The number of professional waiters has become fewer and fewer. These old-line waiters and waitresses didn't see themselves as the equals of the people they were serving; some among them—one thinks of the old contemptuous waiters in Jewish delis who seemed to take especial pleasure in throwing their customers a bit off stride—may well have thought themselves superior to their customers. But they understood that democracy hasn't anything to do with dining out.

No one requires a waiter to mention that he himself just ate the food one is about to eat. Or that he thinks one a man of distinction for ordering the mussels. Or that the desserts in the joint are "to die for." One doesn't want, in short, to be waited on by someone who comes on as if he were one's nephew, the one whose mother recently told you that she was now certain he was never going to take hold and amount to anything. Your entrée may have been an excellent choice, but his becoming a waiter, clearly, wasn't.

Gimme Shelter

(2008)

YOU LIVE, THEY SAY (usually accompanied by a sigh), and you learn. They say it; I don't. You live, I say (with an even deeper sigh), and you yearn. And I generally make it a point to yearn for things that I am certain to be unable to obtain. What's the point of yearning for the merely possible? "I call a person rich," says the character Ralph Touchett in Henry James's *Portrait of a Lady*, "when he can meet the demands of his imagination." I look at my bankbook, I consider my stock holdings, and realize that I am far from meeting those demands, and by now I am confident that I shall never meet them.

What I have found myself yearning for these days is real estate. Real estate may be the new porno. The newspapers are full of it. The back pages of the *New York Times Magazine* contain ads for estates in Connecticut and Virginia with stables and swimming pools and tennis courts and gently rolling lawns. Toward the front of the same magazine are ads for newly erected skyscrapers with condominium apartments starting at $2.6 million.

The Plaza Hotel, I note, is now being broken up into condominium apartments, the great grand Plaza, offering perhaps the most convenient location in Manhattan and lots of history. Everyone has read about that night in the 1920s when Scott and Zelda Fitzgerald, the original fun couple, nicely schnockered as always, jumped into the Pulitzer Fountain in front of the Plaza.

I was once put up for five days in a suite in the Plaza, in lieu of a fee, by a magazine to whose wealthier sponsors I spoke. I felt as if I were living at Versailles, in an apartment down the hall from the Duc de Saint-Simon. I remember heavy red drapes, thick rose-colored carpets, gold-plated faucets in the shape of dolphins in the large bathroom. Unlike the Fitzgeralds, I did not take a refreshing dip in the Pulitzer Fountain but instead walked down to Lexington Avenue, where I bought a hot-pot so that I could make my own tea in the morning. Keeping a pied-à-terre in the Plaza does not seem to me at all a bad idea.

The Weekend Journal section of the *Wall Street Journal* carries ads for four-story townhouses on near-northside Chicago streets named Goethe, Schiller, Astor; 14,000-square-foot palazzos, with eight bedrooms and nine baths (and two half-baths), all for a mere $12 million. Eleven bathrooms might take some getting used to, since I have never lived in more than seven rooms, but I'm sure I could work this out.

Meanwhile I also have my eye on the Hamptons estate of the late Howard Gittis, described in the *Wall Street Journal* as the "right-hand man of takeover artist Ronald Perelman." Along with 15 acres of property, it has a renovated 15,000-square-foot house, with seven bedrooms, a staff apartment, and "a living-room fashioned out of a former ballroom." My staff—not yet hired—would be pleased to have use of the apartment, and would cotton, too, to the tennis court and swimming pool on the property. The only problem I can see is the asking price, which is $59 million. Still, it's lower than the price of the Forbes family ranch in Colorado, which is going for $175 million. Cunning negotiator that I am, I feel sure I could get the Gittis place down to $57.6 million.

Big-time players seem to have apartments and houses all over the world. Apartments in Manhattan and London and Paris, houses in Palm Beach, Barbados, Tuscany. One assumes that, while their owners are elsewhere, there are servants and agents and security firms looking after all this valuable real estate.

I, on the other, much grubbier hand, seem destined to be a single-domicile man. Twenty or so years ago I had the chance to acquire, as a second residence, my late mother-in-law's lovely two-story house on an artificial lake in Michigan for the beggarly sum of $45,000, and chose not to do so. I feared calls in the night telling me that the sump-pump had gone on the fritz, the windows needed replacing, the small pier had sunk.

Which doesn't stop me from noting an ad in the current *Town & Country* for Rendezvous Bay, in Anguilla, in the Lesser Antilles, that has residences in the works for from $3 to $20 million. Sounds promising. When I wake in the morning I shouldn't at all mind looking out on a vast panorama of water and islands and ever changing tropical skies.

Not going to happen, of course. Simplify, simplify, always simplify, is my motto, with the proviso that, while simplifying, it doesn't hurt to fantasize.

Negative Pleasures

(2008)

A FRIEND OF MINE, a highly intelligent lawyer with an interest in human nature, not long ago asked me if I knew any men given over in a serious way to chasing women. When I said I did, he asked if I'd ever noticed that, at the end of a lifetime of doing so, these men seemed to have no regrets? I had to agree that, with the women-chasing men I knew, this seemed to be true.

Not easy to get through life without collecting a hatful of regrets. My own are too commonplace to describe here, but I do count a few items in my life that are the very reverse of regrets. What I have in mind are negative pleasures, the genuine delight found in things avoided or deliberately not done.

I am very pleased, for example, never to have owned a station wagon. At one point, I had charge of four children, and toting them around in a station wagon would seem to have made good sense, yet I resisted. In the early 1960s, I came close to buying a used Volkswagen bus, but when the car dealership (Cliff Packer's Auto Ranch in Little Rock, Arkansas, salesmen equipped with ten-gallon hats and with toothpicks in mouth at no extra charge) wouldn't take cash but would only sell the bus to me on credit, the deal was dead. I have in fact lived in suburbs at various times in my adult life, but acquiring a station wagon would have forced me to regard myself as irretrievably suburbanite, which would have badly dampened my spirits.

Owning an SUV, the station wagon of our day, would be even more dispiriting. Climbing up and into and down and out of one of those monstrous heaps of metal would depress me beyond reckoning. Whenever I am driving behind one, the mortal words of Jackie Mason on the subject return to me: "Sports Utility Vehicle, hell. It's a truck, schmuck!"

Another great negative pleasure I enjoy is not having a PhD. Some of the most deeply stupid people in the country have PhD's. A mediocre student, I never for a moment considered going to graduate school, but I am fairly certain that I couldn't have endured the various tortures that acquiring a PhD entails. I have an AB, *in absentia* (as I always prefer to add), and mildly regret that I have that. I love to hear stories about men and women who never finished, or even entered, college and went on to score great artistic and financial successes, and only wish I could claim to be one of them.

An even greater delight, perhaps the chief negative pleasure in my life, is that I have never golfed. When I was a kid, my friends and I used occasionally to play miniature golf, and sometimes we would buy buckets of balls to hit off driving ranges; one I remember had the name Stop 'n' Sock, after a famous Chicago food emporium of the day known as Stop 'n' Shop. Cleverly, I never went on to acquire a set of clubs. (The initial expense must have deterred me.) Several of these same friends did, and today, it is not going too far to say that golf is close to being the main event in their lives. One of them, who struck it very rich, is said to belong to fourteen golf clubs here and in Europe. Others have settled for that Valhalla of so many commercial warriors, condominiums on golf courses.

I consider golf, like the Soviet Union, good only for the few excellent jokes it has produced, whose punch lines ring in my head: "So for seventeen holes, it was hit the ball and drag Irving, hit the ball and drag Irving." Or, Moses to Jesus: "What do you want to do here—screw around here, or play golf!"

Ah, not to wake early on weekend mornings, and then not to pull on peach-colored pants, shine up one's driver, kiss one's putter for luck, and drive off, to return at dusk one or two strokes better or worse than the last time out—not to do any of these things is for me, as Omar Khayyam had it, "paradise enow."

These trivial but to me genuine negative pleasures may not seem much to brag about, and in the grander scheme of things they aren't. Still, when I think that I shall never drive off, the letters PhD as part of the vanity plate on my station wagon, for yet another round of golf, I realize that, with a surge of pride, I have not lived entirely in vain.

It's Only a Hobby

(2008)

I RECENTLY WENT TO A NEW PHYSICIAN, a dermatologist, for a minor problem, but before seeing her, I had to fill out a longish form setting out my and my parents' medical history. All went smoothly enough until the very last question, which asked about my hobbies. I was frankly stumped. I have no hobbies, yet, chary of leaving the space blank, I wrote in "Cultivating and collecting grievances."

The absence of hobbies from my life, let me quickly assert, is not among these grievances. I never had a hobby, don't have one now, and the notion of finding a suitable hobby has never occurred to me.

The closest I have come is early in the 1950s, when I owned an extraordinarily comfortable pair of trousers known as hobby jeans. Light blue, soft cotton with a thick elastic waistband, they were essentially pajamas that could be worn on the street. Wearing them, I don't recall anyone asking me if he could see my butterfly collection.

In grammar school many of my classmates had hobbies and collections. Some boys had large collections of marbles, or "mibs," as we called them. A few kids had stamp collections. A store opened in our neighborhood called Hobby Models, which sold kits for making model airplanes, electric trains and the rich collection of paraphernalia that went with them, battery-driven racing cars, and all the other stuff that was supposed to interest a young boy but somehow left me indifferent.

Other boys my age could delicately wield an X-Acto blade across balsam to form the fuselage of a model plane. Some found hours of enjoyment in chemistry sets. A boy named Bob Grimm had an impressive collection of miniature cars. Many saved baseball cards, which, if in later life their wives didn't insist they pitch them out, may well be worth vast sums today. I had none of these things, I did none of these things, I had no need of any of these things. I lived, I now see, in that distant country known as my own mind, where no hobbies were required.

I have over the years met people with some out of the way hobbies. I briefly had an editor, acclaimed for his genius in creating the bestseller *Jaws*, who kept bees in his basement in a brownstone on the west side of Manhattan. I have a friend who has a collection of 78-rpm records in excess of 150,000, more than half kept in the basement of his home, the rest in a warehouse. Most every night, after work, he checks into various used-record stores looking for still more. I know another man who pays a pit crew $16,000 on a weekend so that he can enter drag races for a purse of usually not more than $3,000. "It's only a hobby," as the punch line for an old Jewish joke has it.

One thinks of mature hobbies as pure diversion and calm-inducing: an older gentleman cultivating his prize-winning roses, a woman quilting with Mozart's flute and harp concerto playing in the background. A hobby sets off leisure from work, signaling a cooling dive into the pool of tranquility. The pleasure they bring to those who adore their hobbies is perhaps greater than any available to them in their working or family lives. They feel most alive in their hobbies; in them they claim to find their truest selves. I do not doubt that this is so.

Would my having a hobby make me more relaxed, a sweeter character generally? Possibly. But I have to wonder what such a hobby, for me, might be. Collecting matchbook covers? Designing my own clothes? Joining a fantasy football league? Performing complicated card tricks? Artfully photographing grass, sand, and leaves?

The *New York Times* used occasionally to run pieces called Newsmakers, which were profiles of men and women then prominently in the news. Accompanying the profile was a box which set out the main facts of their lives. "Hobbies" was among these facts. People usually used this rubric to establish themselves as cultivated. "Reading and long country walks" was not an uncharacteristic answer to the hobby question. I suppose I could count Reading as my hobby, but I read so much, it is so central to my existence, that, were I to do so, I might as well add Breathing as another of my hobbies.

I wonder if the problem isn't my vocation. A writer's life tends to be seamless, and he doesn't divide it between work and leisure. On the hunt full time for copy, material, something to write about, he doesn't need to collect anything, or play at anything. The writer's work and his play, if he is lucky, are one. How can he have a hobby, really, when the entire world is his hobby?

Vernon

(2008)

THE EVANSTON PUBLIC LIBRARY has a small room devoted to sale books, some donated by patrons, others removed from their shelves because of continuous neglect by readers. I no longer collect books, but old habits die hard, and so I pop in every so often to see if there isn't some neglected book that I might acquire for the negligible price of 50 cents.

In recent months I've bought a couple of slender volumes of the essays of Desmond MacCarthy, *The Collected Stories of Jean Stafford*, *The Benchley Roundup*. Just today I picked up Vernon Young's *On Film*, which has, rubber stamped on its first page, the word "Discard," which must mean that it has had so few readers that it is considered not worth the shelf space it has occupied since the early 1970s, when first published. The book carries the subtitle *Unpopular Essays on a Popular Art*. I guess poor Vernon, who died in 1986, had no notion just how unpopular his essays would turn out to be.

I say "Vernon" with some trepidation. I happen to have edited *On Film* during the year or so I spent in publishing, and I recall his writing to me about the phenomenon of Americans he scarcely knew calling him by his first name. He didn't like it, not a bit. "When people do that to me," he wrote, "I always say to them: 'My good friends call me Mr. Young.

Won't you do likewise.'" He also once asked me what I thought it was
Americans meant when, upon parting, they said, "Have fun." The expression on his face when he emitted these words would have been more
appropriate on that of a swordsman, just before running you through,
uttering, "Die, dog."

Vernon Young was born in 1912, an Englishman but international in outlook. During my editing of his book, and during the time a little later when
I asked him to write a few pieces for a magazine I edited, I addressed all
correspondence with him to Stockholm, c/o Swerlow. I never met Swerlow, but people who knew Vernon said that he was adept at moving in on
women, and I assumed she was one of them.

As befitted his *hauteur*, Vernon's look was aristocratic, slender, coldly
elegant. He had a long neck, and wore high collars to disguise it. In profile, as he is photographed on the back of the dust jacket of *On Film*, he
looks like a handsomer Bertrand Russell. He might have been a character
in an Anthony Powell novel, a friend of X Trapnel or "Books" Bagshaw.

As someone who had arranged for his collection of essays, and who
solicited other writing from him, I suppose I was one of Vernon Young's
minor benefactors. His great benefactor was Frederick Morgan, editor
of the *Hudson Review*, which published his essays over more than three
decades. Fred, an immensely good-hearted man, took it upon himself to
watch out for him. When Princeton invited Vernon to speak, Fred worried about how he would be able to get Vernon back to Sweden.

The only time I met Vernon Young, he stared at me, or so I felt, as if
through a jeweler's loupe. I felt he was testing me, carefully weighing his
judgment, the way he might a suspiciously middlebrow movie. Vernon
was an immitigable highbrow, rigorous, unbending, more interested in
film than in movies. He wrote with great suavity about new films from
Asia, Italy, Mexico, Sweden, France, Italy, England, always with an eye to
capturing the element of national culture at play in the work. Here is a
sample of Vernon's writing:

> If I say that Europeans are frequently more coherent when
> translating the raw material of the American scene into
> movie substance, I don't expect the remark to be taken as
> a finality. But no domestic social realism film I've yet seen,

expressionist or naturalistic, has caught even a reverberation of the polyglot wonder discovered by Francois Reichenbach in his "documentary," *L'Amérique Insolite.*

Vernon was, in other words, not someone you would want to invite to join you to catch Adam Sandler's latest flick. He was also the sort of writer whom as an editor you wouldn't ask to change a comma unless you had good arguments lined up in advance for your request. A friend once told me that he blew a large fee to write some captions for *Vogue* because they wanted him to make some small changes in what he had sent them. A difficult, even an obstinate man, Vernon, but a man with his own kind of unblinking integrity, and lofty critical principles such as we are not likely soon to see again.

I'm glad to own this copy of Vernon Young's *On Film.* Having had a small hand in bringing the book into the world, I figure the least I can do is provide it with a good home.

The Unnaturals

(2013)

MY FAVORITE TENNIS PLAYER is Marcos Baghdatis, who is currently ranked 36th in the world. With a Lebanese father and a Cypriot mother, he has a splendidly Levantine face, framed by his moderately long hair and double-stubble or perma-stubble beard. Baghdatis's best year was 2006; at 21 years old, he made it to the finals of the Australian Open and the semis at Wimbledon, and ended the season ranked eighth in the world. He appears to be in decent shape at present, but I have seen him looking paunchy in the middle and soft in the upper chest; in him a fat man, I should guess, is perpetually struggling to get out.

I suspect that higher-ranked players are not pleased when they draw Baghdatis in the early rounds of tournaments. There is nothing notable about his game, except that he is a scrapper—the sort of player who takes a set or two off bigger, higher-ranked players, and sometimes beats them. In 2010, he defeated both Rafael Nadal and Roger Federer when each was ranked first in the world. He does not take losing easily, and one year at the Australian Open, ticked off by his own play, he broke four rackets during a changeover between games.

What I prize in Baghdatis is that he looks like a rocker, a Fiat mechanic, a cable guy, a terrorist—anything but the very competitive tennis player he is. He is a prominent contemporary member of a club I think of as the unnaturals: superior athletes who do not look the part.

Another is Tony Gwynn, who played 20 seasons for the San Diego Padres and won eight batting-average titles—he is perhaps the best of all the unnaturals. Smallish and pudgy, Gwynn looked more like a short-order cook than the great baseball player he was. He seemed not to run but to waddle, though very quickly. Judged on build alone, he shouldn't have been allowed in the major leagues. What he lacked in natural endowments, Gwynn made up for in instinct and intelligence; he was one of the great percentage hitters in the history of modern baseball.

In his book *Moneyball*, Michael Lewis makes the point that the old-line baseball scouts were suckers for ballplayers with standard athletic bodies. They preferred guys 6′4″ or 6′5″ with deep chests, broad shoulders, and narrow waists: Darryl Strawberrys, Dave Winfields. They tended to pass on the less-godlike-looking mortals. By these criteria, of course, Babe Ruth, with his heavy torso and flamingo legs, would never have made it into the majors. Lewis also wrote about an overweight prospect who played catcher for the University of Alabama. A scout reported that should he run down to first base in corduroys, he could start a fire. The problem was that the kid had an impressively high on-base percentage. Another unnatural.

One of the best athletes I grew up with was a boy named Paul ("Chops") Friedman. Chops was a playground and public-park athlete. He was chunky, with short legs and heavy thighs, and no speed at all. What he did have was high athletic intelligence—he made no mistakes or inept judgments—and a splendid pair of hands. He played third base in softball, where neither grounders nor line-drives ever got by him; and in two-hand touch football he was an unerringly accurate short passer.

The most specialized boy athlete I grew up with was Dickie ("The Owl") Levinson. The Owl—mix metaphors, add salt, and shake well—was a one-trick pony. He came by his nickname through his flat and beaky countenance and soft, stocky body. The Owl had a deadly jump shot and a vertical leap of roughly three-quarters of an inch. His want of mobility didn't matter, for his jump shot always found the basket. His game was two-man half-court—it's difficult to imagine him running full court—at which his jump shot, which must have had more than 90 percent accuracy, made him unbeatable. You never wanted to play against The Owl for money.

When I was a kid, at nearby Tam O'Shanter Country Club outside Chicago, a golf hustler named Marty Stanovich, a short tubby man with an unorthodox swing, made his living gambling. He needed only a few-stroke handicap to beat such pros of the day as Sammy Snead or Lew Worsham. A money golfer, the higher the stakes the cooler "The Fat Man," as Stanovich was called, became. Local mobsters used to follow him around, betting on him. He refused to recognize pressure, and could sink a 15-foot uphill putt during an earthquake.

Charles Barkley was far from a natural. When playing college ball at Auburn, he was known as the "Round Mound of Rebound," a sobriquet earned by the nearly perfect 360-degree circumference of his head and what appeared to be the pudginess of his body. Barkley was smaller than most small or power forwards, the two positions he played during his career. Yet he was a perennial rebounding leader. On defense he was a great shot blocker and ball stealer. He made up for being undersized and overweight through his agility, hustle, and aggressiveness. He was as het-erodox in his opinions as in his play. When a reporter cited a remark made in his autobiography, Barkley claimed to have been misquoted.

Normal by most standards, at 5'10" Doug Flutie was positively dwarf-ish for a professional football quarterback, a mite among mammoths. This made him seem a permanent underdog, and every game he played as a pro seemed a replay of David and Goliath. Flutie often came through in the crunch, usually in a dramatic way. He did so most famously when, as quarterback at Boston College, he threw his Hail Mary pass to defeat the University of Miami as the clock ran out. You had to have a cold heart to cheer against Doug Flutie.

The magic of unnatural athletes is that, through their unorthodox tal-ents, they demonstrate that there is no single, grooved, established way of winning. By eluding the standard formulas for athletic success, unnatural athletes alter one's notion of acceptable form, change the dynamics of play, and widen the possibilities generally. By showing that there is more than one way to do things, they enrich the games they play and make them much more interesting. May they always be in plentiful supply.

Cool Chapeau, Man

(2008)

EARLIER THIS SUMMER, I was discovered to have a basal carcinoma, which sounds terrifying, but is in fact merely a pre-cancerous sore that was easily cut away by a dermatologist. The sore was at my hairline—wasn't it William James who said of Josiah Royce that he showed "an indecent exposure of forehead?"—and was the result of too much sun. I was told to begin using sunscreen and, on sunny days, to wear a hat.

The hat I bought, at a shop too quaintly called The Things We Love, is a straw fedora, with a slender black ribbon running round its base. The brim is of normal size, and it is a fairly serious piece of goods: no Aussie Outback hat or Indiana Jones replica. An adult hat, I call it, and I wear it at an only slightly rakish angle. (Euclid, unfortunately, does not take up rakish angles, a small flaw in one of the great books in western civilization.)

The press this hat has been bringing me all summer is noteworthy. "Nice hat," more than one passing stranger has said to me. "Cool chapeau, man," I've also heard. "Very dapper" is the most frequent comment. So far no one has called me "natty." Dapper I can live with, but natty suggests two-colored shoes and monogrammed shirts. You don't want to be natty—at least I don't.

The reason my hat seems to be garnering so much attention is that it is unusual today to see a man wearing a—how shall I put it?—grown-up hat in a serious way. I suspect that most people who see me approaching from the middle distance ask themselves, "Is this guy in the hat kidding or what?" As a surety of my earnestness, I do my best not to smile as I pass. When I pass people I know, I am not above tipping my hat, or before women taking it off in a sweeping gesture as if it had a plume.

John F. Kennedy is often cited as the man who killed men's hats in America, and perhaps around the world. With his thick head of hair, low-hairline division, a hat probably would not have sat well on Kennedy. One thinks of FDR as, characteristically, wearing a hat and brandishing a cigarette holder; Harry Truman—a haberdasher, after all—also comes most readily to mind behatted. But today there is no politician that one automatically thinks of in a hat.

John McCain is often shown on television walking around Iraq in a baseball hat. A mistake, this, I feel. For the candidate who is supposed to represent gravity and the wisdom of experience, a baseball cap, even one with Navy written across it, is all wrong. McCain doesn't look good in the damn thing. Barack Obama I can easily envision wearing a baseball cap backwards. The picture makes me, in one swoop, lose hope and want to fight hard against change.

The baseball cap marks a steep decline in elegant male attire. Not even baseball players look good in them—just as no Greek fisherman has ever looked good in a Greek fisherman's cap. In his baseball cap, the pitcher Randy Johnson, the Big Unit, looks like a 6' 10" geek. With his cap off, he's more than passable. Yet the baseball cap is endemic in our day, worn forward, backward, or off the side, rapper style. Anyway you wear them, though, they don't come off.

Men of my father's generation wouldn't leave the house without their hats. In the movies, Humphrey Bogart, Robert Mitchum, James Cagney punched thugs out without removing their hats. A *noir* flick is unthinkable without fedoras. Hat shops were a fairly common feature in the cityscape. Many dry cleaners and shoe-shine parlors also blocked hats; blocking was a mysterious steaming process that gave new life to a man's hat.

In my thus far brief return to wearing a serious hat, I discover that doing so entails certain inconveniences. The infrastructure, as we should say today, for serious hats is no longer in place. I shall not, for example, be able to travel on an airplane with a hat, unless I sit with it in my lap through the flight, for surely there will be no room for it in the invariably crowded overhead luggage compartments. Hats also present a problem in restaurants, for the vast majority of even good restaurants no longer have a hat-check facility. Hat racks, too, are less and less common.

I intend nonetheless to persist. I have long owned a green felt fedora that I intend to bring out and wear in the autumn. I may well become known, at least in my neighborhood, as the guy in those strange old-fashioned hats. I shall instead think of myself as among the last men attempting to pass themselves off as grown-ups in America.

Prizeless

(2008)

THE MACARTHUR FELLOWSHIPS were announced some weeks back, and, for the twenty-seventh year in a row, I did not win one. I could have used the half-million dollars, payable at a rate of $100,000 a year, no doubt about that, but I also find I can live without it. At least no one I loathe won; the only person among this year's winners I have heard of is Alex Ross, the excellent young music critic of the *New Yorker*. Even better, none of my friends won it, either.

I haven't had great luck with prizes, which is a gentle way of saying that I haven't won many, and when I have, the satisfaction hasn't been anywhere near as complete as one might imagine.

The first prize I won was, at age fourteen, for sinking twenty-one of twenty-five free throws in a free-throw shooting contest at Green Briar Park in Chicago in 1951. My parents allowed me to nail a basket and backboard to our back porch, and I used to shoot a hundred free throws every afternoon, through all seasons. So I wasn't surprised to win the contest at Green Briar. What did surprise me is that I never received the trophy.

I once won $5,000 for something called the Heartland Prize given by the *Chicago Tribune* for a book of my literary essays, which was gratifying. But when I called my mother to let her know that I had won a prize from the *Tribune*, she replied, "Oh, we get that junk in the mail all the time. I just throw it out." I chose not to correct her.

Early one evening, checking my voice mail, I heard a message from a woman informing me that a book of my short stories had won a prize named after a deceased novelist, and asking me to call back the next day to discuss the details. All that evening I allowed myself to contemplate the amount of the prize: $10,000? $25,000? I went to bed that night thinking myself $50,000, perhaps $100,000, richer. The next morning I learned that the amount of the prize was $250 and that I was expected to travel to Hartford, Connecticut, to receive it and also to prepare a talk to give at the lunch where it was to be awarded. I decided to turn down the prize, with the result that the people who awarded it placed me in their permanent enemies pantheon. Another rainy day in the Republic of Letters.

I've won a few other prizes, been given a medal or two, none of them of sufficient moment to shake me entirely free of doubts about my skill. The problem with almost all prizes and awards in our time is that, even if their sponsors and judges have shown the wisdom to give them to you, they have also, like as not, shown the ignorance to give them to people you know are third-rate. If anyone ever tells you that you are the best at what you do, all you need do to prevent an exaggerated sense of yourself is ask that person whom he thinks is second best.

I have been a judge on a few literary prize panels. The one that gave me most pleasure was that of the Joseph Bennett Award, given by the *Hudson Review*, because we gave the prize to Andrei Sinyavsky, the Russian dissident writer, who deserved it and a great deal more for his physical and intellectual courage in taking on the juggernaut of the Soviet Union.

I was once paid $1,000 to be, for a year, an official nominator for the MacArthur Fellowships, though none of my nominees won a fellowship. Twice I have been asked to serve on the panel of judges for the Pulitzer Prizes and refused both times because the judges' decisions can be over-ruled by the main Pulitzer Prize committee.

Perhaps—who knows?—I could have done some useful preventive work here. Years ago I heard that Gertrude Himmelfarb, a judge for the Pulitzer Prize for Biography, entered a meeting of her fellow panelists by saying, "I say, boys, we're not going to do the commonplace thing and award the prize this year to X [a standard bien pensant who had written a book about a famous American columnist], are we?" And no doubt they would have done, had she not begun the meeting on that aggressively negative note.

The hard fact is that, while prizes are nice and the money that comes along with the prizes even nicer, what most prizes do is stir the hunger for still more prizes. This point was nicely underscored for me one morning when my friend Edward Shils called to say, "Be careful if you speak today with Saul [Bellow]. They've announced the Nobel Prize for Literature this morning, and he's likely to be feeling touchy because he didn't win it for a second time."

Another Season, No Whoopee

(2009)

RETURNING FROM PALO ALTO a few weeks ago, as our plane was about to land at O'Hare, I gazed down at the gray, snow-covered landing field, and braced myself for more of the grim gulagian Chicago winter. The weather in northern California had been in the mid-60s, the skies unfailingly blue and sunny, and, to avail myself of the words with which Bishop Hebert ended his poem on Ceylon, "only man was vile." What, I asked myself, am I doing here?

The answer is not that I don't know any better but that I can't think of any place better. I do not yearn for what are called sunnier climes. Arizona is not a real possibility for me. My friend Robert Nisbet, the sociologist and a Californian most of his life, in his 60s accepted a job at the University of Arizona, built a grand new house there, and after a few years was driven bonkers by the relentless sameness of sunny day after sunny day, and promptly packed up and moved to Manhattan.

I have had short holidays on both coasts of Florida, the Gentile west (Sanibel Island) and the Jewish east (Boca Raton), and in true Judeo-Christian spirit—who are these Judeos, anyway?—found each equally boring. In Florida I saw too many well-dressed older men with funny walks carrying the remainder of their breakfasts in Styrofoam boxes out of restaurants. I don't like to be around so many old people. If I want to look at old people, I have my bathroom mirror. No, Florida, clearly, is not the answer.

But what, as Gertrude Stein is supposed to have said on her deathbed, is the question? The question is, Why should I, a man of many winters, spend yet another one in Muscovite-like Chicago, walking the streets as I do encased in down, wool, leather, fleece, and rubber, trudging along, the roses quite gone from my already sunken cheeks?

The answer is, I like it here. I even secretly believe that undergoing a good spell of rotten weather builds character, if only by teaching how little nature cares about us pathetic humans. "Want to help the environment?" young people on neighborhood street corners with petitions in hand not infrequently ask me. "Why?" I answer. "What did the environment ever do for me?"

I grew up in this wretched climate. So did my mother; and my father, a Montrealer, grew up in an even worse climate. The weather was not a subject much up for discussion in our household. Complaining about it was inadmissible. The weather was what it was, an unalterable given—case closed. "Cold enough for you?" my mother, normally a kindly and always a gracious woman, would sometimes ask, not much sympathy in her voice. The assumption behind the question was, stick around, it's likely to get colder still.

False memory perhaps heightens the coldness of the winters of my youth. I seem to remember winter winds that felt like a slap in the face; not an ordinary slap, either, but the kind that follows a deep insult to one's integrity. I spent a lot of time during those years waiting, in full shiver, on street corners for buses. Under the delusion that I cut a handsomer figure without a lot of extra clothes, I went about in a leather jacket—no hat, no gloves—through most of my high-school winters. I'm lucky I still have both ears and all my toes. Vanity thy name is adolescence.

Vanity has now been replaced by caution. Harsh wintry days suddenly daunt me. I have to work up a bit of courage to go out into them. I leave my apartment as if I'm about to ride through the Eskimo equivalent of Apache territory. The thought of the lengthiness of winter depresses, if ever so slightly, even though Chicago winters are shorter than those in Buffalo, which can, I'm told, run to five-month stretches. (In one of his novels, the fine Indian novelist R. K. Narayan remarks, of a town in southern India, that "eight months of the year the weather is impossible, and during the other four it is worse.") Still, I would rather be here in Chicago, wading through gray slush, than in Scottsdale, Arizona, in a Fila running suit jogging among cacti.

As the president of the University of Chicago, Robert Hutchins, when recruiting scholars and scientists for the school, used to tell them, with the *hauteur* that came so easily to him: "Really you must come to Chicago. The population hereabouts isn't all that interesting. The social life is practically nil. The city's cultural institutions are few. The weather of course is miserable. You'll get so much work done."

The old boy was on to something. Heaven for climate, a character in a James Barrie play says, hell for conversation. But for getting work done through gray winters Chicago can't be beat.

Funny Papers

(2009)

I SEE WHERE MY OLD FRIEND ARCHIE ANDREWS has got his rear-end in a sling. Seems he married the wrong girl, the sleek and wealthy, raven-haired Veronica Lodge, when most people were hoping that he would eventually wind up with the very blonde though less than bombshell Betty Cooper, the girl—or at least everyone's idea of the girl—next door.

Archie Andrews is of course the eponymous hero of the old Archie comic books. As a boy, I loved *Archie* above all other comics books. I could work with *Superman*, *Batman*, and *Captain Marvel*, and was less enamored of *The Green Hornet*, but I much preferred the uncluttered drawings of Archie, with its small cast of regular, entirely predictable characters: the crabby teacher Miss Geraldine Grundy, the high-school principal Mr. Waldo Weatherbee, the slick rich boy Reggie (Reginald Mantle III), and above all Archie's sidekick Jughead, who wore a beanie and the same gray jersey with an S on it.

I also liked, but had to read on the sly, a comic book published for girls called *Patsy Walker*. Once more I was taken by the clear, even more realistic drawings of Patsy, her boyfriend Buzz Baxter, and her rival Hedy. I must have read *Patsy Walker* standing up at the comic-book rack at West's Pharmacy on Sheridan Road, for I couldn't have bought it or taken it home lest I be accused of being insufficiently masculine. (*Patsy Walker*, Google reports, ran out after 124 issues, while *Archie*, begun in 1942, is still alive and in its 605th issue.) What my tastes in comic books showed, I now realize, was an early preference for realism in literature over fantasy and science fiction—a taste I have maintained throughout my reading life.

As with so many others of my generation, my first memory of reading was of reading the comics, which in the newspapers in those days were also sometimes called the funny papers. A radio show in Chicago read the Sunday funny papers over the air, with kids instructed to follow along. In our family, owing to my father's detestation of the *Chicago Tribune*, especially of its publisher, the isolationist Anglophobe Colonel Robert McCormick, the *Tribune* wasn't allowed in the house. This was a personal setback—and the first time in my young life that politics interfered with pleasure—for the *Trib* had easily the best comic strips of all the city's papers, *Dick Tracy* and *Terry and the Pirates* notable among them. The best the *Daily News*, our family paper, could counter with was *L'il Abner* and, on Saturdays, a soap-operaish strip called *Rex Morgan, MD*.

By the sixth grade, I had weaned myself off comic books and began to read the sports books of John R. Tunis: *All-American*, *The Kid from Tomkinsville*, *High Pockets*, *The Kid Comes Back*, *The Iron Duke*, and others. Still, I was far from being a passionate reader. I fell back into the clutches of comic books in the seventh grade, when we had to do weekly book reports, and I did mine courtesy of an enterprise known as Classic Comics. Week after week I reported on one lengthy book after another—*The Count of Monte Cristo*, *David Copperfield*, *The Three Musketeers*, *The Last of the Mohicans*—all cribbed from the 25-or-so-page Classic Comics version of these monumental novels.

My final encounter with comic books came in high school with the item known in Chicago as "eight-pagers," which put comic strip characters through standard pornographic exercises. Eight-pagers were purported to have been created up in the print shop of Lane Technical High School on the city's north side by evil young geniuses whose craft was as impressive as their taste was coarse.

I bring up my rich background in comic-book reading, to say nothing of my love for movie cartoons—I still do a strong impersonation of

Elmer Fudd: "Scroo you, you cwazy wabbit"—chiefly to make the point that today I not only am bored royal blue by comic-book drawing of the kind that appears in so-called graphic novels but cannot watch any television show or film that is done in animation. I have been told by intelligent people that *The Simpsons* is filled with a fine anarchic humor, but on the few occasions that I have attempted to watch it my mind leaves the room more quickly than it does during an early Mahler symphony. Other people my age I know who have been brought up on comic books have told me they find themselves in the same condition.

I recently read that Archie Andrews's marriage to Veronica has been so badly received by the comic book's still substantial number of readers that its creators have had, in effect, to annul it and remarry the amiable redhead to Betty. I have no plan either to attend the wedding or even to send a gift.

Fit To Be Tied

(2009)

I N AN IDLE MOMENT in an otherwise indolent life, I recently counted my neckties. I have, I am slightly embarrassed to report, 86 of them, some purchased as long ago as the late 1970s. The preponderance are bow ties, though I've bought a few brightly colored knit four-in-hand ties in recent years from a Charleston haberdasher called Ben Silver. I also have two four-in-hand ties owned by the poet John Frederick Nims and given to me by his widow, one of which has small red octopuses against a background of forest green. The whimsicality of it is, for those who knew John, very Nimsian.

Eighty-six is a lot of neckties. Since they do not take up much room, I have not felt the need to winnow them, tossing away the more hopeless. None, so far as I know, is stained, faded, or frayed; nor is any of them outlandish. Each of these neckties represents an aesthetic choice on my part. Each tie, I must have thought at the time I acquired it, would make me more dashing, dignified, dandaical, who knows what. As I gaze upon them now, I wonder whether I am likely to wear even half these neckties ever again.

The fact is that the necktie may one day before long go the way of spats, becoming a laughable anachronism. Should this happen in my lifetime, I won't be among those laughing, even though I, too, find myself wearing neckties less and less. Putting on a necktie is not part of my everyday dress now that I no longer go to a regular job. I wear neckties only if I am invited to give a talk or lecture or to go to a dinner party or one of the few remaining restaurants where neckties are understood to be *de rigueur*.

Lawyers still wear neckties in court; so do most physicians when seeing patients. Businessmen seem to be wearing them less and less; casual Friday is increasingly becoming casual every day. A not uncommon photograph in the *New York Times* business section or the *Wall Street Journal* shows two powerful CEOs upon the merger of their companies, both with open collars.

When I began teaching at Northwestern, in 1973, then in my mid-30s, I was faced with two choices: neckties or not, calling students by their first names or not. I went for the more formal option in both cases and never regretted it. My wearing a jacket and tie to class put some useful distance between my students and me, and also gave the impression, or so I liked to believe, that in a crunch I might have a chance of finding work elsewhere.

Until the 1980s, most even moderately expensive restaurants assumed that male customers would wear neckties. This was also true of private clubs. I used to be a member of the Tavern Club in Chicago, and when one night I invited the film director Edward Zwick to meet me there for dinner, Zwick, originally a Chicagoan but long a habitué of Los Angeles, showed up in a black silk shirt open at the neck and a black unconstructed jacket. The Tavern Club made him put on a necktie, of which they kept a few in reserve, which he did in amused good spirits. Not many years later, the Tavern Club dropped its necktie rule. I am not sure that a restaurant or club today could stay in business if it insisted all its male customers wear neckties.

The West Coast has never been necktie friendly. Neither has Israel, a country I have long assumed has only enough neckties for the male cabinet officers of the government in power. The tieless movement has now swept up orchestra conductors, many of whom have turned in their grand white-tie-and-tails for one or another black trousers and tunic get-up. Toscanini, I daresay, would not have approved; Furtwängler would have heaved his cookies.

The only defense for the necktie is tradition, not, in our time, an easy defense to make. I recall an older salesman at Brooks Brothers, a man who had devoted his life to being well turned out and helping his customers do likewise, telling me with chagrin that his 26-year-old grandson did not know how to tie a necktie. His sigh after reporting this reverberated around the shop.

The two movie stars who wore neckties best were Fred Astaire and Cary Grant. They knew that a bit of color at the throat brightens up the countenance of an older player, and they knew which colors did the job most elegantly. Churchill wins in the bow tie division of this competition with his perpetual dark blue bow tie with small white dots. What we can learn from these gents is to button our shirt collars, tie a bit of silk at our necks with a careful crisp knot, and move out smartly.

Sound Off

(2009)

I WAS UP THREE MORNINGS IN A ROW last week and at my post—a comfortable chair next to a lamp table upon which my coffee sat—watching the semifinal and final matches at Wimbledon. Tennis is the sport I played best as a boy and, when played well, the sport I enjoy watching above all others. Nothing unusual about a tennis fan watching high-level tennis played at the grandest of all the grand slam tournaments—except, perhaps, that I watched all three mornings with the sound turned up only high enough so that I could hear the dim pock of tennis balls but not high enough to hear the voices of the various expert commentators, John McEnroe, Mary Carillo, and company.

I once read that one of the signs of encroaching madness is watching television with the sound off. My own sense is that just the reverse is true: The way to madness lies in watching television with the sound on. So irrelevant, so repetitive, so low grade is sports chat that I have, in fact, taken to watching all sports events with the sound off. Baseball, college and pro basketball and football, all are immensely improved bereft of the clichés and cheap sentiments of their highly paid announcers.

Many an evening I feel I can also watch the news with the sound off, so predictable does it all seem. After all, most of the people paid to deliver the news—so-called "on-camera personnel"—aren't there for their wit or powers of formulation but chiefly for their hairdos and wardrobe and calming effect. Their less than penetrating words only obscure a clear view of their neckties, outer coats, coifs, and delicately applied makeup.

Most of the time one knows what these people—"speakerines," the French call them, denoting that for the most part they are devices through whom words written by scruffier characters than they are conveyed—are going to say anyhow. Conventional wisdom, received opinions, false sentiment, dollops of happy talk, such make up their gist. Does one really require sound to pick up the absent nuances of a Keith Olbermann or a Glenn Beck, a Rachel Maddow or a Pat Buchanan? One has only to glimpse the self-satisfaction playing upon their faces to realize that what they know we have no need to hear.

Ezra Pound famously called literature news that stays news. As for the news itself, nothing is more permeable. News, to wring a change on Ol' Ez, is precisely that which doesn't stay news. Much of it requires no comment whatsoever. After a president is in office for more than four months, we know everything he is likely to say. As for presidential press secretaries, their message never changes: The president is, was, and always will be correct, so please don't bother me with contradictions, misquotations, or simple logic. New messages from al Qaeda all come down to the same: You've had the course, Morris. Cures for diseases and announcements of new wonder drugs are generally soon revoked. The weather of course changes, but it can be shown on a crawl.

Things were better in the old days, or so people of a certain age in the business like to think. One wonders. Edward R. Murrow, Eric Sevareid, John Cameron Swayze, and the rest of the major older television figures, were they the real thing or merely a set of empty trench coats? Television news-reading and commentating is not a field notable for attracting geniuses. I make an exception for David Brinkley, who was no genius either, but at least, toward the end of his career, specialized in a cynicism about politics and the politicians of all parties that was bracing.

No exception need be made for Walter Cronkite. During his 19 years (1962–1981) as the anchor for CBS television news, Cronkite was considered "the most trusted man in America." Turns out he could chiefly be trusted never to say anything unpredictable. Whatever the going story—

the walk on the moon, the death of John F. Kennedy, the 1968 Democratic convention riots—he piled on with platitudes. The tag line with which he used to end his show was, "And that's the way it is." The problem is that his version wasn't the way it was at all. He didn't have a clue to the way it really was.

The old joke about Wagner's music is that it isn't as bad as it sounds. The non-joke about television commentary—news, sports, and the rest—is that it is precisely as bad as it sounds. The volume button—there, on the lower left—please, turn it all the way down. Thank you.

Joseph Epstein Has a Cold

(2009)

I N THE APRIL 1966 ISSUE OF *ESQUIRE,* Gay Talese published a famous article called "Frank Sinatra Has a Cold." All I remember of the article is its moral: which was that, when Frank Sinatra has a cold, the world had better stand by with plenty of Kleenex.

I wish to announce that Joseph Epstein also has a cold, one of those full-court, knock-down, lots of coughing, sneezing, nose-blowing, firing from all portals, let 'er rip colds. In my case only my wife is offering Kleenex. Those sub-Sinatrian characters among us are left, I fear, to suffer without people around us tremblingly worried about our health.

I take even minor illnesses hard, not as hard as Sinatra did I'm sure, but hard enough. I consider a cold an affront, a personal insult. Couldn't the damn virus have found a hardier carcass than mine to settle upon? Without ever suffering any serious prolonged sickness, I nevertheless do not consider myself in robust health. Even as a boy athlete, I was never in shape. "When was the last time you felt really good?" a radio commercial of a few years ago asked. I had no problem answering "1950," when I was 13, or just before I began smoking in my 14th year, quitting a mere 26 years later while on a sun-drenched Swan's cruise to the Greek islands and the Dalmatian coast.

A sure sign of my being sick is that I find myself humming some of the worst popular songs ever written: "Cement Mixer, Putty, Putty," "Linda," and the always freshly banal "Tammy." At times of emotional turmoil, I am able to work through what is bothering me, setting it aside as I tap away on whatever I happen to be writing at the moment. But during a cold of any intensity, my mind clicks off: The ole hootie owl, hootie-hoo's to the dove / Tammy, Tammy, Tammy's in love.

A bad cold is especially hard on the sufferer of shpilkosis, a chronic disease I've long harbored. Shpilkosis comes from the Yiddish word *shpilkes*, which means needles or pins in the pants; the opposite of serenity, the chief symptom of shpilkosis is the inability to sit quietly. The victim of shpilkosis needs to be on the go: checking for mail, taking or making telephone calls, popping out to the grocery store or dry cleaners or over to the library, keeping on the move.

A heavy cold masks but does not subdue shpilkosis. Under the cold, the shpilkotic feels the want of energy but does not lose the desire to keep fiddling, noodling, futzing around. The result is mild depression and low-grade agitation that finds no resolution. Not a good thing.

This cold is now going into its eighth day. During two of these days I had actually, as they used to write of women in Victorian novels, to repair to my bed. On both days I slept the day away, awaking near 5:30 p.m., just in time to hobble into the living room to watch the drearily sincere Brian Williams thanking attractive young women named Trish, Savannah, and Kelly for their inadequate descriptions of the latest depredations on the economy. None of this lifted the spirits, either.

The commercials on the network nightly news shows are directed at the sadly aging. Remedies for restless leg syndrome, osteoporosis, arthritis, stomach gas, and more all get their full dismal play, with their always entertaining list of side-effects joylessly iterated. Under the cloud of this cold, it occurred to me that some genius at Pfizer ought to come up with a pill to increase powers of memory and cognition in the aged, Cognagra it might be called, with an appropriate warning that if one has a reflection that lasts more than four hours one should consult a philosopher.

Now going into the second week with this cold, my appetite is back, the snuffling and coughing are less, but my former flow of restless energy refuses fully to return. Normally a 6 a.m. wake-up man, I have been lolling in bed until 7:30 or 8 a.m. This throws off the rhythm of my days. Some people are on a self-imposed schedule, and I am apparently one of them. I feel that I am falling behind in everything, even though no one is in fact waiting for me. Unlike, say, for Frank Sinatra.

"Sinatra with a cold," Gay Talese wrote, "is Picasso without paint, Ferrari without fuel—only worse.... A Sinatra with a cold can, in a small way, send vibrations through the entertainment industry and beyond as surely as a president of the United States, suddenly sick, can shake the national economy." Joseph Epstein with a cold, on the other hand, sends no vibrations anywhere and affects no one except himself, turning him into a red-nosed, wheezing, sneezing general nuisance. Pass the Kleenex, please.

Home Mechanic

(2009)

WHEN I WAS 11 YEARS OLD, my parents bought a two-flat apartment building. The building had a small front and back lawn, the care of which was turned over to me. I was no more than 10 minutes on the job when I found it even more boring than hearing about your children's high SAT scores. I rushed through the rest, and returned to our apartment to let my father know I had finished. Looking around, he noticed the patches of grass I had missed, how uneven I had left the edges of the lawn where it met the pavement, all the little clumps of grass I failed to rake up. "You know," my father said, calmly, "comes another Depression, you are exactly the kind of guy they let go first."

In Chicago grammar schools in those days, girls were required to take a course in home economics, where they learned the rudiments of cooking and sewing, and boys to take a course called home mechanics to acquaint them with tools. In home mechanics, we made bookends and lamps with bowling pins or fancy wine or whisky bottles as their bases. We did a fair amount of work with something called a coping saw. Every so often we used one of the large electric power saws; this was my first and last interaction with the firm of Black & Decker, apart from the few Black & Decker haircuts I've since had.

I did not cope at all well with the coping saw, and broke its slender blades fairly often. I had no patience for careful sanding, no interest in wiring. I took no pride in my ineptitude, as if it suggested that I was cut out for higher things. Nor did I look down on people who were good at home mechanics. I vaguely admired them, but not enough, apparently, to concentrate sufficiently at improving my own skills in this line.

Living in Little Rock, Arkansas, in the early 1960s, I often met men who tuned their own cars or did their own plumbing. My admiration was no longer vague; I wished I had their talent, which, among other things, set them free from having to worry about being overcharged for jobs any normally (oh, hell, let's bring out the word) virile man ought to be able to do on his own but also gave them a sense of independence I lacked.

Over the years, I acquired a tool box. In it I keep a number of screw drivers, a heavy hammer, a long and a flat-nosed pliers, a small drill, a complex wrench I have never learned how to manipulate. I do very minor repairs around our apartment. I hang pictures, I can stop a toilet from running after flushing, I can screw in this or hammer down that. I stay away from anything electrical, and plumbing isn't my specialty either. Fortunately I don't have roofs and air-conditioners and furnaces to deal with. If I had, good chance I would by now be dead.

Of late, a sense of decline and fall has taken over our apartment. Many little things have gone kerflooey, requiring repairs that I cannot provide: a few small chains to secure our casement windows are missing; a bathroom sink isn't draining well, despite all the solvents I've poured down it; a flap is missing from our garbage disposal; a ceiling fixture is out of commission because of a broken off halogen bulb that I have been unable to remove; a toilet requires jiggling after it is flushed; a small portable bathroom heater I bought from Hammacher Schlemmer needs a bracket to attach it to the wall. All this is beyond me and called for the services of a handyman.

The man we hired, an acquaintance of my wife's from the time when they both worked for a reference-book company, arrived in a baseball cap with the name of a lumber company across the front. He wore not jeans but denim workmen's pants and a sweatshirt. His belt had a holster containing a select set of screwdrivers, probes, a small wrench, and pliers.

He carried a clipboard, on which he made notes about the things I asked him to repair.

None of the jobs was unduly complex, at least not for him. He approached each with a nice analytical eye. He handled his tools with strength yet delicacy and respect. He had earlier been a copy editor, straightening out other people's broken sentences; now he was fixing broken appliances and appurtenances.

I didn't want to leave off watching him put our apartment back in order, so measured, so logical, so satisfying seemed his work. I thought I wouldn't mind signing on as his apprentice. Regretting my inability to do what he can, I finally pulled myself away, to return to the repair of my own broken sentences.

A Happy Problem

(2010)

I AM ABOUT TO PUBLISH A NEW BOOK—egads, my twenty-first, which surely qualifies me as a graphomaniac—and the other day twenty-five so-called author's copies arrived. The thrill of holding the artifact, the physical object that is the palpable result of one's lucubrations, in one's hand is still there. So is the slight nervousness entailed in opening it up, and glimpsing the thousands of sentences one has indited. Some of these sentences give genuine pleasure; others one would like to have the chance to rework, ever so slightly but crucially. But, as the old song has it, it's too late, baby, now, it's too late. These 25 books are called "finished copies" for a reason.

Now comes the problem—a happy problem, I admit—of to whom to send these copies and how to sign them. Receiving a signed copy of a book from the author who wrote it is not an altogether unmixed blessing. The late Arnaldo Momigliano, in his day the greatest living historian of the ancient world, once said to me, as we were passing a bookstore on 57th Street in Chicago: "You know, my dear Epstein, the cheapest way to acquire a book is to buy it." I pondered these words for a bit before I came to realize that what Arnaldo meant is that if you buy a book at least you don't have to read the damn thing. But if you are given one as a gift, especially by the book's author, you are under the obligation not only of reading it but of having to respond, preferably in a complimentary way, by letter or by telephone. In sending these books out, then, I am putting their recipients under a heavy obligation.

I have had books sent to me by authors on subjects of the most distant interest to me, some thick enough to qualify as tomes. I generally scribble a note of thanks, adding how much I look forward to reading the book, but neglecting to add that I shall continue to look forward to reading it, well into eternity in fact, since I certainly have no intention of actually reading it while still alive. Contrary to the old maxim, there are some gift horses that need to be looked directly in the mouth.

I am not sure why, but many people feel that there is a certain magic in a book signed by the author. I have myself signed too many books for any thought of magic in the act to linger. Other people feel that a signed copy of a book is one day going to be worth lots of money. I, on the contrary, sometimes warn people who ask for my signature on one of my books that once I sign it they can never return it to the store at which they bought it.

People who see my signed books in the future—if these books are, hope against hope, to have a moderately lengthy future—will no doubt think that many of the signatures are forgeries. This is because my handwriting, as I grow older, is no longer consistent. I have bad handwriting days when I am not in good control of my script. Some days my handwriting is strong and clear; other days shaky and blurred to the extent that I barely recognize it as my own.

While flogging my books in book stores, I generally ask book buyers how they would like me to sign the copies of my books. Some responses are amusing. I once wrote a book of stories called *Fabulous Small Jews*, and at a bookstore a woman, who bought a copy for her husband, asked that I sign the book, "To Jim, An ordinary large Italian." Then there is the baffling complexity of contemporary spelling. "Would you please sign the book to Judy and Edwin—that's Judeye and O-e-d-w-e-n."

I suppose the desire for a book signed by its author is a species of autograph collecting, a passion for which I have little understanding and less sympathy. But the passion doesn't require my approval, so long has it been in force and so intense has it become. Not merely autographs but anything to do with the famous brings down astonishing prices at auction. Imagine what one could get for even one of Shakespeare's socks or Virginia Woolf's aspirin tin or Jacqueline Kennedy's blindfold! Are we talking seven figures here, or eight?

These grumblings, the musings of an ungrateful scribbler, already have more than a whiff of being slightly out of date. I earlier mentioned the fond but less than confident hope that my books may have a long life in print. But the larger question begins to look like whether we shall have books at all. If not, please don't ask me to sign your Kindle.

Adios, Gray Lady

(2010)

T HE *NEW YORK TIMES* used to be called the Gray Lady of American newspapers. The sobriquet implied a certain stateliness, a sense of responsibility, the possession of high virtue. But the Gray Lady is far from the *grande dame* she once was. For years now she has been going heavy on the rouge, lipstick, and eyeliner, using a push-up bra, and gadding about in stiletto heels. She's become a bit—perhaps more than a bit—of a slut, whoring after youth through pretending to be with-it. I've had it with the old broad; after nearly 50 years together, I've determined to cut her loose.

I have decided, that is, to cancel my subscription to the *New York Times*. For so many decades the paper has been part of my morning mental hygiene. Yet in recent years I've been reading less and less of each day's paper. Most days now I do no more than scan the headlines on the front page, check the sports pages for the pitchers in that day's White Sox and Cubs games, then flip over to the Irish sports pages, as the obits have been called, to see if anyone I know has pegged out.

History may not repeat itself, but the news does, relentlessly. Since the *New York Times* began to run more and more feature stories, often on its front page, lots of what appears in its pages hasn't been news, not even close. "Chief Justice Warren Sees No Trend in Burger Court," with its stunning irrelevance, is an old *Times* headline atop the kind of story I have in mind and see more and more.

I long ago ceased reading the newspaper's letters section in the hope of finding a man or woman after my own heart. With the exception of David Brooks, who allows that his general position is slightly to the right of center but who is not otherwise locked into a Pavlovian political response, I find no need to read any of the *Times*'s regular columnists. Every so often I check to remind myself that Maureen Dowd isn't amusing, though she is an improvement, I suppose, over the termagantial Anna Quindlen, whom I used to read with the trepidation of a drunken husband mounting the stairs knowing his wife awaits at the top with a rolling pin. I'd sooner read the fine print in my insurance policies than the paper's perfectly predictable editorials. Laughter, an elegant phrase, a surprising sentiment—the *New York Times* op-ed and editorial pages are the last place to discover any of these things.

I sometimes glimpse the Arts section to see which wrong people are being praised or have been awarded large cash prizes or recognized for years of mediocre achievement by election to the American Academy of Arts & Letters. Arts, of course, are no longer quite The Arts, at least in the *New York Times*, which features hard rock and rap music and video games and graphic novels under the rubric The Arts. Only the photographs of dancers lend an aesthetic dimension to the shabby section.

I lift the Sunday *New York Times* from the hallway outside our apartment with a heart twice the weight of the hefty paper itself. From it I extract the *Book Review*, the magazine, "Sunday Styles," the "Week in Review." For decades now the *New York Times Book Review* has been devoted to reinforcing received (and mostly wrong) literary opinions and doing so in impressively undistinguished prose. The *New York Times Magazine* has always been dull, but earlier it erred on the side of seriousness. Now it is dull on the side of ersatz hipness. The other Sunday I put myself through a long article on the dangers of leaving a record of one's minor misdeeds on the Internet. The article's last sentence instructed that "we need to learn new forms of empathy, new ways of defining ourselves without reference to what others say about us and new ways of forgiving one another for the digital trails that will follow us forever." Yes, I thought, and wet birds never fly at night.

I could go on about the artificial rage of Frank Rich—the liberals' Glenn Beck—or the forced gaiety of "Sunday Styles," but the main feeling I have as I rise from having wasted an hour or so with the Sunday *New York Times* is of what wretched shape the country is in if it is engaged in such boringly trivial pursuits, elevating to eminence such dim cultural and political figures, writing so muddledly about ostensibly significant subjects.

Perhaps one picks up all newspapers in anticipation and puts them down in disappointment. But the *New York Times*, at no extra charge, also leaves one feeling one lives in immitigably dreary times, and it does so daily. I don't need it.

Cancel my subscription, please.

Full Slab

(2010)

I S SOME FOOD, in one of the leading cant phrases of our day, sexist? Food cannot of course take political positions, but some food, let us agree, has a greater masculine than feminine appeal, and probably always will. Try as I might, I cannot imagine the Chicago Bears linebacker Brian Urlacher whispering at half-time to one of his teammates that he cannot wait for the game to be over, because he has a reservation that night at a restaurant where they serve the most divine *salade Niçoise*.

No food is more masculine than ribs. I know women who eat ribs, and even show a genuine appetite for them, but at bottom ribs are a guy meal. What makes them so is their fundamental coarseness. Not always but usually one has to pick them up with one's hands. Many napkins are required to remove sauce from one's hands and around one's mouth. The spectacle of a man eating ribs is reminiscent to me of a 1940 movie called *One Million BC*, starring Victor Mature and Carole Landis. I can still see Victor Mature, who had glistening rib-lips to begin with, gnawing meat off a bone. Men, the movie underscored, are brutes.

Ribs were not served in the home in which I was brought up. Neither of my parents was religious, but my mother clung, culturally, to some of the old habits of keeping kosher with which she had grown up: no pork of any kind found its way to her kitchen, and, along with her belief that all politicians were crooks, she also never veered from her equally firm belief that a kosher chicken was superior to a non-kosher one.

My first ribs were eaten in a neighborhood restaurant called Miller's, owned by a man, a bachelor, in the heating and air-conditioning business, who needed a place to spend his evenings and so opened this restaurant. Beef in its ideal, its all but Platonic, forms was available at Miller's: hamburger, steak, prime rib, and of course ribs.

In Chicago, traditionally a beefy town, even though the city no longer has an active stockyard, many men pride themselves upon their rib connoisseurship. The late Chicago journalist Mike Royko used to run and judge a rib-cooking fest at the end of summer in Grant Park. "It's the sauce," is the motto of a rib joint in my neighborhood called Hecky's, where the ribs served are, as a friend once put it, industrial strength.

Ribs come of course in different forms: beef and pork, regular and babyback, short and now St. Louis, which are alleged to be meatier than traditional ribs. Some ribs fall off the bone, and can be eaten with a knife and fork; some ribs are baked rather than grilled. A few years ago I was taken to a famous—is it still?—New York restaurant called Daniel, after its chef and owner Daniel Boulud, where I ordered short ribs. A mistake. Should have ordered the *salade Niçoise*. The Chinese know how to cook ribs but not the French.

Subtlety has nothing to do with ribs, either in their preparation or their devouring. Ribs come, after all, in slabs, not a subtle word or form. A full slab of ribs—how the very phrase must make vegetarians quiver, vegans faint dead away!

The last place to find either vegetarians or vegans is Mike Ditka's restaurant in Chicago, where I was taken a few years ago by George Will and his son Jeffrey, who was my student at Northwestern and is now in the FBI. ("Betcha can't guess which of us at this table is packing heat?" George asked once we were seated.) A strong notion, if not the actual aroma, of Mike Ditka's, its food and ambience, is available upon my mentioning a single item from the appetizer section of its menu: Pot Roast Nachos. I won't say that every size 50 suit in town was in the restaurant that night, but you would not have found many men in leotards.

Having neglected to major in nutrition in college, I cannot say for sure that ribs are, under the current health-food craze, among the most dangerous foods one can eat, but I should guess that they are probably up there. The cholesterol, the calories, the fat grams in a full slab of ribs—the numbers must be dizzying. Thus far the surgeon general has not pasted a label on ribs warning that they are dangerous to your health, though I suspect they are. Might this make them all the more enticing, at least to men? Men, as I believe I mentioned earlier, are brutes.

Dancing with Wolves

(2012)

I KNEW A MAN WHO ALLOWED HIS WIFE to buy the family car, a fact that always astonished me, and still does. Dealing with car salesmen, if I may say so and still elude the charge of sexism, is man's work. Only men can be so stupid as to get caught up in the hopeless game of trying to defeat car salesmen in getting the best deal possible. This ritual of buying a car, which I myself have recently gone through, I call Dancing with Wolves, and only a man can be so foolish as to think he is likely to come away unbitten.

I once wrote a short story that had a car salesman among its characters. I gave my salesman the name Sy Bourget (né Seymour Bernstein) and reported that he was said to be "so good . . . that he could sell aluminum siding to people who lived in high rises. . . . He was in his mid-fifties, but looked older, especially around his eyes, which were gray and cold. His hair was white, yet his pencil-thin mustache was still dark. He wore expensive suits, flashy shirts, good suits well pressed; he had a blue sapphire pinkie ring and was never without a manicure." By this description I hoped to make him seem quietly menacing, for slightly menaced is how I generally feel when entering a new car showroom.

In my late adolescence and early twenties, I used occasionally to end the evening at one of two local steakhouses in my neighborhood in Chicago:

one called Miller's, the other the Black Angus. Around 10 o'clock, after their dealerships had closed, salesmen from Nortown Olds and Z. Frank Chevrolet would gather over red meat and brown booze, swapping stories about, as I always imagined, the foolish customers who during the day thought they stood a chance to outwit them.

Here's the deal, and I throw in the rear-window defogger and the masculine idiocy at no extra charge: Not only do we men hope to best these salesmen, trained as they are in the arcana of numbers and knowing precisely what we are up to, but we also believe we can do better than their other customers have done. This last point is of crucial importance.

Let us say that you and I are each driving a Volkswagen Passat, with the same so-called extras: sunroofs, leather upholstery, heated seats, sound systems, and the rest. We are both pleased with our cars. One day, over coffee, we begin to talk about the deals we made, and I discover that you acquired your car for two thousand dollars less than I. My car, once a beloved object, is henceforth a symbol on wheels of my failure, a failure of savvy and cunning, and I can no longer look upon it except with a tinge of sadness.

Fraught, that vogue word meaning heavily complicated with the possibility of an unhappy ending, fraught is what everything having to do with buying a car is. Along with the fear of being made a fool of goes that of being treated as if one were a child. Some years ago a car salesman told me that he wanted to find a car for me in which I'd feel comfortable. "What would make me feel a lot more comfortable," I told him, "is if you'd lower your price a few grand." "Right," he said, "no problem," and then scarcely budged on his price.

I believe we may owe car salesmen for the entry and ubiquity of the phrase "no problem"; we also owe them for the word "right" with a question mark at the end of nearly every sentence they utter. "What you're looking for is a car that is both elegant and economical, right? No problem."

On my latest venture into the swamps of car buying, I encountered a salesman who asked me a series of perfectly irrelevant questions—where did I live?, at what did I work?, what car was I currently driving?, etc.— and to each of my answers he replied, "Great." This brought back to me the time when, working on a film script, I gave a young woman at Warner

Bros. who worked for my producer my phone number. "Wonderful," she said. "We're very excited," she invariably said about this film script that never got made.

In the end I bought the car, though with no great confidence that I'd made an especially good deal on it. My salesman—and here is a new twist—asked me if I would please go online and rate his performance. He hoped I might give him all 5s, the highest rating. "You want all 5s, right?" I said. "Great! No problem," and I drove off with that intoxicating new car smell in my nostrils and a glint of doubt in my heart. Don't ask what I paid for the car. I'd only lie to you.

Bye, Bye, High Five

(2011)

TIME TO DECLARE A MORATORIUM on the high five. That combination salute and handshake has been around for more than 30 years, and is now entering the stage of the perfunctory, perhaps even the otiose. The other evening, watching a White Sox game, I saw a player hit by a pitch replaced by a pinch-runner and returned to the Sox dugout forced to undergo from all his teammates a full round of high fives, with a few head rubs and bottom pats thrown in at no extra charge. Perfunctory, I call that, otiose.

I am equally eager to see an end to the low five; the side five; the high-low five; the fist bump; the handshake and shoulder bump; the handshake, half hug, and double-back pat (President Obama's masculine greeting of choice); and the leaping chest bump. I have myself participated over the years in perhaps 20 high fives, a few of them with strangers at sports events, but never without a nagging feeling of falsity. I am a straight handshake man, and a handshake man I wish to remain.

"You call that a handshake?" I can recall my father saying to me when I was five or six years old. "That's a dead fish you just gave me. A real man shakes hands with firmness." And he grasped my hand, lost in his much larger one, with a reassuring squeeze. The simple masculine handshake is not quite gone, but one senses that it has become a touch drab, square, yes, honky.

Google recounts the controversy over who threw the first high five. Some claim it was between Dusty Baker and Glenn Burke, then both of the Los Angeles Dodgers, in late 1977. The University of Louisville Cardinals are said to have widely popularized it during their run to the 1980 NCAA basketball championships. A man, Lamont Sleets, was reported to have first used the high five in the 1960s, when greeting his father and his four buddies from Vietnam, exclaiming, "Hi, Five." Later the Sleets story was revealed to be a hoax. But whoever invented the wretched thing should not be any prouder of it than, say, those false geniuses who gave us the electric hand dryer and the hospital gown.

The high five and its variations are part of the empty triumphalism that has overtaken sports and spread to life outside sports in recent decades. In an earlier time, people saved strong congratulations for truly momentous victories: winning the final game of the World Series or the Stanley Cup, Wimbledon, an Olympic marathon run, the Kentucky Derby, and a few other select events.

Now we have the touchdown dance, the sack dance, the Tarzan-of-the-apes scream after the slam dunk, the triple fist pump and knee raise after winning a mere point in tennis. They go too far, all of them. A good winner has felt, and thereby understands, the funk of defeat; he knows that the best man doesn't always win; and so he is therefore generous in victory. Gracious winning was part of what used to be called sportsmanship.

Difficult to say exactly when sports decided it could do without sportsmanship. Perhaps it began with football, professional football especially, where a team can get a 15-yard penalty for excessive celebration. In college football, one can celebrate but not taunt an opponent, but players, feeling it worth the penalty, do it anyhow.

In baseball, at the conclusion of each game, the winning team parades onto the field, and the players form a double row to exchange high fives with one another. During the game itself, there is the home-run trot, the finger pointing to heaven demonstrating that the player has God on his side, the double-leg stomp at home plate to signify scoring the winning run. All that is missing, really, is a net and trident.

Tennis was a game that once had an etiquette for victory and for close calls. Enter those stinkers Jimmy Connors and John McEnroe. Connors stirred up crowds with yells, fist pumping, and pelvis grinding. McEnroe treated linesmen and umpires as if he were a Russian count and they his incompetent serfs. Exeunt the elegance of good manners. In basketball, trash talk is now a regular part of the game.

Golf may be the last game that still values sportsmanship. Players have been known to disqualify themselves for using the wrong ball or having too many clubs in their bag. In recent years, a bit of fist pumping, usually after making a lengthy or tricky putt, has come into play. But there is nothing of the mean-spiritedness of triumphalism in golf that one finds in other sports.

As for the high five, the next time anyone offers you one, meet his upraised hand with the small end of your fist while extending your thumb outward. The meeting forms a perfect picture of a turkey, a word—"Turkey"—you then call out. He'll never throw another high five without giving it a serious second thought.

Kindle at the Cleaners

(2011)

THE OTHER DAY I asked my five-years-younger-than-I brother—the wit in our family—if he had taken to using a Kindle. "My Kindle," he said, "is at the cleaners." I'm not sure why I found that funny, but I did, and still do, and take it that he means he would never think of using this new aid to reading with which so many people are so very pleased.

If I owned a Kindle, I, too, would take it to the cleaners but never bother to pick it up. I'm sure that this miraculous new device has lots to be said for it in the realm of convenience (many books can be stored in it at once) and ease of handling (it's much lighter than most hardcover books), but electronically is not the way I prefer to read books.

Some of my own books are available on Kindle, though I have never attempted to glimpse them in digital form. Years ago I had a few books on tape and thought what a pleasing snack it might be to my XXL ego to drive around town listening to my own scribblings being read aloud by an out-of-work actor. I listened to one for about three minutes and couldn't bear it, so different were the actor's reading rhythms from those I heard when writing the words he was now, so to say, misspeaking.

I doubt that I would fare any better reading myself on Kindle. I wonder if I am alone in finding digital printing an invitation to skim. When

I have a book or magazine in hand, I generally read every word, attentive not alone to meaning but to style. In digital form, prose has a different feel; style gives way to mere communication. If I discover an essay or article on, say, artsandlettersdaily.com that runs to more than 25 paragraphs, by the fifteenth paragraph or so I feel a tug of impatience I rarely feel with printed prose. The idea of reading serious poetry online doesn't even qualify as an abomination.

The bias of ebooks, at least for now, is toward bestsellers, contemporary books, and standard classics. Most of the books I read are old, many of them out of the mainstream. At the moment I happen to be reading Primo Levi's *The Periodic Table* and Emmanuel Ringelblum's *Notes from the Warsaw Ghetto*. I haven't checked, but I suspect both are unkindled, or unkindleable.

I read books with a pencil in hand and a few small pieces of paper, on which I make occasional notes, for a bookmark. I make light markings— sidelining, it's called—alongside what I think significant passages. None of this can be done on a Kindle. I keep books in my bathroom, others on my night table. I like the look of books, the heft of them in my hands, their different sizes and various fonts and dust jackets, the smell of them.

Mine is a neighborhood with a small number of excellent used-book stores, which the Kindle, should its use continue to spread, will eventually help put out of business. The supermarket bookstores, in a similar way, helped put the independent booksellers out of business; and now the online booksellers are putting the supermarket bookstores out of business. Thus do big fish swallow smaller ones, until in the end one large fish—let us call it Amazon.com/kindle—will remain. Sometimes, as Adam Smith failed to point out, the invisible hand of the market has jagged and dirty fingernails.

If more and more books are sold online and read on Kindles, Nooks, and other such devices, a serious source of education will be obliterated. My friend Edward Shils once set out the four main forms of education in the modern world: the classroom, the intelligent conversation of friends, serious magazines and journals, and new and used book shops. In my education, the latter two—magazines and journals, new and used book shops—have been more important than the others.

In bookstores, especially used-book stores, one discovers books and writers one never knew existed in a way one can't on a Kindle. One day in a dingy local bookstore, I found a book called *Rome and Pompeii: Archeological Rambles* by a writer named Gaston Boissier, a nineteenth-century French classicist. Opening it, I came upon the following sentence about Horace: "He desired retirement with a passion which cannot but surprise us in a sage who professed to wish for nothing with too much ardor." This sentence sold me on the book, which I bought straightaway. I have gone on to read other of Gaston Boissier's books, always with pleasure and, I like to think, intellectual profit. Such discoveries through sampling aren't likely to be made digitally.

The cheerful choreography of progress proceeds: one step forward, two steps back. "Get thy Kindle," as a latterday Hamlet might have said to Ophelia, "to the cleaners."

At Moral Rest in
Old New York

(2011)

TOURISM, IT HAS BEEN SAID, is a condition of moral rest. On a recent trip to New York—where I was lent a two-room time-share apartment on 56th Street across from Carnegie Hall—I invoked this maxim time and again. I ate what I pleased, saw what I wished, did no work of any substance, and achieved nothing whatsoever in the way of self-improvement.

I enjoy New York's hum, the cacophony of foreign languages I hear on its streets, the high quality of its food, the frankly sexual get-ups of its female denizens. For these reasons, and for the wondrous variety of its shops, New York is one of the world's great walking cities. Walk in it I did, every chance I got, yet scarcely was I able to take in all the rich tumult—the rhooshey-booshey, in a fine neologism of my mother's—there on display.

Moral rest includes cultural rest. One of the things I did in New York was drop my highbrow standard and take myself to a musical comedy. I saw *Jersey Boys*, the story of Frankie Valli and the Four Seasons, which has been running for five years. Without a dead moment, the show is well-made, which in part explains its long run. The music isn't my music—

I am of an age that puts me well on the other side of the rock 'n' roll divide—but not without its charms: "Can't Take My Eyes Off of You," "Silhouettes," "Walk Like a Man," and the rest.

The great moment in the show for me, though, was the quiet one when the actor who plays Frankie Valli announces that the Beatles came along and wiped every other group out, but not the Four Seasons. The Beatles, he says, made music for people who protested war; the Four Seasons made music for people who went to war, for the soldiers and the truck drivers and the hamburger flippers. What made this all the more interesting was that the people in the audience, many now in their fifties and early sixties, were preponderantly these people, now grown older but still enamored of the music.

To rinse the Four Seasons' songs from my mind, the next day I took myself to the Metropolitan Museum. I spent my time there in the Greek and Roman collection, at the end of which was the installation of the third-century AD Roman floor mosaic found in Lod, Israel. I ended this with a quick walk through a small collection of Cézanne drawings and sketches for his famous painting "The Card Players." Still, all this high culture could not stop me, once I hit the street, from humming "Silhouettes."

Food in New York is as good as it is because of the sheer demanding-ness of New Yorkers. Poor restaurants die quickly there, where in other cities they live on for three generations. I stopped to pick up a salad at a place called Chop't on West 51st Street, the unrelenting energy of whose workers, servicing a perpetually lengthy line of harried lunchers, is of a kind difficult to imagine encountering elsewhere in America. I had two lunches at Cellini, on East 54th Street, my favorite restaurant, where even the water tastes good. One, accompanied by much laughter and rich gossip, was in the company of two old friends, one a native New Yorker, his wife a naturalized one.

I could have become a naturalized New Yorker myself. I lived there, in my middle twenties, for a few years. When I was young, if one felt one had talent, New York was the only place to test it. Certainly this was—and remains—true for the performing arts: acting, singing, dance, classi-cal music performance. One night I attended three ballets put on by the

Juilliard School and was impressed by the professional level attained by its young dancers in works by three very different choreographers: Nijinska, Eliot Feld, and Mark Morris. Nowhere else in America but in New York was this possible.

For writers the beneficence of living in New York is less certain: So much energy is used up in the sheer exercise of living. Nor is it clear that the city is the best place to find the ripest material for either fiction or nonfiction. New York, in a strange way, isn't really America at all; it has been described—not inaccurately, in my view—as a European city but of no known country.

Had I remained in New York, I would have got less work done. Whether the quality of what I have written would have been better under the forcing house of endlessly vibrant New York is not something I can judge.

I remain, then, a visitor, a man come to see the sights and seek the odd week's moral rest.

Katie in Kabul

(2011)

B Y THE TIME YOU READ THIS, Katie Couric will no longer be the anchorwoman on the CBS Evening News. She could not do what she was paid $15 million a year to do: bring up the ratings for CBS prime-time news and with them its advertising revenues. Both fell further during her tenure. While advertising revenues are down 9.1 percent for prime-time news shows generally, CBS's revenues fell, according to the *Wall Street Journal*, a full 23 percent.

I have been among Katie Couric's dwindling audience, and, in perhaps a slightly perverse way, I shall miss her. Prime-time news in Chicago goes on at 5:30 p.m., which is drinks time *chez* Epstein: specifically, time for a glass of cold Riesling and a handful of Paul Newman pretzels, which, as the spoonful of sugar did to the medicine, helps the news go down. My demographic cohort, to use the charming advertising phrase, is the chief audience for prime-time news, or so I judge from all the Viagra, Plavix, Boniva, and other older players' medicines, palliatives, and panaceas hawked on all three news shows.

I have a dim memory of a stern gent named John Cameron Swayze (great portentous name) doing prime-time news. I recall Edward R. Murrow, broadcast journalism's Mother Teresa, demeaning himself on a show called *Person to Person*, in which one night I heard him ask, "Fidel, is that a baseball bat in the corner there?" "That's right," the genial dictator replied, "love de game of baseball, Ed." I remember Huntley and Brinkley, and enjoyed Brinkley's subtle hints that politicians were not to be taken entirely seriously.

By the time Walter Cronkite came along I was old enough to realize that behind his avuncular omniscience was a man who knew even less than I about the way the world works. The blandness of Tom Brokaw made me doubt even the greatness of his Greatest Generation. Peter Jennings I thought a nice enough looking *shaygetz*, but unduly soft on Araby.

In the era AC (after Cronkite), I began watching Brian Williams, who easily had the best tailoring. But Williams ended his show with a segment called "Making A Difference," which usually entailed some retired steel magnate teaching ghetto children how to make lanyards, and, frankly, I could never see the difference it might make. I tried a guy named Charlie something or other on ABC, who was substituting for the deceased Peter Jennings, though it was evident that he had neither the requisite hairdo nor smile for the job. When ABC brought in as its new anchor Diane Sawyer, with her heavy-breathing empathy, I was out of there.

That left me as part of Katie's diminishing audience on CBS. In the meanwhile, progress being our most important product, I had acquired a television set with a DVR, which allowed me to record shows and movies to watch when I wished. Best of all, a pre-recorded show could be fast-forwarded. This meant that, by recording beforehand, I could eliminate all the commercials on the evening news and all those weepy stories that they all go in for: stories about veterans missing limbs, young children with cancer, old people whose homes have been wiped out in floods. (Television news likes people crying on camera; if it weeps, it keeps.) The happy effect has been to get the formerly 30-minute evening news down to roughly 12 minutes.

For a while I thought myself rather grand in overlooking all the standard prejudice against Katie Couric: that she was a light (make that a bantam) weight, syrupy, a dope generally. I would sometimes tell people that whoever was editing her show was selecting more interesting stories than were available on ABC and NBC, and for a while I think that may have been so.

But soon Katie, like all television anchors people watch with any regularity, began to get on my nerves. Given her widely known salary, it was hard to credit her sympathy for people suffering mortgage foreclosures or other economic hardships. She had acquired two physicians as medical reporters, always ready with news about the latest false cures for hideous diseases, who resembled no one so much as aging Barbie and Ken dolls. One night when she wasn't on set, a man named Harry Smith announced, "Katie's in Kabul." Katie in Kabul, Katie in Kabul—I couldn't get the phrase out of my mind; it reminded me of Eloise at the Plaza.

Katie's replacement on CBS News is a man named Scott Pelley, who has the mien of a ticked-off Niles Crane, from the *Frasier* sitcom. Pelley threatens more hard news under his—is there such a word?—anchorship. He, I suspect, will drive me back to Brian Williams; to Diane Sawyer I cannot return. But, then, what does the news matter if the Riesling is good?

The Divine Miss H

(2011)

A S I TAP THIS OUT ON MY COMPUTER, there resides in my yellow wooden inbox a sleeping three-month-old female Calico kitten named Hermione. I acquired her this past Friday evening, and spent the better part of the weekend in her company. Jolly company it was, too, all fun and games. In the most famous moot question in literature, Montaigne asked if he were playing with his cat or if his cat were instead playing with him. I failed to ask this question of the divine Miss H, but I can attest that the two of us had a swell time.

I have had a pair of Siamese cats (Ralph and Clara) and, more recently, a quietly affectionate tiger-striped cat (Isabelle), who used to sit beside me at our kitchen counter during my coffee and early morning reading. When Isabelle died, I thought her irreplaceable, and therefore made no attempt to replace her.

A few weeks ago, at a local pet store called The Fish Bowl, I saw a sign in the window advertising rescued animals. Among them was a litter of kittens whose mother was killed and not around to raise them. The runt of the litter was the not-yet-named Hermione. She was still too young to be taken home, as I probably would have done, so immediately enamored of her was I. I made a mental note to stop back to see her again. I did, and found myself no less nuts about her, but, somehow, delayed making the decision to bring her to our apartment. On a third trip, at last ready to make my move, I learned that someone had come earlier that same day and whisked her away.

We have here a tragedy with a happy ending—William Dean Howells's formula for a successful Broadway play—for the person who took the kitten had another cat in his house who had territorial rights and wanted no new animals on the scene, and so he had to bring Hermione back to the pet shop. At this point—maestro, please play the heavily violin-laden finale to the movie *An Affair to Remember*—Hermione and I permanently entered each other's lives.

Hermione immediately found her food and water dishes, and straightaway used her litter box. Well-trained dogs offer their owners uncritical adoration, as J. R. Ackerley, author of *My Dog Tulip*, learned to his contentment. Well-trained is never an adjectival phrase one would think to place before the noun cat. In place of uncritical adoration, cats offer elegant sangfroid, fits of passionate intensity and affection, and, when the mood strikes them, a fine go-bugger-off-pal independence that makes the phrase cat-owner an imprecision. Nobody, finally, owns a cat. Cats are instead superior house guests.

Calico means mottled and multicolored, and in Hermione's case the multicolors are caramel, black, gray, white, and, on her left side, tiger striping. Nothing the least bit symmetrical about the placement of any of these colors, either, with the exception of her paws, all of which are white, though with differently shaped gray markings above each. On her, as they say, it looks good. I, at least, cannot take my eyes off her.

In dreams begin responsibilities, and the same might be said about pets. Equipage has to be taken on—in the case of a cat, a litter box, bowls, a carry-box—food provided, the ample bills of veterinarians paid. One cannot travel without making arrangements for their care. A pet—even a single goldfish—does not simplify one's life. "Simplify, simplify," said that self-approving nudnik Thoreau. In my own life, I have never come within hailing distance of being able to do so.

When I look at the three-month-old Hermione capering about our apartment, the thought occurs to me that this charming creature, with the luck of good health, could easily outlive me. Was I right to have brought her into my life? Did I need to add to my list of morning errands the cleaning of a litter box? Have I joined the ranks of the pet-goofy who make up much of the clientele at PetSmart, where the other day I paid my first visit, to purchase a scratching mat? That mat and others of her toys are for the moment strewn around the floor of our formerly orderly living room. Shall I end my days as—groan—a cat-person?

And then I hear the galloping clatter of Hermione's paws, as she races along the wooden floors of our long hall, a run that sometimes ends with her popping onto my lap, causing my heart to leap and to conclude, without hesitation, that simplicity and good order are vastly overrated.

Bring It on,
Fyodor Mikhailovich

(2011)

A T **English department parties** of many moons past, or so I have been told, once all had become properly snockered, a popular game commenced in which everyone confessed to what he or she hadn't read. The game had a crescendo quality as the intellectual stakes rose. "I've never read Christopher Marlowe," a Renaissance English specialist might admit at the outset. "That's nothing," a Romantic poetry man might add, "I've never read, and won't allow in the house, Wordsworth's *Prelude*." "*Paradise Lost*—forget about it!" Finally, as things continued, escalating nicely, someone would admit to never having read Homer or *Hamlet* and everyone could go home.

What I thought interesting about the game is that everyone, no matter how well read, is certain not to have read something he or she ought to have read. As for that phrase "well read," I long ago decided that no one is genuinely well read; there are merely some people who have read more than others. I am probably one of the latter, or at least I am taken for one of them. Which is why, without the aid of alcohol or a boring English department party, I wish to confess that I have never read—wait for it, wait for it—*The Brothers Karamazov*.

I am about to remedy that deficiency. A few days ago, at a library book sale, I acquired, for two dollars, a clean Penguin edition, translated by a Scotsman named David McDuff and running, with notes, to a mere 920 pages. I am off presently on a three-day trip and plan to take the novel along. (I hope American Airlines hasn't begun to charge extra for thick Russian classics in one's carry-on bag.) Not that I shall come near finishing it in three days, for I am a slow reader, always, like all writers, on the lookout for something I can steal from better writers. I shall be further slowed by the fact that I find it uncongenial to read dark works late at night, lest they disturb my already fragile sleep. I could well be a month or more reading *The Brothers Karamazov*, which I have promised myself never to call *The Brothers K*.

I write about a great deal of what I read, but I shan't be writing about *The Brothers Karamazov*. "Joseph," my friend Edward Shils once said to me, "we have each read a fair number of books. We are also reasonably civilized fellows, civilized enough, at any rate, to know that there is no point in our ever getting into a discussion about Shakespeare." And we never did. Edward's point, or so I took it to be, is what is there left to say about genius? The same applies to Dostoyevsky, or at least to this greatest of his novels, if its vast advance press is any guide.

For decades people have made a great fuss about the translations of Russian novels. One of the victims of this fuss has been Constance Garnett, who, as a one-woman translation factory, single-handedly imported Russian literature into the Anglophone world. The gravamen of the criticism against this amazing woman was that she "englished" the novels by including too many English idioms and thereby made all 73 of her translations of various Russian writers sound alike. I must say that, as a young student, so blown away was I by the sheer power of the storytelling in these novels and stories, I never noticed, and didn't much care. If two Russians met on the Nevsky Prospekt and greeted each other as "old chap," that was all right by me.

George Steiner wrote a book called *Tolstoy or Dostoyevsky: An Essay in Contrast* (1960), but I see no "or" about it. Why not both? Forced to choose, I would take Tolstoy, if only because even when he is writing about dark things the light flows through his work, whereas with Dostoyevsky's fiction it really is lights out. Not that Dostoyevsky can't do amusing bits: His novel *The Idiot* is replete with them, and his parody portrait of Turgenev as "the great novelist" Karmazinov in *The Devils* is a wickedly funny take down of the type of the older liberal sucking up to the young.

In one of his letters to Harold Laski, Justice Holmes remarks that conscience drove him to finish every book he ever started until the age of 75, when he could finally quit an inferior book without finishing it. He claimed to fear St. Peter would test him on all he had read, and he was fearful of being caught unprepared. My simpler fear in failing till now to read *The Brothers Karamazov* is of missing out on something magnificent. I have now reached the age to read the novel with the tranquility and, I hope, the thoughtfulness it requires. So bring it on, Fyodor Mikhailovich; give me the best you've got.

Down the AmaZone

(2012)

NO GREATER FANTASTS EXIST than writers, who are able to bring an extra dollop or two of imagination to their unreality. About no subject are they more fantastic than the potential commercial success of their books. When I publish a book with the least chance of popular appeal, I am unable, even after all these years, to suppress dreams of shekels raining down upon me. ("I can stand a lot of gold," said Henry James, who was himself subject to these fantasies.) I imagine villas in Tuscany, apartments in Paris, a nicely understated Bentley in my garage. Not, let me hasten to add, that I am in the least need or want of these items—ownership of any one of them would make me even nuttier than I now am. But a boy—quite an old boy, as it turns out—can dream, can't he?

I once came close to achieving serious commercial success with a book. David Brooks, who reviewed it in the *Wall Street Journal*, declared it would be the book every intelligent person would be reading on the beach that summer. A full hour was devoted to the book by the NPR show *Talk of the Nation*. Presto, I found my book on bestseller lists: seventh on the *New York Times*, second for several weeks on that of the *Los Angeles Times*, and on other bestseller lists in Chicago and San Francisco.

Thrice the editor at my publishing house called to announce that they were going back to print another ten thousand copies. Radio shows and newspapers sought interviews with me. Someone told me that my book was number 11 on Amazon.com. I didn't hitherto know about Amazon.com ratings. Nor did I know about the brief reviews from readers who fancied themselves critics, of which my book received quite a few, the majority pleasing, a few suggesting, in effect, that perhaps I would do better to quit writing and get a job at Jiffy Lube. One has only to have one's book slammed on Amazon to appreciate the journalist Lars-Erik Nelson's remark that the Internet is "a vanity press for the demented."

The success of my book didn't sustain itself long enough to get me out of the financial wars with an honorable discharge. To be the eleventh-bestselling book at Amazon.com was lovely. The problem is that the position of one's book on Amazon.com is always changing, inevitably heading downward. After one flogs a book on one NPR station or another, the book's Amazon standing can radically improve—by ten or twenty thousand places—but this gain, too, is soon lost as the book continues its inevitable plunge.

Of all that might be said about the Internet, the invention of the age, the one undeniably true thing is that it is a momentous distraction. With a book freshly out in the world, a writer awaits Google alerts bringing fresh news of reviews, or mentions in the press, or on blogs and Twitter. He checks Amazon numbers hourly. He dreams of a dazzlingly approving review that will jolt one's Amazon.com number to two digits. The approving review appears, yet the Amazon rating scarcely changes.

Henry James wrote of the "benefit of the *friction with the market* which is so true a one for solitary artists too much steeped in their mere personal dreams." James was himself savvy about marketing his writing, but all his savvy brought him insufficient commercial success. He wanted, as most writers do, artistic and commercial success both, but had to content himself with achieving, sublimely, only the former.

As one's book's Amazon.com ratings fall, slowly at first, precipitously a bit later—going from the hundreds to the thousands, to the tens, then hundreds of thousands—one realizes what a dope one has been, and what a mug's game is hoping for huge commercial success with a book. In the current day, new books have roughly the shelf life of yogurt; the shelf life of books may be shorter. With the world offering so many distractions—

smartphones, iPads, cable television, social media—the book itself is beginning to take on the feel of a specialty, or niche, product. As someone a good part of whose life is devoted to writing books, I have begun to feel as a blacksmith must have done in the first decades of the twentieth century when the automobiles were beginning to crowd the streets.

As my own most recent book sinks into the west—it is at this moment number 188,812 on Amazon—I feel I can relax and let go of my fantasy of a great commercial score. What a relief to be out of the AmaZone! Now I can concentrate on the prospect of mere immortality for this and all my other books.

The Proustian Solution

(2012)

FIVE OR SIX YEARS AGO I found the seats at classical music concerts becoming uncomfortable. I blame the seats, but in fact I had lost the *Sitzfleisch*—in German literally "seat meat," in looser translation "bottom patience"—to sit through a concert. In concert halls my mind wandered, I counted the people around me who had fallen asleep, searched the audience for anyone under 40, frequently checked my watch. Time seemed to pass more slowly than in a laundromat.

I used to go to from 12 to 20 concerts a year. With my loss of attention at concerts, and given the expense of concert tickets, it finally occurred to me that I was wasting time and money in dragging myself to these events. I love serious music; it was only at concerts that I couldn't seem to enjoy it. My condition was not unlike that of the English journalist Malcolm Muggeridge, who once wrote that he couldn't take his mind off thoughts of God, and it was only when he entered an Anglican church and the vicar began speaking that for him God was gone.

George Santayana late in life also found he could no longer bear to attend concerts. Going to hear serious music, he reports in one of his letters, had come to resemble an act of piety instead of one of pleasure. In Rome, where Santayana was living at the time, there was lots of good street music, and he achieved a useful compromise by listening to this music out-of-doors and standing up. I listen to most of my music on CDs driving around the city in my car.

I recently attempted a concert-hall comeback. An all-Mozart program was scheduled a few weeks ago by the Chicago Symphony Orchestra, with Mitsuko Uchida, the foremost Mozart interpreter of our day, playing and conducting two Mozart concerti. Uchida was splendid, the CSO turned in its usual smooth performance, and as the program ended to a standing ovation for Uchida, I said to myself, "Please don't let her play an encore."

Two weeks later, I went to a Dame Myra Hess Memorial Concert at the Chicago Cultural Center. The program, played by a youthful woodwinds quintet, was roughly 45 minutes long. The crowd, like most classical music audiences, was less than sprightly. The man seated to my left fell asleep just before the performers were introduced and woke—refreshed, let us assume—only at their finish. I found myself rising to my feet to applaud, and went happily off to lunch with friends afterwards. Successful as this outing was, I feel no urge to return, at least not soon.

No, the best arrangement for me is what I think of as the Proustian solution. Marcel Proust was a regular concertgoer, and his interest in music was intense and highly intelligent; his fictional composer Vinteuil of *In Search of Lost Time* attests to that. He was especially enamored of the music of Beethoven and César Franck, and in particular of Franck's String Quartet in D as played by the Poulet Quartet.

One night around 11 o'clock in the winter of 1916, wanting eagerly to hear the Franck quartet, Proust paid a call on Gaston Poulet, the leader of the Poulet Quartet. When Poulet came to the door in his pajamas, Proust informed him that he would like very much to hear his group play the Franck composition that very night in his apartment on the Boulevard Haussmann. Lured by the high fee Proust offered, Poulet agreed, and he and Proust in a cab rounded up the other members of the quartet. They arrived at Proust's apartment near 1:00 a.m.

As they began the César Franck quartet, Proust listened with his eyes closed. He enjoyed it so much that he asked the musicians to play it again, and then went to a small Chinese box from which he extracted a stack of notes redeemable for 45,000 ordinary francs, a sum grand enough for the Poulet Quartet to play the piece a second time without diminution of energy. In subsequent months, Proust called on the Poulet Quartet to play others of his favorite compositions in his apartment, Mozart, Ravel, and Schumann among them, each time one assumes for a similarly lucrative fee.

I should mention that when Proust's mother died, in 1905 at the age of 56, she left her son the equivalent of roughly $4.6 million in current dollars, a sum that allowed him to tip waiters at the Ritz 100 percent and more and to listen to live music in the ideal conditions of his own apartment.

If only I could adopt Proust's solution to my concert-hall problem. How I should like to have the Chicago Symphony perform for me alone in my living room! And perhaps someday I shall, once I figure out how to do so without dipping into capital.

The Great Apartment Hunt

(2012)

I SPENT A GOOD PART OF THE LAST THREE WEEKS helping a young friend look for an apartment, and the experience was revealing. Among other things, it made me realize that so much has changed in the city where I grew up and have lived most of my life that I scarcely know it. The experience also showed the crucial role of computers even in such fundamental activities as finding shelter. And it revealed, finally, the pressure that the current economy has put on the stock of available rental property.

My friend is in her early twenties, attractive and intelligent, a visual artist by training. She has been renting an apartment on the twenty-third floor of a building overlooking Lake Michigan with a spectacular view of Chicago's downtown skyscrapers. Views, though, even magnificent ones, will take a person just so far. She has felt isolated in this apartment, and longed to live in a livelier neighborhood among her contemporaries.

Her demands were straightforward enough: She was looking for a one- or two-bedroom apartment, with hardwood floors, a secure parking space, a safe neighborhood, and decent light. Central air-conditioning and an in-unit washer and dryer would be nice, but not absolutely essential. She had between $1,200 and $1,500 a month to spend on rent, and five weeks in which to find a place.

Her first choice of neighborhood was one located in the north central part of the city called Wicker Park/Bucktown. I knew Wicker Park but had not been there for many years. My father's place of business, a one-floor factory manufacturing costume jewelry, was located in Wicker Park when I worked for him as a boy. The neighborhood then was drab and ethnically dominated by Poles. The novelist Nelson Algren, who was militantly unfashionable, lived there.

Were Algren alive he would be as repulsed by his old neighborhood as I was amazed by it. Wicker Park today is filled with galleries, vegan and other restaurants, yoga centers, bike and clothing shops, and no one walking its streets seems to be above 30. Much of the housing on its side streets has been handsomely rehabbed. A not uncommon sight as one drives through the neighborhood is that of a young mother in spandex jogging behind a stroller containing her infant child or a man out walking his two pugs. At my age, I felt in this neighborhood like a visitor from another country, if not another planet.

One of the first things my friend and I learned is that there is not a great stock of rental property available. This is owing to the fact that relatively successful people in their late twenties and early thirties are not moving out of their rented apartments to buy condominiums and houses, as they normally would, because they feel that the drop in real-estate prices has not yet bottomed out. My friend, whose own career is just beginning, had no wish to buy an apartment, for she wanted the freedom of movement that renting allows. The problem was there was not that much to choose from.

As once one went to the classified section of one's newspaper to look for an apartment, today one goes to Craigslist or other real-estate websites. Along with descriptions of the apartments up for rent, there one often finds wildly deceptive photographs, which make rooms look larger, things generally brighter and newer. Telephone calls help to clear some of this up. The second bedroom of an oddly inexpensive two-bedroom apartment I inquired about was 7′ x 10′—in other words, the late Wilt Chamberlain could not have lain down in it.

We saw six or seven apartments. Some were preposterously narrow, some had wretched and not easily altered paint jobs, a few had spooky landlords: One of these that we encountered was a powerlifter with a German accent who wore his black cap backwards and patent-leather slippers. We found a few excellent apartments, but in shaky neighborhoods. An elegant apartment in Logan Square, a neighborhood to the west of Wicker Park/Bucktown, met my friend's every criterion and had a lovely view off its fourth-floor balcony. But it was located in a neighborhood in which walking around seemed risky. (The reigning fear in Chicago at present is of youth gangs, black and Puerto Rican gangs chiefly. "The nice thing about Jews," a witty acquaintance of mine remarked, "is that they don't form gangs until they get out of law school.") The rental agent's emphasis on the excellent security in the building only made things seem more frightening.

On her own, my friend found an apartment on the edge of Bucktown, one meeting her desiderata and within her price range. Out of her front-room windows her view is of one-story factories; from her ample patio and back porch, the leafy tranquility of a neighborhood on the rise prevails. As she showed me around the place, I thought it was nice to be rich but even better to be young.

Weepers Keepers

(2013)

A N OLD JOURNALISTIC AXIOM HOLDS, "If it bleeds, it leads." This means that stories of violence—of murder and arson, tornadoes and hurricanes, floods and carnage—always get primary attention in newspapers and on radio and television news. They still do, but coming up fast on the outside, especially on television news, are stories of deep personal sadness. So regular a feature of nightly television news has the spectacle of heartbroken people become that a new axiom is needed: "If it weeps, it keeps."

I have in mind those stories that cause people, in response to the coarse questioning of journalists, to break down in tears. I saw one the other night about a couple who were in the advanced stages of adopting a Russian child when Vladimir Putin decided to outlaw American adoption of Russian orphans. Pictures were shown of the couple playing with the child during visits to Russia. The story ended with the journalist asking the husband how he felt about this setback. He answered that Putin's edict would cause great distress for many orphans, tears streaming down his face as his voice broke.

"What was on your mind when this disaster occurred?" "Did you ever think you would be unemployed this long?" "How do you feel about your horrendous luck?" These seem to be among the most frequently asked questions in television journalism. Inspired by the soppy success of Barbara Walters and Oprah Winfrey, television news shows, local and national, now go directly not for the jugular but for the tear ducts.

"How do you feel, knowing that the bank has foreclosed on your mortgage on the house that your grandfather built when he arrived here from Poland 75 years ago?"

"What were your first thoughts when you saw the tornado was headed straight for your home with your 3-year-old twin sons in it?"

"When you learned that your 14-year-old daughter, an honor student, was killed in the crossfire between gangs, what went through your mind?"

Two questions of my own: Why do the people on whom all this sadness has been visited agree to talk to jerks with microphones in their hands and cameramen in tow? Second, Where do television stations find journalists vulgar enough to ask such questions?

Journalists, to be sure, have never been known for their sensitivity. In *A Child of the Century*, his autobiography, Ben Hecht recounts that his first job in Chicago journalism was to get photographs of recently deceased people to run with their obituaries. One family, valuing its privacy, refused to speak to him. So Hecht climbed up to the roof of their house, clogged their chimney, and when the house filled with smoke, causing the family to evacuate it, ran in to steal a portrait of the deceased from its place over the mantle.

In the 1980s, the *New York Times Magazine* ran a weekly column about the psychological problems of contemporary men. Contributors to the column told of complicated relationships with their fathers, or with their children, or of experiences in which they had to abandon the standard responses of traditional masculinity. Among editors at the magazine, the column was known as "Wimps."

I shouldn't be surprised to learn that, at the planning sessions of current television news shows, the question arises daily of what stories are lined up in which people break into tears. Easy to imagine a scene where the local news anchor asks the managing editor what weepies he has scheduled for tonight's six o'clock news. "We've a choice of three," the editor tells him. "We've got a woman whose uninsured house burned down, the widow of a recently shot cop, and a kid whose puppy was run over by a fire engine." The anchorman pauses, then says: "Let's go with the cop's widow and end with the kid and his dead puppy. Animal stories are always good to close on."

Why have these insensitive, indelicate-because-altogether-too-personal questions asked of people who have undergone loss become a staple of television news? Is having the victims of tragedy break down on television supposed to make the rest of us feel good by comparison? (There but for the grace of God . . .) Are we supposed to feel bucked up for not having our own houses blown away or flooded out, or for having managed our personal finances more carefully than those now out of work and in danger of losing their homes through foreclosure, or for not having lost people we love to acts of arbitrary violence?

Far from feeling lucky, or elated, or in any way superior, the effect on me of watching people brought to tears on television is much simpler. It confirms me in my belief in the low-grade cynicism and irretrievably bad taste of television journalism.

Audio-Dismal Aids

(2013)

A YEAR OR SO AGO, I took part in a conference in Mexico for which I, along with several other intellectuals, academics, and writers, was paid an excellent fee to talk for 10 minutes. The proceedings took place over three days. They were held in a movie theater and were well attended. I was distinguished at this conference, near as I could tell, in being the only one who did not avail himself of audiovisual aids. The reason I didn't is that I don't have any; nor have I any wish to possess any. I am a word man, a writer, a mere scribbler, and in me what you read or hear—not see—is what you get.

The conference generally was high-tech, if that word is still in vogue. Each speaker was introduced with a light show of sorts, with musical accompaniment, and stood behind a series of boxes that were raised at the end of a dramatic-sounding introduction delivered in Spanish. I remember feeling foolish when all these pyrotechnics were over, and there I stood. I felt like the Jewish woman who used to shop at the same Greek greengrocer's I did who, when her turn came, used to say, "You got me now."

Of those talks—I suppose they are more precisely regarded as presentations—I did attend, I recall how unimpressive the visual portions seemed. A speaker mentions Einstein, and up on a big screen is a picture of the old boy, hair disheveled, in a sweatshirt, the standard shot. ("Yo, Al, what's sha-kin'?") Another speaker mentions the universe and—*click*—there is a wash of stars and planets on the screen.

Another man, with the aid of his PowerPoint, enumerated six kinds of betrayal in relationships, all of which left my mind as soon as he clicked new information onto his screen.

But the talk that did stay in my mind was that of an evolutionary psychologist who compared the human brain to a smartphone. When we consider man, he began (*click*, on the screen appeared a human skull in profile), and his brain (*click*—lo, a brain appeared inside the skull), we come to see that the human mind is like a smartphone (*click*—picture of a smartphone). The brain itself, he continued, is in many ways like a smartphone (*click*—apps show up where the brain was). We have, for example, an app for morality (*click*—app that says "morality"), and another app for self-preservation (*click*—self-preservation app), and so on, app added after app, *click, click, click.*

One might say that is brilliant, except that it is stupid. The human brain isn't in the least like a smartphone. A smartphone doesn't have courage, isn't capable of evil, knows nothing of altruism, cannot innovate or create, and of that great human capacity for wondering and mental wanderings called consciousness, it is completely void. It can send a text and play chess with you but knows nothing about loyalty and mental wanderings, love and principle.

All that is interesting about the human brain, in other words, you aren't going to find on any smartphone, not now or in the future. But up there on that big screen, with the speaker clicking and app-ing away, for a moment or two it seemed an interesting connection. The human brain, the smartphone—yeah, baby, it all seemed to make sense—except that it doesn't.

During this presentation it occurred to me that audiovisual aids, far from being an advance in pedagogy, may well be nothing more than another form of dumbing down. One of the reigning clichés in pedagogy for some while now has been that current generations are visual-minded; they cerebrate not through words but pictures. So, the argument runs, it makes sense to appeal to them visually. Some learning can doubtless be accomplished visually. But that it can doesn't necessarily mean that the visual is the best way to accomplish it. The visual has its limits, and they may be more extreme than devotees of the audiovisual know.

Many years ago I was at another conference, where Irving Kristol was one of the speakers. He spoke sitting down. Behind him happened to be a large screen. The man who introduced him joked that Irving was here today with his usual full panoply of audiovisual aids. Everyone in the room laughed.

The joke was that Irving Kristol was the last man in the world to require audiovisual aids. He didn't even require a note. He set out his argument with lucidity, wit, and undramatic but genuine force. What made a talk by Irving Kristol impressive was that when he spoke you saw a man thinking. The sight of a man or woman of high intelligence in the act of thinking—there can be no more compelling audiovisual aid.

Go Google Yourself

(2013)

I WAS NOT LONG AGO INTRODUCED before giving a talk by a woman who, to authenticate my importance, said that she had Googled my name and found more than twelve million results. She didn't, thank goodness, go on to say what some of these results were. If she had, she might have mentioned that a few years ago I was, in the blog of a minor academic, "Blowhard of the Month." More recently I have been a "wuss," an "old pouf," and a "homophobe." (An old pouf *and* a homophobe? On the Internet, the law of contradictions, like many other laws, has long ago been abrogated.) Had she checked more closely under Amazon.com she would have discovered that some of the books I've written have been deemed "mediocre," "deeply biased," and (a favorite) "a waste of paper."

"To write a book," said Stendhal, "is to risk being shot at in public." I used to compare having a book out in the world to walking down a deserted street, when suddenly a window opens and from behind a curtain someone yells, "Fool." Twenty or so steps farther a second window opens and out of it another person shouts, "Fraud." Not too much farther on, yet another window opens, and someone screams, "Hey, Emperor. Forget your trousers?"

This was in olden days, BI, or Before the Internet. With the advent of the Internet, the feeling of having a new book in the world is more like driving a buckboard and sighting, on the rim of the hill in the near distance, an endless lineup of Apaches, armed not with bows and arrows but computers and smartphones. On the Internet anyone can say anything without need of argument or authentication. A reader of one of my books gave it the lowest possible rating on Amazon.com even though he allowed he had never read it, but he agreed with another reviewer who thought the book "disappointing and annoying." Better this, though, than to be called, as I recently have, a "hack" and a "bigot."

"The Internet," Molly Haskell wrote, "is democracy's revenge on democracy." I take Ms. Haskell to have meant that there are places where democracy has no place, and in those places where it puts forth its snouty nose, disarray is likely to follow. Fifty million Frenchmen, to reverse an old cliché, are frequently wrong. Does this sound elitist? If so, that is only because it adamantly is. Many are the things on which one opinion is not as good as another, and culture is high among them.

The Internet gives writers too much information about reactions to their own work. Over the past 40 years, I have been reviewed perhaps 2,000 times. I have been much more praised—sometimes lavishly, unconvincingly so—than attacked. Some of the attacks are perfectly understandable, due as they are to fundamental disagreements about literature, politics, the way people ought to live. In literary criticism, injustice isn't all that hard to take. As H. L. Mencken noted, only true justice stings.

I have even forgotten the names of some of the professional reviewers who have attacked my books. This suggests that I do not suffer from Irish Alzheimer's, a condition, a friend named Pat Hickey tells me, in which one forgets everything but one's grudges. But the off-the-cuff remark from someone without any intellectual pretensions can hurt more. Because of this, when in my local library I never look at copies of my books, lest I pick one up and find something insulting written in the margins.

The problem in Googling oneself—"Googling oneself," the act sounds vaguely obscene—is that a writer does so in the hope of finding himself extravagantly praised from unexpected quarters. Or he hopes to find that his slowly dying book, ranked 682,567th on Amazon.com on Tuesday, has leaped forward and is ranked 9th on Wednesday because adopted by the entire public school system of Calcutta.

Not everything a writer finds about himself on Google is a kick in the pants, a stick in the eye. On occasion a hitherto unknown blogger turns up showing not only appreciation but genuine understanding of what he is trying to do. Or he might find others rising to his defense after he's been unjustly slammed.

Yet for writers, who are by nature fantasts, Google functions as a reality instructor. In its devastating randomness it reminds them of what the world thinks of them. "Every time I think I am famous," the composer Virgil Thomson once said, "I have only to go out into the world." For writers, this might be altered to read, "Every time I think I am admired, I just Google myself."

Pretensions à la Carte

(2013)

F IFTY OR SO YARDS from the apartment building in which I live a new restaurant has recently opened called Found Kitchen and Social House. It's doing land-office business: Lines of people awaiting tables gather in the foyer, its bar stools are perpetually filled, hustling valet car-parkers are kept on the run. The food, I'm told, is quite good. I have no plans for going there—ever.

All I remember of its menu, placed in the window during its opening days, is an appetizer of arugula and white beans and a main course of chicken-liver mousse with bacon marmalade and toast. Looking in from outside, I could see a number of tables, chairs, and couches set up among large plants and globes, giving the impression of a vast living room. (The furnishings were all found, hence the name of the restaurant.) "This space is really a personal expression of my full evolution," declares the owner, Amy Morton, a woman of 50, long in the restaurant business. A friend who recently dined there told me that the waiters, arriving at one's table, ask, "May we feed you?"

Pretension has become an inescapable part of contemporary dining. Some of this pretension entails phony familiarity. Increasingly young waiters and waitresses—now known as "servers"—address customers as "guys." The reason they fall back on "guys" is that they are unsure how to address female customers. "Ladies" these days, in the rigid etiquette of political correctness, could be taken as an insult, and the neutral "guys" is a way around that.

After reciting the day's specials, these waiters and waitresses frequently tell you their first names. "I'm Kimmie [or I'm Tyler], and I'll be your server." Hope I don't seem sniffy, but I should prefer not to know their first names. I wonder if Kimmie and Tyler know that the origin of filling customers in on their first names comes from the sexist-to-the-highest-power Playboy Clubs, where bunnily dressed girls, before taking drink orders, announced: "Hi. I'm Carol, and I'll be your bunny this evening."

The pretension to democracy—that is, the notion that we are all equal—follows naturally from the phony familiarity. Someone orders the veal limone, and Kimmie says, "Oh, that's my favorite." Another person orders the mushroom-barley soup and a Caesar salad, and Tyler replies, "You ordered very intelligently." I am glad that my mother, who was something of a *grande dame*, is not around today, for she would have been utterly mystified by Kimmie and Tyler. Why, she would have asked, should we possibly be interested in knowing Kimmie's favorite dish? And how, she might have inquired, one eyebrow raised, is Tyler in a position to judge the intelligence of my order? And just who are these guys to whom they refer?

Young men and women have for a long while now taken up waiting as a stopgap until they find work in their chosen fields. Many of them are would-be artists, lots of them actors. In Los Angeles, a friend tells me, when someone announces he or she is an actor, the response is, "Really? At what restaurant?"

The job of professional waiter is all but gone. Often it was filled by immigrants who had no other training, or middle-aged women who could find no other work. I sometimes have lunch at a nearby Greek restaurant where the same middle-aged women have been working for decades. They do not tell me their names or their favorite dishes or that I have ordered very intelligently. Nor do they come to my table seven or eight times to ask if everything is okay. Friendly though they are, they know that I have come to the restaurant to eat, and not to establish a relationship. I make it a habit to over-tip them.

Kimmie and Tyler could learn a thing or two from these women. They would, in fact, do well to spend a few weeks at Jewish delicatessen waiters' school, if only such an institution existed. There they might meet up with the waiter who, when asked by two genteel women to see the sommelier, replied, "Ladies, if it's not on the menu, we ain't got it." Or the waiter who told a customer that, if he wanted the cabbage soup, he should've ordered the borscht. Or the waiter who, in response to a question about how the restaurant prepares its chicken, answered, "First thing is, we tell it it's going to die."

A shame that Found Kitchen and Social House can't avail itself of one of these crusty old Jewish waiters as its maitre d'. He'd give the joint the tone it much needs.

The Greatest Story Never Read

(2012)

I HAVE NEVER READ THE BIBLE. When I was a small child, my father read portions of a child's Bible to me. I recall the story of the Garden of Eden, of Abraham being asked to sacrifice his son Isaac, of Jacob outwitting his brother Esau for his father's blessing, of Joseph's brothers mauling him and leaving him for dead, of David with his slingshot defeating Goliath, of Solomon's decision about the two women disputing possession of a child. At 13, a bar-mitzvah boy, I read a few paragraphs of the Bible, my Torah portion, to the northside Chicago synagogue congregation of Ner Tamid. In later years, I read bits of the Bible, when studying *Paradise Lost* or reading Thomas Mann's *Joseph and His Brothers*. But that is as far as it went.

Until six or seven weeks ago, when I determined to read the Bible straight through, which I am now doing. The dreariness of the so-called New Atheists—Richard Dawkins, Sam Harris, Daniel Dennett, the late Christopher Hitchens—may have been an unconscious motive for my doing so. The Bible is advertised as the greatest story ever told, and, as a literary man, I would be foolish to depart the planet without having read it straight through. Is the Bible the greatest story ever told? I'll let you know when I get to the end at page 1130; I am currently only at 251. Miles to go, as the poet said, before I sleep.

I generally read three chapters a day, with my breakfast, and just this morning I have come to "The Book of Judges." As a literary snob, I am of course reading the Bible in the King James Version. Marvelous stuff, though there is a small price to pay. What one gains in lilting rhythm and elegant vocabulary, one sometimes loses in repetition. A brief example from "The Book of Joshua," where one reads: ". . . Joshua waxed old and stricken with age. . . . And Joshua called for all Israel, and for their elders, and for their heads, and for their judges, and for their officers, and said unto to them, I am old and stricken with age."

Longueurs there are in plenty. One must gird one's loins and keep one's mind on the job when the begats begin, or when the land of Canaan is divided among the 12 tribes of Israel, each portion of land specified in a thicket of proper names. Preparation of animals for sacrifice is set out in detail of a kind likely to drain the color from a vegan's cheek.

Violence can be swift and unremitting. Should Israel not obey the Lord in all his commandments, "they shall be snares and traps unto you, and scourges in your sides, and thorns in your eyes, until ye perish off this good land which the Lord your God has given you." The God of the Old Testament does not, unlike American democracy, offer much in the way of second chances.

When encouraging people to read the great but formidably long books—Gibbon's *Decline and Fall of the Roman Empire*, Proust's *In Search of Lost Time*—I tell them they have to read them religiously, by which I mean in small portions, but relentlessly, showing up at the same time every day for the job.

Have I been reading the Bible religiously in the word's more fundamental sense? Although I intend to read through both the Old and New Testaments, in the Old Testament I can, as the kids used to say, identify; these are my people being written about. I feel a small but real satisfaction when I get through my morning's Bible reading, as if I have done the right thing. Thus far I cannot say that I have felt that special frisson that is associated with religious emotion.

As someone more and more impressed with the mysteries of life, and less and less impressed with science and human explanations of those mysteries, I find a certain comfort in reading the Bible, with its miracles, feats of endurance, and obedience to a higher power. Reading my daily portion, I like to think that I have not given up on God. More important, while reading it, I hope that God has not given up on me.

Toting a Dumb Phone

(2013)

ELL PHONES TODAY IN AMERICA are of course endemic, if not epidemic. On one of the thoroughfares in the youthful neighborhood in which I live, I can sometimes walk an entire block without passing anyone not on or gazing down at or thumb-pumping his or her cell phone. Everyone has seen three or four people sitting at a restaurant table, each one of them on a cell phone. Or a young couple who should be looking longingly into each other's eyes looking instead into their cell phones. Just yesterday a homeless man, in front of the Whole Foods in our neighborhood, his cup extended for change in one hand, was talking loudly into the cell phone held in his other hand. Contemporary America might have a homelessness but certainly not a phonelessness problem.

The homeless man's cell phone was not a smartphone, but a flip phone, rather, I am a touch nervous to confess, like my own. My nervousness derives from my being so out of date as still to be toting around a flip, or what I have taken to calling a dumb, phone. Taking out a flip phone in some circles is tantamount to carrying an ear trumpet—it's almost quaint.

Weeks go by in which I never use my dumb phone. Still, I don't often leave the house without it. I carry it around in case some strange emergency should occur in which I would need a phone: I get a flat tire in a distant part of town, I fall and injure myself, I lose my wallet. The one thing I don't have to worry about is thugs mugging me in order to steal my phone, at least not when they notice it isn't a smartphone.

I bought my first cell phone roughly 20 years ago. The point of having the cell phone was security. I kept the cell phone, on which I paid a monthly fee of $36, or roughly $400 a year. Then someone told me that I need pay only $25 a quarter if I went into a nearby AT&T shop and "refilled" my phone every three months, at $25 a shot. At $100 a year, I acquired a second dumb phone—one for me, one for my wife. But the bargain isn't what is at stake.

The truth is that I am wary of having a smartphone. I already feel sufficiently enslaved by computers and digital culture. I can no longer write at more than a few paragraphs' length except on my computer. I must check my email 20 times a day, including first thing in the morning. I do not myself tweet, but I read the tweets of a few friends and also their Facebook pages. I spend roughly 40 minutes early in the day getting my (mostly unsatisfactory) news online. My computer pings and I rush over to learn the *Wall Street Journal* has discovered another hedge-fund guy guilty of insider trading, or three bombs have gone off in downtown Islamabad, news that could have waited. Digital life, with its promise of keeping one up to the moment, is very jumpy—and generally unsatisfactory.

So why, then, do I need to carry a computer around with me, for smartphones have of course become portable computers. Do I require Google in my pocket, a permanent aid to memory, so I can check something as important as who pitched the fifth game of the 1945 World Series? Do I really need apps that will give me stock-market quotations, or let me play video games, or provide Baroque string quartets while I am in the bathroom? I have no need for these artificial distractions.

The mind, the rabbis tell us, is a great wanderer. In its wanderings it often comes upon memories of dear but now dead friends, interesting connections between dissimilar notions, random observations, ideas for stories and essays. No app exists to organize the wandering mind, thank goodness.

Think I'll stay with my dumb phone.

Nostalgia Organized

(2013)

A REUNION MARKING THE HUNDREDTH ANNIVERSARY of the founding of my high school—Nicholas Senn, on the north-side of Chicago—is to be held this month, and I shall not be attending it. I am one of those people who had a good run in high school. A minor athlete, a member of most of the school's better clubs, a boy who went out with pretty and pleasant girls, I had mastered the arts of conformity, and in high school they brought me much happiness. So much so that I sometimes think I may have peaked around the age of 17, and it's been slowly but relentlessly downhill since.

After some hesitation, I went to my high school class's fiftieth reunion, which did not do much for me. I did, though, make one notable discovery: that some of the people who as kids were on the periphery of high school social life went on to have interesting lives as painters, drama teachers, entrepreneurs, while the most popular kids in the class tended to take up ordinary jobs, move out to okay Chicago suburbs, and hold unexceptional views.

Members of the class were invited to send in a paragraph about their lives for our reunion book. Most people responded in an earnest way, expressing gratitude for their good luck in life, or remarking on how much they were enjoying their retirement, or mentioning their eagerness to see old classmates. One woman announced that, after marriage and children now grown up, she has been spending the second half of her life in a lesbian partnership. A more standard entry, though, might report that the classmate and her husband "enjoy golf, bridge, photography, and traveling," and end, "We have seven lovely grandchildren, and next year we're planning a trip to Indonesia."

My entry read: "I've written a few books. For thirty years I taught in the English Department at Northwestern University, and remain on the football team coaching staff there, working exclusively with Jewish wide receivers, which leaves me lots of free time for my writing. I've no complaints at present, but am confident something will turn up soon."

An Italian restaurant on the outskirts of the Loop was the scene of our fiftieth high-school class reunion. When I walked into the restaurant, I immediately hit a wall of disorientation. Just who were all these fat bald guys, these white-haired women? Did I actually once have rivalrous feelings toward some of these paunchy men, harbor adolescent fantasies about some of these grandmotherly women?

Roughly 400 attended the reunion. Dance music from our high school days blared. A few people stood at a microphone to utter cliché-laden remarks. Nobody noted what a fortunate generation we were. Born in the late 1930s, we missed the Depression, and the men among us, though subject to the draft, did not have to go off to any wars, being too young for Korea and too old for Vietnam. We lived through decades of unbroken prosperity in the most powerful and culturally interesting nation in the world. We have strong memories of American life before the center ceased to hold, which has given some of us a touch of perspective on the dizzying changes that technology and our radically altered social mores have wrought.

At such functions one can either table hop or let others hop to one's own table. I chose the latter. A few old friends, some from grammar-school days, came up to say hello, briefly filling me in on their lives over the past half-century, then wafted off, probably never to be met again in this life. Two women I much liked when they were girls, both named Roberta (shortened, in the fashion of the day, to Bobby), came up to tell me that they enjoyed my books of short stories. I was pleased to see how still recognizably themselves they looked, how little time seemed to lay a glove on them. In the crowded, noisy room, I tried to identify faces, to rediscover the boys and girls in the now often overly ripened faces of people milling about. At evening's end, I returned home with a melancholy sense of disappointment.

"The future," noted Paul Valéry, "isn't what it used to be." Neither, one might add, is the past. I enjoy a warm bath of nostalgia as much as the next person. But I prefer my nostalgia spontaneous, not organized and crudely sentimentalized, which is what school reunions tend to do to it. The sociologist Robert Nisbet called nostalgia "the rust of memory," and so it often is. School reunions, though, tend to sand down and shellac memory, which is even worse.

I may one day change my mind about all this and decide to attend my hundred-and-fiftieth high-school reunion, but between now and then, thank you all the same, no further reunions for me.

A Condition in Need of a Label

(2013)

THE NOBEL PRIZE IN MEDICINE has already been given for this year, but I should like to get a jump on next year's prize by describing and naming a mental condition from which untold millions suffer. The condition is not anything so devastating as dementia. Most people who have it manage to work around it.

For the most part the condition attacks people in their fifties and beyond, though the young can acquire it in an early onset version. Consider a single, if far from singular, case—mine. I encounter with mildly irritating regularity the problem of forgetting names, both common and obscure. In sports, the Mets' catcher Gary Carter's is a name I not long ago forgot. The other day I could not call up the name Eric Blore, the comic character actor in lots of Fred Astaire movies. From culture I lost the name Reynaldo Hahn, the composer who was a friend and some say lover of Marcel Proust. With a few clues, of course, one can locate all these names on Google.

Less bearable is forgetting names of acquaintances, recent and old. I could not remember the name of the girl, the tallest in my grammar school class, so shy when young, who turned out to be an extraordinarily sweet character (Doris Weisbrod). People at the university at which I taught for 30 years, both administrators and fellow teachers, their names—poof!—have disappeared from my mental Rolodex, gone, I assume, where notes of music go.

I can list movies—*Match Point, The Odessa File, The Freshman*—in which I can name the principal actor but cannot recall a shred of the plot. Sometimes, in a nice reversal, I remember a fair amount of the plot of a movie but cannot come up with its title. I'll sit down to a movie shown on television, or on a DVD, and halfway through realize that I've seen it before. More worrisome, though, is when watching a movie with my wife, who is my contemporary and the person with whom I have watched every movie I've seen over the past 40 years, one or the other of us is certain we have seen this movie before and the other certain that we have not.

I do not misplace my glasses, nor do I lose my keys and wallet. Yet every so often I will unconsciously break with decades-long routine and neglect to place one or the other in the pocket in which I traditionally place it. A brief moment of panic results when I put my hand in my left-hand pocket and find my wallet isn't there, relieved a nanosecond later to discover it's in my right-hand pocket. Whew!

I go to the grocery store to pick up four items. Four measly items, I decide, do not require a shopping list. I arrive at the store, and I cannot remember the fourth item. Cottage cheese? Pretzels? Possibly sparkling water? I buy them all. When I return home the item I couldn't remember turns out to have been bananas.

Then there is the problem of not being able to recall the things I forgot earlier in the day and hoped to remember or look up later. These are usually bits—notions, conceits, ideas—that seemed dazzling when they occurred to me on the edge of sleep or in the shower or in my car, yet they depart my mind quite as mysteriously as, unbidden, they arrived.

None of this stops me from functioning. I continue to work, pay taxes, lunch with friends, maintain family life, get riled up about politics, harbor preposterous fantasies. Still, why have so many small, usually quite unimportant items slipped from memory? Why do I so often find myself doing once-routine things ass backwards: putting my cell phone in my night-table, a necktie in my shirt drawer, a salt-shaker in the refrigerator.

The cause of this condition is unclear. As with all conditions with no known causes, I suspect there is no cure. A label for it, though, would be helpful. Attaching a label to a mental condition can be, if not necessarily explanatory, highly comforting. Without such labels the Diagnostic and Statistical Manual of Mental Disorders would be out of business. The condition I have been describing—forgetting mostly unimportant things, falling out of once-secure routines—badly needs a label, and I have decided to call it Assbacker's.

Assbacker's—it does have a nice lilt to it, does it not? When next I cannot recall the name of the manager of the Tampa Bay Rays, or the director of *The Postman Always Rings Twice*, or two names of the French composers known as *Les Six*, I shall say to myself: "Not to worry, kiddo. It's only Assbacker's. It's not fatal. Merely mortal."

Hold the Gluten

(2014)

MEN, IT IS SAID, do not like to go to doctors. Clearly I qualify here. I have long considered myself a Christian Scientist, minus the Christian part. A realist in my taste in fiction, I am a fantasist in my views about physiology. I prefer, that is, to pretend that I do not have such organs as a liver, spleen, and kidneys, and like to think of the duodenum as a doo-wop group from the late 1950s.

My problem with doctors is that when I go to them, they tend to find unpleasant things wrong with me, but not always the right things. They send me for tests, which fairly often prove inconclusive. A few years ago my then-gastroenterologist informed me that blood tests revealed that I had celiac disease, a condition that damages the lining of the small intestines and prevents one from absorbing food properly. He suggested I go on a gluten-free diet. At the time I was suffering from a skin-blistering problem called—and best pronounced in a W. C. Fields accent—bullous pemphigoid, which was all the medical trouble I could handle at the moment, and so I ignored his advice about the diet. Nothing untoward happened, and six months later I called him to tell him so. "The analysis wasn't really definitive," he said. "Is that so?" I answered, and made a mental note to leave him, which I did.

Three or so years later, I encountered stomach trouble. Along with all the usual inconveniences stomach problems bring, I had lost seven or eight pounds, which I, already so lithe and dazzlingly beautiful, could not afford to lose. I went to my primary physician, who suggested I go on a fat-free diet. On a fat-free diet I couldn't seem to regain the lost pounds. Only then did it occur to me that I might after all possibly have celiac disease, long delayed, and so I put myself on a gluten-free diet, which seems to be working.

Gluten, Wikipedia informs me, is "a protein composite found in foods processed from wheat and related grain species, including barley and rye." Gluten-free has in recent years become a fad diet. Middle-class supermarkets now stock much gluten-free food. Some have entire shelves devoted to it, and one can easily enough acquire gluten-free breads, crackers, pasta, and even (flourless) cakes and cookies.

Being on a gluten-free diet has not been all that difficult, except for eating in restaurants. I meet weekly with three friends from high-school days at a deli in Chicago called The Bagel, which has never heard of cholesterol let alone gluten, and there I can no longer order sandwiches or chicken soup with matzo balls, kreplach, or noodles, which is a deprivation. I don't much mind taking a pass on cakes, pies, danish, and pastries, and liken my situation here to that of a reformed alcoholic I knew who told me that after 40 years of serious drinking he gave up alcohol because he felt he had had his share.

After so many years of eating whatever I wanted, suddenly being diet-conscious feels strange. I used to mock, at least in my mind, health-food faddists. They seem, for one thing, so unhealthy-looking. I go into a health-food store in my neighborhood called J. D. Mills, run by an east Indian gentleman named Mr. Prakash, who drives a sleek gray Mercedes sedan. I go there to buy salted almonds and dried apricots. "Non-organic," I always instruct Mr. Prakash. The one small smile I've ever got from him was when I recently whispered to him that "that organic stuff will kill you."

I never used to read labels on packaged food or cans, though now I tend to do so. Labeling on food is clearly going to become more and more prevalent. I note that a government regulation requires vending-machine operators to label the number of calories in the various snacks in their machines. Liberals, I have heard it said, don't care what we do so long as it is mandatory.

The other night I was watching on television the movie *You've Got Mail* and in one of its final scenes noticed that Tom Hanks is eating a pretzel. I would not have noted this before I went gluten-free. This made me wonder if the day will come when movies, along with being graded X, R, PG-13, and the rest, will also have to announce that they contain scenes with gluten.

In the best of all possible worlds, the one that Dr. Pangloss inhabits, one will eat exactly as one pleases with no ill effects. Until that day arrives, though, I shall stick to my gluten-free diet, hoping it will temporarily ward off the *angelo di morte* and keep me out of the offices inhabited by those all too imperfect artists who go by the name of physician.

The Reluctant Bibliophile

(2014)

I'M PLEASED TO REPORT that I've just returned from the Evanston Public Library saleroom empty-handed. The saleroom is off the main lobby and contains used books, donated to the library, which sell for a mere fifty cents. Not all the books in the saleroom are serious—junky novels predominate—but a fair number of superior books show up. The library is less than a block from my apartment. When passing it, I find it difficult not to step inside to check the saleroom for a book I don't need but nevertheless buy.

The reason I say I'm pleased to have returned empty-handed is that I already have enough unread books around my apartment, as the English say, to see me out. Old habits, though, die hard; and my habit of acquiring books doesn't seem to die at all. How can I not check the saleroom? I mean, fifty cents, for heaven's sake, and for some genuinely splendid books!

Before I mention some of them, I ought to make clear that it feels slightly odd, not to say antiquated, to be buying books nowadays. Collecting books in the age of the Kindle, the iPad, and the smartphone—I have a friend who read *War and Peace* on his smartphone—begins to feel a little like collecting buggy whips or anvils.

I love books, their feel, smell, design, but I do not require a large personal library. Twice, in fact, I have broken up my library, lest it take over the apartment. I told myself that for every new book I brought home I would get rid of one already in my possession. I haven't quite lived up to this rule. I do, though, continue to eliminate books that I've read and am fairly certain I shall not need to read, or even consult, again. I don't believe a book has any special value because I happen to have read it. I'm not, that is to say, in the least sentimental about books.

My rough guess is that I currently own 700 books. Among serious bibliophiles this is small beer. (When my friend Edward Shils died in 1995, he left a library in his Chicago apartment of 15,000 books, and had another 6,000 in his house in Cambridge in England.) I've kept 90 or so volumes from the Library of America, the books of my favorite writers (Gibbon, Tolstoy, Henry James, Proust, George Santayana, Max Beerbohm, Thomas Mann, and Hugh Trevor-Roper), and books on subjects in which I have a continuing interest (Greek history and philosophy, French literature, modern poetry up to 1960 or so), and the books of friends. Enough here, one would think, to keep a fellow busy.

Why, then, does a small marimba band begin playing softly in my heart when, at the Evanston Library saleroom, I see a paperback copy of J. P. Nettl's biography of Rosa Luxemburg? Why am I so pleased on another day to discover Isaac Bashevis Singer's *In My Father's Court*, which I read perhaps 30 years ago, and *The Rape of Tamar*, by my friend Dan Jacobson, which I've never read? Two volumes of Lewis Namier show up— irresistible. Ah, me, a clean hardcover copy of Eugène Fromentin's *Les Maîtres d'Autrefois*; I already own a copy of the book in English, but you can't have too many copies of a minor classic, I always say. (What do you always say?)

Am I likely to read the two thick Liberty Press volumes of Adam Smith's *An Inquiry into the Nature and Causes of the Wealth of Nations*? A good chance not, though I buy it all the same. What have we here: *The Collected Stories of Caroline Gordon*, the wife of Allen Tate, and the travel writings in paperback of Bruce Chatwin. Go for it, a small wicked voice within me cries out, and I do.

Clearly, I am a man with a problem. How else would you describe someone who has taken home from the Evanston Library saleroom at least five copies of H. W. Fowler's *Modern English Usage*, three of which

I've given away to people sensitive to language who have not hitherto heard of Fowler. These are books, I reason, that deserve a good home.

The remainder of my reading life should be devoted to filling in the gaps of the great books I've not yet read or rereading those I read too young and with too little understanding. Yet I continue to acquire new books. At what point does bibliophilia turn into bibliomania? I fear I may have reached it. So if you happen to see a mild-looking little man descending the steps of the Evanston Library, a copy of Tarn and Griffith's *Hellenistic Civilization* and of Michael Millgate's hefty biography of Thomas Hardy under his arm and a complacent smile on his face, proceed cautiously. He is probably not dangerous though undoubtedly mad.

Making a Spectacles of Myself

(2014)

O F LATE, THE LAST FOUR YEARS OR SO, I rarely go out for
long without being praised. I am praised not for my writing,
my perspicacity, my elegant bearing, my youthful good looks,
my extreme modesty, but for my eyeglasses. "Nice glasses," strangers say
to me. "Like your glasses," they say. "Love those glasses," is a refrain I hear
at least once a week. "Where did you get those glasses?" people wearing
glasses of their own often ask me. "Thank you for your kind words about
these glasses," I have taken to answering. "They are my best feature."

The frames of my glasses are round, large, heavy, and dappled with an
emphatic tortoiseshell. Although they are bifocals, I do not need them
full-time. I work at my computer without them. I don't need them to
watch television. I sometimes leave my apartment without them. Clearly,
though, when I do wear them they dominate my face. Were I to commit
a crime, they are probably the first thing that witnesses to it would recall
about me.

A few Sundays ago, I was walking in the neighborhood when a middle-aged woman, in tights and doing a power walk, paused to say, "Love
your glasses." I told her I much liked the glasses she was wearing. She told
me she has several pairs of glasses at home. "Glasses are jewelry for the
face," she said, and humped and pumped her way down the street.

Some glasses make one look forbidding. I think here of those rimless spectacles that suggest an older banker foreclosing on one's mortgage. Other glasses make one look owlish. As an older man, Cary Grant wore black-framed glasses that made him even more elegant. Senator Carl Levin of Michigan wears half-glasses low on the nose that do not work well with his sad comb-over.

When I grew up, wearing glasses of any kind was considered a serious detraction, a handicap of sorts. "Men seldom make passes," Dorothy Parker wrote, "at girls who wear glasses." Men who wore them were thought bookish, make that bookwormish, nerdy *avant la lettre*. "Foureyes" was the put-down term of choice used against those who did. As if to illustrate how much this has changed, For Eyes is today one of the nation's leading optical franchises. Naming a company after an insult— only in America.

I did not need to wear glasses until my mid-forties. I have not in the least minded wearing them thereafter. Thirty or forty years ago, many people still did mind. For those who could afford them, contact lenses were the first solution. The solution was not always a successful one. People who wore them seemed fairly regularly to lose a contact lens. I've seen professional basketball games stopped while players, down on their hands and knees, hunted for a teammate's lost contact lens. Contact lenses are more efficient today, and some people wear them purely for cosmetic reasons to change the color of their eyes, a touch that has always struck me as positively Persian Empire in its decadence.

Not many movie stars have worn glasses. Harold Lloyd, the silent-film star did; and so, too, does Woody Allen, the too-talky film star. No women regularly wore glasses in movies. A standard movie bit, though, had a female star playing a spinster, perhaps a librarian, until at the appropriate point in the story her glasses would come off, the bun at the back of her head would be loosed to release a luxuriant growth of hair, and— presto change-o—she turns into a sexpot.

Monocle-wearing men used to appear in English movies; Adolphe Menjou might have donned a monocle in a flick or two. Did Margaret Dumont use a lorgnette, glasses on a stem, in the Marx Brothers' *A Day at the Opera*? The University of Chicago philosophy teacher Allan

Bloom, who went in for lavish haberdashery, affected a pince-nez late in life, which even with his florid personality did not quite come off.

In the 1970s, I was on a cruise of the Greek Islands on which the political journalist I. F. Stone was a fellow passenger. Stone wore Coke-bottle-thick lenses in rimless glasses. Magooishly, he made his way among monuments and sculptures. At one point, in the museum at Olympia, I watched him inspect the detail of a dazzling Hermes statue from a distance of three feet through binoculars.

As for my own glasses, a friend who hadn't seen me for a few years remarked that they seemed to be getting bigger and bigger. Is it possible that eventually they will take over my face and then my personality, and I shall become little more than tortoiseshell on legs, which sounds like the perfect donnée for a story by Kafka? I haven't yet written it, but its working title is "The Man Who Made a Spectacles of Himself."

Portnoy's Children

(2013)

SUCCÈS DE SCANDALE if ever there was one, *Portnoy's Complaint*, Philip Roth's fourth book of fiction, will soon be 45 years old. At the center of the novel's scandalousness, which recounts the 33-year-old Alexander Portnoy's reporting to his psychoanalyst the emergence of his repressed desires growing up in a middle-class Jewish home, was its emphasis on masturbation, or "the secret vice," as the Victorian medical encyclopedias used to call it. The novel's last sentence, spoken by the analyst, Dr. Spielvogel, reads: "Now veee may perhaps to begin. Yes?"

Roth ends things there, and never takes up the character of Alexander Portnoy again. The author wrote several novels told through a character he named Nathan Zuckerman, and a series of others told by a character called David Kepesh, but he left Alexander Portnoy to wither and die on the analysand's couch. Isn't it, one wonders, time for a sequel? Roth has announced his retirement and so clearly isn't the man for the job. I don't claim to be that man, either, but I thought I might leave a few notes for anyone interested in taking up the task.

The sequel, which might be called *Portnoy's Children* or *Putting the Kid Back in Yid*, would begin after Alexander Portnoy's successful psychoanalysis has come to an end. The psychoanalysis is considered successful insofar as it has diminished his libido and deprived him of all powers of sexual fantasy. Portnoy gives up on chasing *shikses*, or gentile women, and soon marries a perfectly bourgeois Jewish woman named Lilly Spitzer. Before long, they have a son they name Eliot, a good student type—he will go on to Princeton and Harvard Law School—but with something a touch odd about him. Portnoy notices, for example, that his supply of Viagra is short, and he detects Eliot putting it in his milkshakes.

After five or so years, Portnoy realizes that in marrying Lilly he has really married his mother—the nightmarish, relentless nudge Sophie Portnoy—with a crippling standard of high maintenance added. He and Lilly undergo a bitter divorce in which Lilly wins custody of their son, whose affections for his father she alienates totally.

In the years ahead, Portnoy watches from the sidelines as Eliot, after departing Harvard Law School, launches a successful financial career and goes into New York politics, first as a crusading attorney general, then as governor. All comes tumbling down when Eliot, a married man, is caught availing himself of $2,000-an-hour prostitutes, for whose services he pays with a credit card. *Was he going for airline miles?* Portnoy wonders, as he recalls the boy's drinking those Viagra milkshakes.

Not long after his divorce, Portnoy remarries, this time to a less aggressive woman named Louise Weiner. She is pudgy, meek, and not particularly attractive. They, too, have a son together, named Anthony. Portnoy is determined not to lose the love of this boy, whose affection he sedulously cultivates. He coaches the kid's little league and hockey teams. He takes the boy along on camping trips. The kid strikes Portnoy as clever— not the good student his older brother was, but with street smarts and a good heart. So Portnoy is all the more shocked when he is called by the principal of his son's high school and learns that Anthony has been found to have obscene postcards in his locker. What is it with these children of his? Are the sins of the father being visited upon the sons?

Portnoy discovers he is not an ideal husband when his second wife begins a divorce action against him, charging sexual neglect. "I had no notion she was interested in sex," Portnoy tells his lawyer. As with his first wife, Louise wins custody of their son. Father and son drift apart, and this boy, too, becomes enthralled by politics, serving as a New York City councilman and later as a popular congressman.

Anthony is riding high when a sexual scandal his father does not quite understand—something to do with his sending photographs of his private parts over the Internet—brings him down. The humiliation ratio is added to by Anthony's long before having taken his mother's maiden name, and weiner jokes abound. Portnoy thinks to call his son to offer comfort, but then thinks otherwise.

The denouement of *Portnoy's Children* entails both of Portnoy's sons attempting comebacks after their disastrous scandals. Eliot is planning to start slowly on the road to rebuilding his career by running for New York comptroller; Anthony, a higher roller, runs for mayor of New York. Portnoy finds himself appalled by the effrontery, the sheer chutzpah, of his children. On Election Day, he votes against both his sons. On the last page of the novel, Alexander Portnoy, now 80 years old, goes back into psychoanalysis.

The Issue Issue

(2015)

I HAVE AN ISSUE WITH *ISSUE*—with the word, that is. It pops up everywhere, meaning everything and meaning nothing. One hears of a pitcher who has rotator-cuff issues, of a landlord who has issues with pets in his buildings, of a bill up before Congress that poses jurisdictional issues. A weather reporter informs me that dressing warmly in a snowstorm is the main issue. The issue over reinstating the draft is whether soldiers serving only two years can be of serious military use. Can a word having so many different meanings, capable of being plugged into so many various contexts, finally have any useful meaning whatsoever? That, you might say, is the issue, though if you did you, too, would be misusing the word.

I first became aware of the proper use of the word issue sometime in the late 1960s. I was a senior editor at *Encyclopaedia Britannica*, sitting in lengthy, often goofy meetings presided over by Mortimer Adler, who was redesigning—and not at all by the way destroying—the old *Britannica*, turning it from the world's best straightforward reference work into a Rube Goldberg device of monstrous complexity. Mortimer was many things—clown, tyrant, force of nature—but he could also chop logic finer than they chopped liver at the old Katz's Delicatessen on Second Avenue. In one of these meetings someone described an item up for discussion as an issue. Mortimer, his always-racing mind causing him to stammer, shot back: "That's not an is-is-issue. It's not even a qu-question. It's a problem. The difference is a problem calls for a solution, a question for an answer, and an issue, an issue is something in the fl-fl-flux of con-controversy. Got it?"

As the only useful thing I ever learned from Mortimer, I not only got it, but I have never forgot it. Being in the flux of controversy, an issue doesn't allow for an easily settled conclusion, even though one might have strong opinions about it. Whether the federal government should fund abortions for the poor is an issue, at least if one is not morally opposed to abortion. Whether there should be a Nobel Prize for the dubious science of economics is an issue. Whether the news can be presented over television in a bipartisan way and still gain high viewer ratings is an issue.

The crucial distinction is among question, problem, and issue. Whether Jay Cutler will start at quarterback next year for the Chicago Bears is a question. Whether the team can afford to cut him loose and forfeit the cost of his enormous salary is a problem. Whether they ought to keep him at all is an issue.

"'The question is,' said Alice, 'whether you can make words mean so many different things.'

"'The question is,' Humpty Dumpty said in a scornful tone, 'when I use a word it means just what I choose it to mean—neither more nor less.'"

The problem (not the question or the issue) is that, according to the Dumptian school of language, which just now is dominant in the world, fairly soon all words will mean everything, and no word will mean anything—at least fewer and fewer of them will mean anything with the precision required to get a purchase on reality. Let one word after another lose its meaning, its common usage, its precision and soon everyone becomes his own Tower of Babel.

Dictionaries, those cowardly institutions, prefer to describe the way people use words instead of setting out the core meaning of those words. Here and in England dictionaries increasingly define an *issue* as something that people are thinking or talking about—so that an issue becomes a hot topic, little more. People meanwhile pick up the new meanings of words with cheerful readiness. Something pleases them about saying that they have foot issues rather than trouble with their feet; issues somehow seem more elevated than troubles. A happy vagueness resides in the loose use of the word *issue*. Remarking that one has issues with one's children is much to be preferred to ranting about one's kids' unreasonableness, the result, doubtless, of one's having spoiled them in the first place. Better to have issues with children than to have, what is more likely, wretched children.

Need anyone but a proud pedant give a rat's rump about keeping in mind the distinction among a question, a problem, and an issue? The likelihood of convincing many people of the importance of doing so is less than that of the return of Prohibition and vaudeville on the same weekend. The only argument I can think to mount, apart from that of a taste for precision in language, is based on political correctness. Misuse the word *issue* and you are likely to offend members of a small but touchy minority group, some would call them an endangered species—I refer, of course, to the educated.

How I Learned to Love the Draft

(2015)

As the struggle with the Islamic State, or ISIS, grows more intense and the Obama administration's air-attack strategy—if the experts turn out to be correct—proves unavailing, the calls for boots on the ground in Syria and Iraq are likely to become more insistent. Despite the coalition of nations aligned against ISIS and other terrorist groups, no one doubts that any such boots will be preponderantly American. Our current volunteer military will fill those boots.

Which prompts a question: Should the burden of defending America be exclusively theirs? When one watches those heartbreaking segments on the national news of men and women returning from Middle Eastern wars with missing limbs, and reads accounts of their suffering from mental-health problems as a result of their experiences in battle, one feels an essential unfairness about current military arrangements. True, these men and women volunteered for battle, yet in a democracy it somehow feels wrong for a small segment of the population to be charged with the responsibility of defending the country in foreign wars.

The remedy for this fundamental unfairness is of course at hand, and it goes by the name of the draft.

The draft was legally halted in 1973, toward the close of the Vietnam War. The effect was to relieve citizens of having to fight their country's battles. A reinstated draft, or compulsory military service, would redistribute the burden of the responsibility for fighting wars, and engage the nation in military conflicts in a more immediate and democratic way.

The first effect of restoring the draft would be to make the American electorate generally more thoughtful about foreign policy. It's well and good to call for boots on the ground, but all of us might make a mental adjustment if some of those boots were to be filled by our own youthful children and grandchildren. A truly American military, inclusive of all social classes, might cause politicians and voters to be more selective in choosing which battles are worth fighting and at what expense. It would also have the significant effect of getting the majority of the country behind those wars in which we do engage.

The last war fought by America that had the enduring support of the nation was World War II. This was so in part because of the evil nature of the enemy. But the war was also vigorously supported because the troops who fought in it, owing to the draft, came from all social and economic classes. Everyone had a husband or brother or son or uncle or cousin in the war; everyone felt a stake in victory. People old enough to remember World War II remember the small flags with blue stars in the windows of people who had relatives fighting, and gold stars for families who had lost close relatives in the war.

The draft was still in effect for the Korean War, but public support was less, chiefly because the objective was far from clear and not very many troops were needed. During the early years of the Vietnam War, when the draft was still intact, a great many middle-class Americans avoided serving by going to graduate and professional schools and obtaining deferments. Vietnam was the first of our wars to be fought almost exclusively by an American underclass and, in part because of this, at no time did it have anything like the full support of the American people.

The great example of a successful conscription army is in Israel, where nearly all eligible young men and women serve. Israel exists, of course, in a state of perpetual peril; as has often been said, it cannot afford to lose even one war. But the glory of the Israeli army, and its support by all but the most pacifist Israelis, surely owes to the fact that everyone serves, or has served, in it.

Under the draft, the American social fabric would change—and, judging from my experience, for the better. I write as a former draftee who served in the Army from 1958 to 1960. I was, in other words, a Cold War soldier, and never for a moment in danger. Much of my time in the military—I worked on the post newspaper at Fort Hood, in Texas, and later as a clerk, typing up physicals, in a recruiting station in Little Rock, Arkansas—was excruciatingly boring.

Yet I am grateful for having served. Doing so took me out of my own social class and ethnic milieu—big-city, middle-class, Jewish—and gave me a vivid sense of the social breadth of my country. I slept in barracks and shared all my meals with American Indians, African Americans from Detroit, white Appalachians, Christian Scientists from Kansas, and discovered myself befriending and being befriended by young men I would not otherwise have met. I have never felt more American than when I was in the Army.

Memories from my two years in the Army retain a 3D vividness. I shall never forget Andrew Atherton, a Korean War veteran and my platoon sergeant in basic training. A tall, lean black man with a highly mobile Adam's apple, he was, in starched fatigues with an ascot at his throat, more elegant than most men in white tie and tails. In dealing with us, he adopted a deliberately comic style, a combination of high pomposity and profanity. "It behooves all Christians among you," I recall his bellowing out on our first night of training, "to get your sorry asses to church services on Sunday. As for those of you of the Hebrew persuasion, it is mandatory for each and every one of you young troopers to get his swinging dick to Friday-night services. Am I clear?"

At Fort Leonard Wood, in Missouri, where I did my basic training, I remember a guy from Tennessee named Flowers, whose ex-wife turned him over to the draft for failing to make alimony payments, and who joked about renegotiating the terms of his divorce when first issued his M1 rifle. At Fort Hood, I worked in the Public Information Office with a Wharton Business School graduate, a private first class named Carl Kershler III, who drove a current-year black Cadillac convertible around the base, causing full-bird colonels, taking him for the post commander, to salute him when he passed. In Little Rock, I remember Sergeant Wilson Duncan, whose drinking never got in the way of his kindness to the men under him, including me. None of these are men I would have encountered outside the Army.

In contemporary America, if one is born into the middle or upper-middle class, one is unlikely ever to have to step outside that class. One stands to go to school with people from the same social class, marry into that class, raise one's children within it, live out one's days among its members. Members of the working classes are more cruelly class-bound and isolated. The ingredients in the once famous American melting pot thus remain frozen.

The hiatus the draft brings can have a decisive effect on one's future. Certainly it did in my case. By drawing me at the age of 22 out of the workaday world for two years, the draft gave me space to think about my life and what I wanted to do with it. But for the draft, I might, God forfend, have gone to law school simply out of the need to appear serious, and today have been a perhaps wealthier but undoubtedly much less contented man.

During the years the draft was in effect, it was not uncommon for judges to let young criminal offenders choose among reform school, prison, and the Army. Most chose the Army, a decision I should like to see made by the gang members who now menace the streets of my city, Chicago, and other major American cities. As a totalitarian institution—that is, one that has total control over the people in it—the Army in my day had a remarkably high success rate in rehabilitating young offenders and even wayward jerks. In the Army, you shaped up or—well, there really wasn't any alternative but to go to prison or have your life permanently stained by a dishonorable discharge.

Arguments against reinstituting the draft, though not trivial, are mainly technical. Training volunteer soldiers is said to be hard enough, given the complexity of military hardware—training reluctant conscripts would be even more difficult. Yet far from all military tasks are technological; clerks, cooks, infantrymen are always needed. Having lots of soldiers who have gone through college and professional schools would also leaven the enlisted ranks in a useful way.

At a time of defense-budget cutting, as military bases are threatened with closure and new weapons systems are abandoned for lack of money, the Pentagon may not be interested in having to increase personnel dramatically with conscripts who would serve for only two years. Yet President Obama has said, and no one of any authority has disagreed with him, that this war is going to be a long one, a matter not of months but of years, possibly even decades. The reinstitution of the draft would make our country's participation in this lengthy struggle not merely more just but possibly more efficient, by conscripting better-educated young people. Time, I would argue, for a serious consideration of returning to compulsory military service in America.

Unsentimental Journey

(2014)

I N PAST YEARS I HAVE TAKEN TO PRINT to attack two words—*focus* and *icon*—that drove me bonkers. *Focus*, a metaphor from the world of cameras and microscopes, replaced the words *concentrate* and *emphasize*. Suddenly everywhere ballplayers lost their focus, students were encouraged to find theirs, schools, companies, nations began focusing on this or that problem. Hocus-pocus, I used to mutter to myself, please, drop the focus. Nobody did, and the word today has still not lessened in popularity.

In its original meaning *icon* was a small religious painting used as an aid to devotion. In its new meaning, persons, cultural events, inanimate objects became iconic. To be an icon was, apparently, a step up from being a superstar, as superstar was a step up from being a mere star. The word *icon* became part of the vocabulary of hype, and was used so often that it no longer carried any weight or absorbed the least truth. Awesome, you might say, but then again the matter mightn't be of any interest to you. Whatever.

Focus, *icon*, *awesome*, *whatever*, all are among what H. W. Fowler, in his great but surely not iconic book *Modern English Usage*, calls vogue words. According to Fowler, every now and then a word emerges from obscurity, or even from nothingness or a merely potential and not actual existence, into sudden popularity. It is often, but not necessarily, one that by no means explains itself to the average man, who has to find out its meaning as best he can. . . . Ready acceptance of vogue words seems to some people the sign of an alert mind; to others it stands for the herd instinct and lack of individuality. The title of this article is perhaps enough to show that the second view is here taken.

On the way to becoming a vogue word an ordinary word is often transmogrified into a metaphor. Consider *window*, which appears frequently these days in the trappings of *window of opportunity*, a metaphorical bit of glass that, you will have noticed, keeps endlessly opening and closing. Or the new meaning of *narrative*, which used to mean a connected account of events but now means, roughly, my story the way I want it told, or rather spun. In a recent issue of *Vanity Fair*, poor Monica Lewinsky writes, "I've decided, finally, to stick my head above the parapet so that I can take back my narrative and give a purpose to my past." In the same article she blames the Clinton administration, Kenneth Starr, and the media, who "were able to brand me. And that brand stuck." *Branding* is of course another vogue word; it means something like setting your own image (a vogue word of an earlier day), deciding how you or your candidate or corporation wish to appear. Talk to any recently minted MBA for more than 10 minutes and branding, like a Tourette's tic, is sure to pop up.

The latest vogue word to ignite my ever flammable ire is *journey*. I first noted the voguish use of this word four or so years ago when the 37-year-old daughter of an acquaintance of mine was undergoing the tortures of breast cancer: chemotherapy, nausea and weakness, hair loss, depression, the full catastrophe. When I asked this man how his daughter was doing, he answered that it was "a journey." Having cancer in one's thirties is no journey; it is instead wretched luck, horrible and hope killing.

When he used the word *journey* to cover the torments his daughter was going through, it was evident that for this man the word was, somehow, consoling. *Journey*, in its vogue word incarnation, is of course pure psychobabble. The advent of the word in its voguish form comes from the false wisdom holding that the effort to attain them is more important than any goals one might reach in life. How much easier for this man to say that his daughter's suffering is a journey than to describe in sad detail the nightmare she was going through. Some words, Fowler writes, owe "their vogue to the ease with which they can be substituted for any of several different and more precise words," and *journey* is surely, is egregiously, one.

"Enjoy the journey," advises a television commercial for a resort and spa in Lake Geneva, Wisconsin. The word figures to show up a lot more before long. Watch for it. Its detachment from reality recommends it to those who fancy themselves deep thinkers. Life, be assured, ain't no picnic; and it ain't no journey, either. What it is is much too complex— a thick purée of fate, luck, will, character, historical circumstance, and much more—to be captured by the word *journey*. Those who use it to do so may not know it, but they themselves are intellectually traveling in steerage.

Everyone Has His Price

(2014)

I JUST BOUGHT A BOTTLE OF WATERMAN'S INK for $11.34, tax included. The bottle contains 50 ml, or less than two ounces, of black ink. This makes ink far more expensive than wine, even quite superior wine. I would have complained—or at least exclaimed—about the price, but the man who sold it to me was so pleasant and so knowledgeable about fountain pens that he quite took the whine out of my sails.

I can remember when a bottle of ink cost 15 cents. Memories of much lower prices of an earlier day are a standard complaint of—shall we call them?—the no-longer young. I remember when this hit my father, a remarkably generous man but a man who, in old age, would be shocked at the price of a restaurant check, an item of clothing, downtown parking. One comes into one's maturity with a certain set of numbers prevailing, and when the numbers change, inevitably upwards, the phenomenon known in the car business as "sticker shock" hits hard.

I remember in my twenties buying excellent Brooks Brothers oxford-cloth, button-down shirts for $7.50. Those same shirts now sell for $92. One has to grimace and bear it—or, in the case of these shirts, go topless. I remember when candy bars were 5 cents and so were Cokes. Cigarettes, now something like $10 a pack in Chicago, were 25 cents when I began smoking at the age of 16. That I don't buy candy bars or drink Cokes and long ago quit smoking is beside the point. Gasoline when I began driving was around 30 cents a gallon. In 1970, I bought a new Volvo for $3,000. Today cars I wouldn't care to own are priced in the 20-grand range. It's not the principle, you understand, it's the money.

Everyone has his price, beyond which he cannot go. I remember having dinner with a friend in the Oak Room at the Plaza. We ordered a bottle of wine, salad, and Chateaubriand for our main course. When the waiter asked if I cared for a vegetable, I thought about peas, but glimpsing the menu, I noted that they were $8. I couldn't do it; I could go $4 for peas but not $8. I went without a vegetable.

I wrote a short story in which my main character, a well-to-do physician, is taken by his lady friend and her circle to a restaurant in Los Angeles where his share of the check comes to $680, tip included. Afterwards he tells her: "I'm not a $680 dinner guy. It's not that I can't afford a dinner like that from time to time. It's just that I feel there's something intrinsically wrong about it. People lie and cheat and even kill for money. This being so, I've always felt that the least I can do is respect it. Spending that kind of money for a meal isn't, in my opinion, respecting it."

I steer clear of immensely expensive restaurants. My taste buds aren't worthy of them. A few years ago, though, I was taken to Daniel, then the restaurant of the moment in New York. My host remarked, "Didn't I read somewhere that you were opposed to expensive wine?" I corrected him: "Not at all. I am only opposed to paying for it. I'll have a bit more of the red, if you please." More recently I was taken to Charlie Trotter's in Chicago, a restaurant where the fixed-price dinner was $175. With a bottle of wine, tax, and tip, that makes for a $500 dinner for two. The next morning the man who took me sent me, via email, one of the most charming compliments I have ever received. He told me that he was angry with me because he enjoyed our conversation so much that he forgot what he ate.

Some people are of course much freer with money than others. These others, like the character in my story, like me, feel they mustn't blow it frivolously. Are we merely cheap, unsporting, or instead careful, responsible? In his poem "Money," Philip Larkin writes: *And however you bank your screw, the money you save / Won't in the end buy you more than a shave.* By that shave Larkin means the undertaker's shave of one's corpse.

Which is a darker way of saying that you can't take it with you, the first and truest maxim about money.

Still, while alive, one doesn't want to leave it just anywhere. In money matters, lines must be drawn, proportion maintained, measure observed. "Only the gauche, the illiterate, the frightened and the pastless destroy money," says a character in *The Mansion*, the final novel in Faulkner's Snopes trilogy. I agree, and wonder if my new $11.34 bottle of Waterman's ink will see me out, so that, at these prices, I won't have to buy another.

Incommunicado

(2015)

THIS PAST WEEK I decided to change living arrangements *chez* Epstein. I turned my office into a den and our spare bedroom into an office. Sounds simple enough. I soon realized that I would have to hire professional movers to lug a couch, a weighty television set, and several bookcases and a few file cabinets from one room to another in our apartment. I was prepared to do so, and to pay the expense, which came to $288 plus $60 in three $20 tips for the men who did the lugging. I wasn't prepared for two days' loss of the use of my computer, television set, and landline phone, due to the loss of my cable connection, which rendered me, apart from the flip-phone I carry around, essentially incommunicado.

I don't use a smartphone because I would be checking it too regularly for emails, texts, and other information. I already do too much of this on my computer when at home. I am, I'm embarrassed to report, a man who checks his email 20, perhaps 30 times a day. What do I expect to find there? The usual things, I suppose: extravagant offers for my modest services, announcements of my having won grand literary prizes, news of vast inheritances, feelers for university presidencies in gentle climates or possibly for an obscure cabinet post. That none of these items has shown up hasn't stayed my optimism.

I should have but hadn't quite realized how strong a role these three machines—the Internet, television, and the telephone—have come to play in my life. Was it Emerson or some other Waldo who said "man rides machine"? Whoever it was, he got it wrong. Our dependence on these three machines has, if anything, grown greater and greater. I write "our," but perhaps I really mean "my" dependence.

I rise at 6:00 a.m. and, with tea and toast before me, begin my day reading a serious book. I also turn on the television set, with the sound off, and read the crawl, which gives me the weather and news of murders, fires, and political scandals in Chicago, none of which ever seems to be in short supply. At 7:00 a.m. I turn up the sound for *CBS This Morning* with Charlie Rose (*Il est Charlie*), which begins with a segment called "Your World in Ninety Seconds" that provides national and international headlines, and 90 seconds of it is all I can bear. An hour later, just before rising from my chair, I check the day's listings on my movie channels, hoping there is something worth recording to watch that evening or later in the week.

The television doesn't go on during the day, but at 5:30 p.m., a glass of Riesling in hand, I watch the evening news. I could never stand Diane Sawyer's false empathy, or Brian Williams's false earnestness, and so settle for Scott Pelley's false seriousness. (It helps that I refer to Pelley, if only to my wife, as Chuck E. Cheese.) Sometimes I will turn to the soulful ladies of the *PBS NewsHour*, or flick on Fox News for the amusement of watching my friend Charles Krauthammer, wearing his game face, give the president of the United States his daily shellacking. Two days without these divertissements, I have to confess, threw me.

Email has gone a long way to replacing telephone calls for me, though I continue to get a few from friends, between the various calls asking me to donate my car, check my credit, or have my ducts cleaned. Only two people, my wife and granddaughter, have my cell phone number, and it rarely rings. The main drawback to being without a landline was that I couldn't ring in people who called from our lobby.

I missed the Internet most sorely. Apart from my tic-like checks of email throughout the day, I spend forty or so minutes every morning reading a few blogs (*Anecdotal Evidence*, Bill Kristol, Jonathan V. Last, etc.), checking a few websites (*Arts & Letters Daily*, *Mosaic*, *The Daily Beast*), glimpsing the headlines and obituaries in the *New York Times*, reading John Podhoretz on Twitter. I am a Facebook friend to 10 or 12 people, but a one-way friend only, since I have never put an item on Facebook, nor ever intend to do so. Occasionally I'll Google myself, to see who has freshly insulted me.

When my telephone, television, and Internet were restored, I had six calls waiting, none of them of any importance, and 70 or so emails, only one of which was significant; no shocking items had appeared in the *New York Times* obits; Scott Pelley was as pompous as ever; and Charles was still kicking the president's butt. Might it make sense, I begin to wonder, to take two such days off every week, in the name of good intellectual hygiene?

That's a Nickel

(2015)

I ONCE APPEARED ON A PANEL at the National Endowment for the Humanities with two women who talked about the importance of their secondary education. One was German and spoke reverently of the *gymnasium* she was fortunate enough to attend. The other, an American, spent her adolescence in France and mentioned her deep debt to the *lycée* that gave her so sound a grounding in the classics. When my turn came, I remarked how I envied them, and allowed that I had myself gone to a public high school in Chicago notable for its disadvantaged teachers.

I remember older women teaching in house slippers; a red-faced biology teacher who put the more bosomy girls in the front row, wrote out the pages of the textbook we were to read and which exercises at the end of the chapter to do, and promptly nodded off; gym coaches reeking of nicotine who did scarcely any coaching whatsoever. They represented the rich fruits of tenure in a public-school system.

One teacher I do remember fondly was Dr. Branz, a German émigré who taught a course called Commercial Law. He must have been a refugee from Hitler, with a doctor of laws degree; by the time he arrived in this country, I assume, he was too old to practice law, and so had to fall back on teaching the barbarian young of my high school. I cannot recall a single thing he taught. What I do remember is his instituting a system of fines for our misbehavior. If he caught any of us talking, or nodding off, or chewing gum, or not having read the day's assignment, he would say, in a sing-song, heavily Teutonic accent, "That's a nickel." He used the nickels to pay for a picnic at the end of the term.

"That's a nickel" is a refrain much heard over the past month or so *chez* Epstein. My wife and I, two not always successful Couéists—Émile Coué being the French psychologist who said, "Every day in every way I am getting better and better"—have set out on another of our self-improvement programs. We are trying to eliminate the word "yeah" from our speech. Each time one of us fails, we pay a nickel fine, dropped into a large tin coffee mug, and announce, "That's a nickel."

A modest enough program, trying to eliminate a single word from one's speech, or so one might think, and yet our success has been less than spectacular. I'd estimate that we currently have more than $15 in our cup or, in the good Yiddish word, *pushkeh*, and that's a lot of yeahs. When first we set out, the nickels were flying. We are now down to lapsing into error as seldom as one or two times a day. Few are the days when neither of us gets off without making a contribution or two to the *pushkeh*. Later in the evenings, our guards lowered by fatigue, our lapses tend to be more frequent. When the *pushkeh* is full, perhaps we'll treat ourselves to a bottle of champagne.

One of the things this little campaign of self-improvement reveals is how often the word "yeah" comes up in the talk of others and in the dialogue of movies and on television. The English now use it quite as much as we gringos do, though I haven't yet noted any yeahs on *Masterpiece Theatre*. Imagine how much the Beatles would have been fined for their song "She Loves You, Yeah, Yeah, Yeah." The singer Joe Nichols has a full song called "Yeah," which is about the affirmation a man feels for a beautiful woman—like, yeah!

A small enough improvement, this attempt to eliminate a single slurry word from my speech, yet I would nonetheless like to achieve it. Some years ago I gave up, with reasonable if not complete success, profanity, which was threatening to take over my speech. (I still require a certain amount of profanity for my thoughts.) I long ago eliminated psychobabble from my vocabulary. I attempt to speak in full and grammatical sentences, not to mix metaphors, to divest myself of clichés, even to eliminate split infinitives, so with all this grooming of my speech, yeah, I feel, also has got to go.

Yeah is of course a synonym for yes. In German and Dutch, *ja*—much closer to yeah than to yes—is standard. Is yeah the more natural word; is the synonym more sensible than the original? In some idiomatic phrases yeah seems irreplaceable. "Yeah, right, sure, you believe *that* you'll believe anything" is much better than "Yes, right, sure . . ." So is "Yeah, go for it" better than "Yes, go for it." For my own touchdown dance, followed by three vigorous fist pumps, I find only a concluding yeah will do.

Sometimes you just have to spend the nickel.

Funny, But I Do Look Jewish

(2003)

FUNNY, BUT I DO LOOK JEWISH, at least to myself, and more and more so as the years go by. I'm fairly sure I didn't always look Jewish, not when I was a boy, or possibly even when a young man, though I have always carried around my undeniably Jewish name, which was certainly clue enough. But today, gazing at my face in the mirror, I say to myself, yes, no question about it, this is a very Jewish-looking gent.

The article "Types, Anthropological" in the old *Jewish Encyclopedia* (1901–1906), written at a time when the Jews were anthropologically still considered a race, notes that "persons who do not have the Jewish expression in their youth acquire it more and more as they grow from middle to old age." True enough in my case, apparently, though much material in the rest of the article now seems comically antique: such as that Jews commonly wear their hats on the back of their heads because of the need to put their phylacteries on their foreheads, or have posture of a kind known as the "ghetto bend" from studying Talmud so relentlessly.

The remainder of the *Jewish Encyclopedia* article, which is accompanied by illustrations ("Composite Portrait of Ten Jewish Lads, New York"), works around the notion that the precise nature of the Jewish expression "is very difficult to determine with any degree of certainty or accuracy." Admitting all exceptions—Theodor Herzl, the founder of Zionism, "was not distinctively Jewish [in appearance], all observers drawing attention to his resemblance to the Assyrian rather than to the Jewish type"—the article nonetheless insists there is a "Jewish expression."

Against much scientific evidence to the contrary, I happen to believe there is one, too. Noses used to be considered the defining Jewish physical characteristic—"chosen noses," in the phrase I myself sometimes use. High arching, aquiline, hooked, long, nostril-flaring, sometimes bump-bearing noses have generally been taken for Jewish. My own nose is fairly regular, in shape and in size, though its straight bridge now seems a touch high and it has become a tad beaky and, in profile, begins to seem more prominent.

I somewhere read the phrase "Jewish ears," implying large and fleshy appendages, and, if such Jewish ears exist, these I indubitably have. My ears have always stuck out, but now they seem to be growing larger, in proportion to my head, and a bit pointy into the bargain. Gershom Scholem, the great scholar of Jewish mysticism, had such ears. So, more famously and pointily, did Franz Kafka, giving him the look of a bat, or other member of the order Chiroptera.

Where I think I may look most Jewish is in the eyes. Once dark brown, my eyes are now more mottled, even containing bits of blue. The skin over my right eye is beginning to sag slightly—my mother's right eye did something similar late in her life—and my eyebrows are growing grayer and bushier, more unruly. But it's the look in my eyes that strikes me as most Jewish: It seems to me worldly, not to say a trifle world-weary, melancholy, if not mildly depressed.

The human face, we now know, is not symmetrical, a fact that painting seems to capture better than sculpture. Of my two sides, the right is the more lined, weather-beaten, battered-looking. I think of this side of my face as even more Jewish than my left side, which, to be sure, I don't exactly think of as Swedish. Am I equating suffering here with looking Jewish? I hope not, because not only have I never knowingly suffered in America for being Jewish, but I also take genuine pleasure in thinking myself a Jew, or member of what I, perhaps chauvinistically, prefer to think the most lively minority group in the United States.

A man named Sam Profettas, a Greek Jew from Salonika, photographed in 1991 by Frédéric Brenner for *Diaspora*, his two-volume photographic study of Jews, has the face I may have a chance of attaining. Mr. Profettas has thin lips, deep-sunk, pouch-underlined eyes, a straight but prominent nose, and no fewer than seven deep furrows in his forehead, with white hair brushed straight back. If I can survive another fifteen or so years, I shouldn't at all mind having a face approximating his, thoughtful, ironic, melancholic.

If one of the contributors to the text volume of Brenner's *Diaspora* were asked to read a photograph of my face, he might well find in it a longing to return from my post-exilic existence in America. How perfectly, absolutely, delightfully wrong he would be! Proudly Jewish though I may be, pro-Israel though I shall always remain, I have never wished to live anywhere else than in America. I can recall one evening in Jerusalem, awaiting the performance of Shlomo Mintz and the Jerusalem Music Center Chamber Orchestra, thinking that everyone else in this room could, theoretically, be Jewish. Rather than feeling that I was home at last among my people, I thought how, given a choice, I preferred instead to be among a small minority in a larger, free country. Perverse? I don't believe so; this position might even be considered a natural one for a writer who longs for objectivity, which is to say to be a little distanced from the life around him.

A French social anthropologist, Frédéric Brenner has been photographing Jews in their diasporic condition over the past twenty-five years, in what began as a search, as it was described in a *New York Times* article about him, for "the quintessential Jew." He has photographed Jews in fifteen republics of the old Soviet Union, in Yemen, India, Israel, Iraq, Iran, Greece, Tunisia, New York, along the Amazon, in Brazil, Argentina, China, Hong Kong, Africa, Germany, Holland, and most other countries of Europe. Among other things, *Diaspora* demonstrates the demographic ubiquity, if not everywhere the density, of Jews worldwide and in countries where they are often deeply rooted and not in the least cosmopolitan.

Brenner might be called the Jewish Diane Arbus, if Miss Arbus herself weren't Jewish (having been born a Nemerov, sister of the poet Howard). He has, that is to say, a taste for the stark and even the freakish; grotesquerie seems to light his fire. He provides photographs of a midget Jewish hatter in the Ukraine, rabbinic couples (men and women rabbis) on beds together at a bargain furniture store in New York, a Jewish drag queen stretched along the sandy ground in Johannesburg, South Africa. Some of his photographs are distinctly "in your face," or, to use the pro-football term, "smash mouth." An example of this aspect of his work is seen in a photograph of ten defiant-looking young female rabbis and cantors at the Jewish Theological Seminary, in prayer shawls with phylacteries, or *tefilin*, wrapped round their forearms. None of Brenner's photographs carry titles or captions, but this one might have been entitled "Not Your Mother's Judaism."

The photograph in this book for which I do not possess a proper introductory adjective—shocking? devastating? desolating?—is one of six Jewish women from Los Angeles with their blouses off who have had mastectomies (five single, one double). I am not sure how one is supposed to react to this photograph. Powerful it is; that is beyond question. But to what end? How was Brenner able to get the women to pose for it? They sit at a table, each holds the hands of the women on both sides of her. Some attempt a smile, but without much success. "Posing for this picture with these women was a very intense experience," one of them remarks, and then, alas, breaks off into psycho-babblish jabber about meditation and the sense of connection required to summon the bravery for allowing the photograph. One can perhaps see the possibly cathartic effect of having done so. Only the motives of the photographer are really in question here.

Is iconoclasm part of Brenner's project? One picks up bits of anti-Israeli feeling, for example, in some of his photographs. A set of photos, taken roughly a decade apart, shows a perhaps six-year-old, earlock-wearing Yemeni Jew, Lewi Faez, studying a Jewish book in his grandfather's jewelry workshop, a room that does not seem far advanced above a cave. Years later Brenner photographed the sixteen-year-old and now married Lewi Faez and his wife and infant child in a nearly empty modern apartment in Israel in a manner meant to suggest his loneliness in his new country—the implication here being that Yemen, with all its primitiveness, may have been better. The camera, it is said, does not lie, but the man behind it can have his devious subtexts and political agendas.

The text—contained in the slenderer of the two volumes of *Diaspora*—includes what Brenner calls "Voices," or commentaries on smaller versions of many of the full-page, sometimes two-page-wide photographs found in the photographic volume. The "voices" are in fact brief passages written by novelists, poets, historians, scholars, and critics stirred by particular photographs; sometimes these passages entail a reading or interpretation of the photograph, sometimes they occasion autobiographical sorties suggested to them by the photographs. The passages written by André Aciman (a Jew born in Alexandria, Egypt), Julius Lester (an African-American who many years ago converted to a Judaism he takes seriously), and Tsvi Blanchard (an American orthodox rabbi) are easily the most penetrating. Jacques Derrida, a Jew born in Algeria, is interesting only when he is autobiographical and is otherwise his old charmless, obscurantist self. The Harvard philosopher Stanley Cavell, another frequent "Voices" contributor, is reliably disappointing. Thousands of words are in this text volume that aren't worth a single one of Brenner's pictures.

As for that quintessential Jew, Brenner allows that he has never found him and suggests, as does the impressive variety of his photographs, that he may not exist. Who might he be? Surveying the immensity of Jewish types, might he be the philosopher Martin Buber, the gangster Meyer Lansky, the comedian Woody Allen, the sports announcer Howard Cosell, the operatic singer Beverly Sills?

Is the authentic Jew an earlock-wearing, tsitsit-on-the-undergarments-bearing Hasid in the Mea Shearim neighborhood in Jerusalem, a merchant originally from Iraq living in Calcutta, a Marrano praying in an attic in Portugal, a golfer in plaid pants and peach-colored shirt teeing off at the Lakeshore Country Club in Glencoe? The answer is of course all and none of the above.

And yet Jews remain, at least to most other Jews, identifiably, unmistakably Jewish. "Gaydar" is a word, formed from "radar," that describes the ability to discern a gay man, especially one attempting to pass as heterosexual. If there is an equivalent power of discernment that allows one to spot Jews, even where they do not conform in any obvious or even subtle way to stereotypical notions of the Jew—let us call this "Jewdar"—I like to think I possess it in reasonably good working order.

I feel that I can see through the occasional name change, cosmetic surgery, or sad attempts to pass oneself off as something other than Jewish that come within my purview. "Ah, a *landsman*," lights up on the screen in my mind when I encounter a person I take to be Jewish. A name can sometimes be more suggestive of Jewishness than physical appearance. Names, too, can give to Jews an odd sense of worldwide connectedness. Brenner, in this collection, provides Cohens from Venezuela, Kushners from Birobidzhan, Aarons from Calcutta, Bermans from Paris, and Hershs and Freys from Antwerp.

On the other hand, I have always wondered what it might be like not to be Jewish but to have a Jewish-sounding name—Sarah Jacobson, Norman Davis, Mark Steyn—and often be taken for Jewish. First, there would be the worry that someone might hold your being Jewish (when you're not) against you; and, second, there is the discomfort entailed in getting special treatment from another Jew or philo-Semite because that he or she thinks you are someone you are not. I once saw a man who was a dead ringer for the old actor Cesar Romero wearing a bright red T-shirt with bold white lettering that read "I Am Not Cesar Romero." Perhaps people with Jewish-sounding names ought to wear T-shirts, or at least carry business cards, that read, "I'm Sidney Ross, But Not Really Jewish." Glenn Gould, whose name and face and manner all falsely suggest Jewishness, could have used such a T-shirt.

The first time he saw troops from the Israeli Army, so in shape and formidable did they seem, Jackie Mason claims that he thought they were actually Puerto Ricans. One of the points Brenner attempts to make in *Diaspora* is that it's no longer so easy to tell Jews from non-Jews. In the photographs that he took of Jews in Italy, for example, especially those of men, none looks especially Jewish: They seem purely Roman or Venetian or Florentine. Yet my Jewdar rings even when I gaze upon most of the Chinese Jews in his photographs from Beijing. Brenner seems to play off this point with a photograph of a group of black and Hispanic moving men seated by a truck in Palm Beach, Florida, on which is written the company's name: Nice Jewish Boys. Only one actual Jewish boy, Jerry Burnstein, the driver of the truck and perhaps one of the owners, is in the picture. "Gee," remarks Julius Lester of this photograph, "but they don't look Jewish." What—or on whom—is the joke here?

Brenner supplies a variety of Ashkenazi and Sephardi Jews, and his selection of photographs emphasizes more the distinction between them than between German and Eastern European Jews (both of whom are Ashkenazic). The rivalries and little snobberies among these three divisions of Jewry are themselves of humorous interest to those who consider themselves connoisseurs of Jewishness. Traditionally, the German Jews held themselves to be above—more assimilated, more cultured—Eastern European Jews, while the Sephardi Jews, who were exiled from the Iberian Peninsula in 1492, held themselves to be more aristocratic and hence above both. Some of them even claim the cachet of having been exiled in 1492 in the same way that some old-line American WASPs used to claim coming over on the *Mayflower*.

Eastern Jews referred to German Jews as *yekkes*, probably from the German word for "jacket" and a metonym for the notion that the stiffer, more formal German Jews never took off their suit jackets. What is the difference between a virgin and a *yekke*? an old joke asked. The answer was that a *yekke* remained a *yekke*. In a novel called *Café Berlin* by Harold Nebenzal, I came across the amusing generalization that the real division between Sephardi and Ashkenazi Jews is that no true Sephardi, at least one raised in the Middle East, can abide *gefilte* fish, an Ashkenazi dish. An often-disputatious people, the Jews, and never more so than among themselves.

Brenner frequently attempts to score subtle jokes with his photographs. His better ones usually come by way of the settings he arranges for many of his subjects. Consider his photograph of fourteen Jewish shrinks, in a tight grouping off to the left, shot in the library at the New York Psychoanalytic Society. Books and busts and photographs of Sigmund Freud are scattered throughout the room.

But dominating all—even the fourteen shrinks—is a large psychoanalytic couch at the picture's center, which, in the context of the photograph, resembles a mastless Egyptian boat. Might this couch stand for the boat that all these shrinks, still working away at their now quite dead ideas, seem to have missed? I don't know the state of Brenner's belief in psychoanalysis—though anyone who has read my previous sentence now knows the state of mine—and so I could be wrong about my interpretation of this photograph. But the brilliance of his arrangement makes it certainly possible, amusing, and, to me at least, persuasive.

Another of Brenner's photographs has sixteen actors all in Groucho Marx makeup and poses. Tsvi Blanchard remarks that "this photograph nearly convinced me that Groucho Marx was the official logo of Jews in exile." Underlying this is the notion of the Jew as someone who is skeptical, quick in response, verbally menacing. The Jew as witty radical is also suggested, for almost all the Marx Brothers' movies are attacks on what were once established American WASP institutions: Ivy League higher education, the opera, first-class ocean travel, thoroughbred racing.

The New York Jew may be a spin-off from the Groucho, wise-guy-son-of-recent-immigrants Jew. When you're in love the whole world's Jewish, was an old joke line. Closer to the truth is that when you're in New York, everyone seems Jewish, sometimes including Irish cops and Italian priests. By their combination of knowingness and aggressiveness—a combination that is not everybody's cup of caviar—is how New York Jews are generally characterized. Among the earliest anti-Semitism I encountered as a boy came from Chicago Jews returning, in the early 1950s, from Miami Beach, saying that the chief thing wrong with the place was that, as far as they were concerned, it had too many New York Jews. I have myself been taken for a New York Jew, and once read, in a biographical note accompanying an essay of mine reprinted in a college reader, that I had attended CCNY and then Columbia, when I've never set foot in either. Funny, I don't seem to myself New Yorkish.

But there is also the cerebral Jew (J. Robert Oppenheimer), the sensitive artistic Jew (Yehudi Menuhin, Vladimir Horowitz—this one comes in handsome and homely versions), the genius Jew (Albert Einstein), the infuriating Jewish woman (Barbra Streisand, she should only mind her own business), the Rebecca-by-the-wells beautiful Jewess (Marisa Berenson), and a full typology of other Jews, enough and more than enough, really, to go round.

Frédéric Brenner's point is precisely that there may be no quintessential, authentic, absolute Jew. He makes this point, over and over, by showing Jews in unexpected connections. A photograph of the members of a Jewish motorcycle club in their leather and on their bikes before a synagogue is a notable example. Another is a Chaplinesque little Jewish man, with yarmulke and cane and cavalry mustache and bemused smile, standing against a blank wall in Calcutta. More in his smash-face mode, he provides a picture of a Passover ceremony at a maximum security women's correctional facility in Bedford Hills, New York; in case you missed the message, this photograph says, there are dangerous Jewish criminals and they aren't all Jewish men, either.

Brenner does not emphasize the Holocaust in this collection, though it was Hitler who sent more Jews off into a second diaspora than did the Romans when they destroyed the Second Temple. One extraordinary photograph, shot from above, shows a circle of twelve women, six Holocaust survivors, back to back, arms entwined with their lesbian daughters.

What, one has to ask, is the moral of this picture: You survive the Holocaust, and you still get a lesbian for a daughter? Or might Brenner have intended that women who have gone through the Holocaust and lesbians, mother and daughters in this instance, share equal status as victims? I fear that our photographer intends the politically correct, drearier, and much more boring second interpretation.

Most of Brenner's photographs in Israel are not of the appealing Israeli young that characterize the place for many of us but of Hasidic Jews. Tsvi Blanchard remarks of a photograph of two, dark, bespectacled, spindly-legged Hasids: "How curious this is! We can only imagine the Jew as people we do not wish to be." Whether in the Catskill Mountains, Mea Shearim, on 47th Street in New York, at a study or dining table, or out in an open field, the Hasidim bring their complete world with them, which perhaps accounts, at least in part, for why they are as photogenic as any subject going.

Brenner provides a rigged up photograph of Jewish American celebrities, each appearing in a nineteenth-century gold gilt frame, out of which some place a hand or even their full head. The people in the photograph range from Henry Kissinger to the swimmer Mark Spitz, from Isaac Stern to Betty Friedan, from Philip Roth (the frame in which he appears is set horizontally on the ground) to Lauren Bacall. Different as they all are in the quality of their minds and outlook, all look distinctly Jewish. Saul Bellow, who also appears in this photograph, here resembles nothing so much as an ancient parrot, but, it must be added, a distinctly Jewish one.

"Over time," Tsvi Blanchard remarks, "Brenner's work will increasingly undermine our conscious belief that there is only one way to be Jewish." Perhaps so. Hasidic Judaism harks back to the eighteenth century. Much modern Judaism, in its liberal strain, makes a conscious attempt to be as inclusive as possible; a visit to many Reform Jewish synagogues today can sometimes make one feel as if one has just attended a platform session of the McGovern wing of the Democratic party. Above all there reigns the paradox that, as some branches of Judaism make more and more concessions to modernity—female rabbis being the most notable step in this direction—more and more young Jews seem to be returning to Jewish orthodoxy. Go, as the Jews say, figure.

And yet . . . and yet . . . and yet . . . despite and perhaps because of all this, why is it that I continue to feel that I can recognize a Jewish face at twenty paces, no matter what its possessor's politics, nationality, personal history? "Numbers of Jews are found," the *Jewish Encyclopedia* notes, "who possess none of the characteristics here noted, and yet are recognizable as Jews."

Jews come in all shapes and sizes, tastes and temperaments. They can be garish and vulgar, pushy and wild, sensitive and cerebral, artistic and conservative, but they are rarely dull, except of course when trying to pass themselves off as something other than Jewish. Sometimes I think I can have had no better luck than to have been born Jewish, even though I am in my religious belief a pious agnostic and far from a sedulous practitioner of the Jewish religion. At other, rarer times, the complication of being Jewish seems heavy, or "fraught," as is nowadays said, and what it is fraught with, I believe, is the feeling of never quite feeling altogether at home anywhere.

"What are you doing here?" is a question that plays somewhere in the back of every Jewish person in whatever country he or she takes up residence. ("A Jew," André Aciman remarks "is always someone about whom one asked: Why on earth isn't he where he belongs?") The pressure of history makes it a tough question to block out. It was supposed to have been put to rest with the founding of the State of Israel, but, just now, a good part of the world seems to be asking the Israelis and their nation precisely this question: What are you doing here?

Aggressiveness can sometimes mask this feeling of outsiderishness on the part of Jews, sometimes irony can attempt to do the same thing. And on occasion, so can a measured distancing of oneself from full participation in the life around one. But anyone dedicated to being a person on whom little is lost will notice it playing somewhere in the expression of almost all Jews. Careful scrutiny will inevitably reveal that, funny, but they really do look Jewish.

Cuppa Joe

(2015)

FROM MY LIVING-ROOM WINDOWS, I can see two of the three coffee shops within a block of our apartment. Within less than a mile, there are five other coffee shops. In America the coffee shop has for the most part replaced the neighborhood bar, the country club, it used to be said, of the working man. Bars have never been my idea of a good time. Hemingway was, I think, correct when he said that there were only two reasons to go into a bar: the search for complaisant women and the yearning for a fight. Looking for neither, I tend to steer clear of bars.

I do, though, tend to steer into coffee shops. For a good while I met friends and acquaintances and a few strangers down the block at Peet's, the coffee shop begun at Berkley in 1966, and now itself franchised round the country. But Peet's is frequently crowded, and, as a neighborhood character, I am too often recognized by people who come up to greet me and have to be introduced to whomever I'm with. I still take out coffee from Peet's, but otherwise avoid the place.

I've noticed that a number of people spend a good part of their day in Peet's. Some, who don't need to go into an office to earn their livings, bring their laptops, legal pads, and whatever else they require and set up shop there. Others I assume come to Peet's to escape the loneliness of isolation in their apartments. They use Peets the way people once used neighborhood bars. Ten or eleven such people, more men than women, are regulars in my local Peet's, members, as I think of them, of the Occupy Peet's Movement.

Over the years I have become friendly with some of the young baristas working at Peet's. Many are young men and women just passing through. A nice feeling of toleration reigns among them and their customers; they are often tattoo-bearing, pierced, with day-glo colored hair. Nobody seems to mind, nor does anyone suggest this might slow them in their efforts toward getting a different job. Before long, as the country continues to alter both its etiquette and its expectations, it may well not do so. The *Wall Street Journal* not long ago reported that many large corporations, the Ford Motor Company and Boeing among them, allow their executives to bear tattoos and piercings; about day-glo hair the word hasn't come down.

My current coffee shop of choice is called Coralie. A Nous Sommes Charlie sign is in the front window. French songs often play lightly in the background. I enjoy at Coralie the presence of an attractive woman, young enough to be my granddaughter, who works there named Sarah Adams, with whom I have a running joke. The premise of the joke is that she is my long-divorced first wife. After introducing her as such to whomever I'm with, I sometimes add, "The sex was terrific but we found nothing to talk about." Other times I say, "The sex wasn't much, but the conversation was dazzling." Playing along nicely, she inquires, in a complaining tone, about yet another of my late alimony checks. How I have come to acquire the reputation of a neighborhood character I shall never know.

I claim no connoisseurship in the realm of coffee, and cannot tell you on which side of the hill outside Lagos the beans for my coffee were grown. I take a pass on all designer coffees, lattes, capuccinos, half-calfs, mocha-boca ratons, skim milk, four Splendas lightly marinaded in cinnamon, and order only plain coffee, regular in the mornings, decaf later in the afternoons.

I've still not got used to the steep price currently charged for coffee. I come from the time when Henny Youngman used to tell a joke about a bum asking him for fifty cents for a cup of coffee. "But coffee's only a quarter," Youngman says. "Won't you join me?" the bum replies. Today that joke, with the bum banished for political correctness, would go:

A homeless man asks for $6 for a cup of coffee. But coffee costs only $2.50, he is told. "I was thinking of adding a chocolate croissant," the homeless man replies.

My friend Edward Shils once asked the Christian socialist R. H. Tawney, author of *Religion and the Rise of Capitalism*, if he had noted any progress in his lifetime. "Yes," said Tawney, "in the deportment of dogs. In my youth dogs seemed so much more unruly than they do now." I wonder if Professor Tawney, were he alive today, might wish to add the replacement of the neighborhood bar by the coffee shop as another bit of small but genuine progress. The neighborhood bar was dark and xenophobic, the coffee shop light and welcoming. For those still looking for complaisant women or a fight, I recommend Google or the Yellow Pages.

The Divine Miss H, Revisited

(2015)

ROUGHLY FOUR YEARS AGO I reported on the acquisition of a Calico kitten named Hermione. I began by writing that she was asleep in my inbox. Now four years later, too large for my inbox, she sleeps in the chair next to mine in the room in our apartment I call my office. I ended my earlier scribble about her by saying that whatever disorder she might bring into my life I judged to be worth it. I now have to report that she has brought no disorder whatsoever, and instead her becalming company has brought only contentment, pleasure, and delight.

In all the time she has lived *chez* Epstein, Hermione has caused no destruction of any kind. She has knocked nothing off any counters or tables. She never attempts to eat any but her own food, with the exception of her taste for tuna, a small amount of which I parcel out to her when I prepare tuna salad. On the it's alimentary, my dear Watson front, she has never failed to use her box, and, given her constant bathing, is doubtless cleaner than I. Her only known vice is a passion for rubber-bands, which I prevent her from indulging out of fear of her swallowing one.

Hermione is a house, or in our case a sixth-floor apartment, cat. Apart from a few trips to the veterinarian, since living with us she has not been out of doors. Only once has she been left, for a week, in a vet's kennel for cats, and, though she survived the ordeal well enough, with luck she will never have to do that again. I have decided that she is the feline equivalent of a Christian Scientist, at least on that religion's medical aspect, which is to say, I have determined to dispense with regular visits for her for check-ups, shots, and the rest. She is—touch wood—bountifully healthy.

When I first saw Hermione, she was the runt of a litter of eleven kittens, all of whom had lost their mother and were lodging in a local pet store as what were called rescue animals. Runtish no more, she is, without being overweight, a full-figured girl, though with a small and elegant head. Hermione is lengthy, and gracefully passing from room to room she sometimes reminds me of one of those accordion-connected double buses.

Hermione sleeps a lot, in various locations. (Is this, I wonder, because I bore her?) One of her favorite locations is atop our kitchen counter in a square box, now filled with tissue paper, that once contained a pair of boots. Although she is not a lap cat, she will squiggle up at the feet, or sometimes, atop my head when napping. Evenings, when we are watching television, usually some old BBC drama now on DVD, she joins us on the couch, and agrees to allow petting, which she prefers behind the ears and under the chin, though she will accept strokes along her back. She spends most nights asleep at the foot of our bed.

Apart from a dish of dry food, and a quarter can of moist food served twice daily, and a bowl of cold water (known locally as Walden Pond) set out to the right of the kitchen sink, she has no other regular requirements. Some mornings she will appear at my desk, mewling lightly, a signal that she wishes to be brushed. Other times she will roll over on her back, paws raised, which means she wants to play with the toy called Cat Dancer: a length of wire with bits of rolled cardboard at each end, with which she tussles and rolls about.

I cheerfully accede to Hermione's few demands not only because of my deep affection for her but because I sometimes worry that she has had a bad deal in life. Here, as I see it, is the deal. Hermione has been spayed and for company been restricted to two adults, who, though quite mad about her, can communicate with her only in a limited way. In exchange for the loss of freedom and a life among her own species in the larger world, she has been given warm shelter, a guaranteed supply of food, and safety from the harsh depredations of nature and malevolent humankind. In this deal, she is likely to live three or four times as long as she figures to do out on her own in a cold climate. In short, she has been offered a gentler if more extreme version of the welfare state, in place of the life that Hobbes described as nasty, brutish, and short. Would you take such a deal? I'm far from certain that I would. That's why Hermione, for all her days, has only to ask for a brushing or a cat dance workout and she shall receive.

Remembering Torelli

(2015)

IN 1991 I WROTE AN ESSAY CALLED "The Ignorant Man's Guide to Music," in which I was both the ignorant man and the guide. The essay was about my love for classical, or serious, music, and my hopeless inability to get beyond the stage of a coarse admiration of it. Midway in the essay I remarked on the vast quantity of great music available from the past, and as an example mentioned a composer I had not hitherto heard of named Guiseppi Torelli (1658–1709). At a concert I had heard Torelli's *Sinfonia for Two Trumpets in D Major*, and thought it splendid. This Torelli, I noted, was no ordinary Guisseppi, adding, "yet, a month from now I shall have quite forgotten his name."

Turns out that I have not been allowed to forgot the name Guiseppi Torelli. Nor, as I shall explain, will I ever. The reason is that, since writing the essay, I have, for nearly twenty-five years now, every month received a postcard on which appears the name, writ large, TORELLI. Sometimes the composer's first name also appears. Always the name is set out in an interesting design from the school of high doodling.

Two of these postcards are before me. The one from last month has the name Torelli printed vertically and on its side, outlined in red, filled in with yellow against a blue background, surrounded by stripes of red, yellow, and blue on both sides. This month's card shows four large T's, in red, one pointing up, one pointing down, two horizontally on their sides, all nearly touching, the four forming an unenclosed box with the letters O R EL LI set out around the cap T's. The other sides of the postcards are invariably noteworthy. Last month's showed the Civil War Ruins of Montgomery Blair's House in Silver Springs, West Virginia; this month's card has a lovely madonna from the Museo de Tavera in Toledo. The postmark, which never varies, reads "North Texas, Dallas. 750."

I have toted up the cost of this project to my unknown correspondent. Assuming an average postage over the years of 40 cents per card and another 50 cents for each postcard, the sum, over a twenty-five year period, comes to roughly $270 and, as they say, counting. Rather expensive, I'd say, for a joke the response to which the joker isn't around to register.

Who is the person doing this? And with what intent? Is it a man or a woman sending out these cards? I suspect a man; no woman would be so *meshuggi*. How old is he? What impels him to continue over so long a period? All I know about this person is that he combines a sense of humor that relies heavily on repetition and that he is a man of astonishing diligence. As I think of him, sending out these Torelli postcards month after month, does he wonder what my reaction to them might be? Winging off another of his postcards, does he think that this will teach the old boy— me—to forget the great Torelli? Is he wondering if I am going out of my gourd trying to discover who is sending all these cards? Does he ever think about one day revealing himself to me, and letting me in on the joke?

Is my correspondent aware that I once wrote a story called "Postcards?" The story is about a man, a poet *manqué* named Seymour Ira Hefferman, who each month buys and sends off postcards to cultural figures, novelists, critics, poets, angry feminists, college presidents. On these postcards he tells them off for their toadyism, pretensions, arrogance, stupidity, and foolishness generally. Unlike my correspondent, the character in my story does not send off his postcards anonymously but instead signs them with false names. One day he sends off one of these poisonous little missives on which he has mistakenly affixed his correct return address, which leads to what I hope are interesting complications.

That is fiction, but my Torelli man exists in real life. Might the moral here be that one can't invent anything and that life, as advertised, really is stranger than fiction?

I should like my anonymous correspondent to know that each month, as I shuffle through mail consisting of bills, useless catalogs, and letters requesting I help save the armadillo, and discover another of his Torelli postcards, I smile and think the world is not without its charm. Unlike Queen Victoria, who was famous for saying "We are not amused," I am amused, highly so. The only question is with whom do I get in touch at the *Guiness Book of World Records* to report this surely most longstanding of impractical jokes.

Original Publication Information for Essays in this Book

(listed by page number)

Index